Just off the Autoroute

Interesting places, beauty spots, good food and accommodation in France

by

Monique Riccardi-Cubitt

CADOGAN BOOKS LTD.

ISBN 0 946313 01 6

Published by Cadogan Books Ltd 1983
Imprint of Gentry Books Ltd
15 Pont Street, London SW1

Typeset in Great Britain by
M.C. Typeset, Chatham, Kent
Printed and bound by
Biddles of Guildford

Acknowledgements

I would like to thank the following people for making the writing of this Guide possible:

Mrs Helen McCabe, without whom this book would never have been, for her continued support.

My husband, Michael Riccardi-Cubitt, for his encouragement and help in every way with the research in France.

The French Tourist Office in London for its courteous and efficient service.

And last but not least, Paula Levey, my editor, for her understanding and enthusiastic assistance.

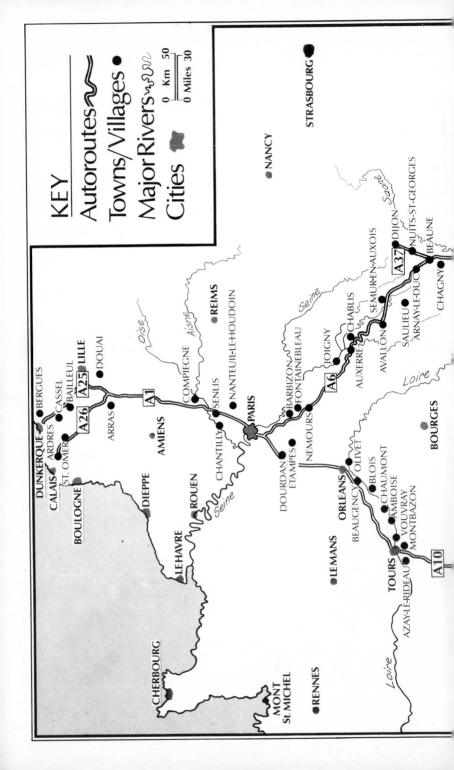

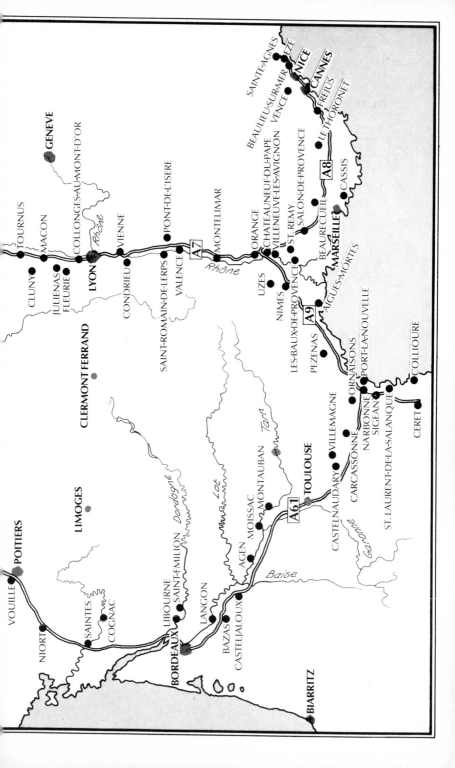

Contents

Introduction

Often when motoring through France on the *autoroute*, I have longed to stop at a good, friendly restaurant not too far out of my way, to relax and relieve the strain and tedium of motorway driving. On many a long journey, the thought of the comfort of a quiet hotel, easily accessible, waiting for me in the deep peace of the countryside, would have soothed me and kept me going a little while longer.

Wading one's way through the Michelin is not much help, as after a frantic search on the map for a possible halt, the relevant village or town is often not included in the listed hotels and restaurants. The idea of *Just off the Autoroute* was born.

Why not have a clear, easily consulted guidebook listing and describing hotels and restaurants within a given radius, say 20–25Km, under the names of the *autoroute* exits?

It would include luxury hotels with gourmet food and simple two-star or unlisted family hotels with comfortable rooms and delicious food at reasonable prices, all bearing the unmistakable hallmark of a warm provincial French welcome.

Enlarging the concept of a food and accommodation guidebook, I thought of providing enough information for the motorist to enjoy a longer visit for those with time to take in the sights and explore the region. Thus *Just off the Autoroute* became a companion guide as well as a practical hotel and restaurant guide.

As a Frenchwoman eager to share the love I have for my own country, I wanted to give the modern British traveller an insight into France's rich culture and heritage. Within the clear-cut formula of separate entries in this book, I aim to introduce the historical, artistic and gastronomic wealth of France. I have given particular emphasis to the wine regions, the various *crus* and where to taste them in pleasant and often historical surroundings.

While planning your journey, or at the end of a long tiring drive, you should be able to consult *Just off the Autoroute* quickly and easily, with its maps giving the names of the entries, distances and simply charted directions.

However, when refreshed by a delicious dinner and a good bottle of wine, you may want to know more about the region in which you are staying. Therefore I have written the beginning of each chapter as my own personal introduction to the region described, outlining its natural heritage, the richness of its historical past and the many delights of its table, for your enhanced enjoyment.

It only remains for me to wish you *Bon Voyage et Bonne Route!*

Practical Information

When selecting the entries for *Just off the Autoroute* I have always kept firmly in mind the *ease of access to the village or town* mentioned and *its distance from the autoroute* within the given radius. However, as far as the criteria of natural beauty, history, art, and gastronomy are concerned, I have made a personal choice of what I, as a Frenchwoman, thought would appeal to and interest British travellers through France. Obviously I have given precedence to food, wine and accommodation, but a small town or village will only have one or two hotels and restaurants worth mentioning, while a fairly large city, like Dijon will have been chosen not only for its hotels and outstanding restaurants, but because its very structure is a microcosm of the region's art and history, and for the beauty of its monuments.

As for the South of France, so full of hotels and restaurants and fascinating places of all sorts, I have deliberately selected the lesser known, unusual places, most revealing of the true heart and soul of Provence, rather than those on the more obvious well-trodden paths.

Hotels and Restaurants

The standards of accommodation and cuisine vary from region to region. Some parts of France abound in hotels and restaurants of very high quality whereas others are not so well endowed. I have therefore aimed to select the best of what was available in any particular region.

Hotels and restaurants come under various guises in France. There are four-, three- or two-star hotels with restaurants, of gastronomic or more ordinary standard. I have given a full description of the range of facilities offered by each listed hotel. In these hotels the traveller will normally be required to take the evening meal at the restaurant of the hotel, particularly during the season. If in any doubt it is better to enquire when booking, *Le dîner est obligatoire?* (Is dinner compulsory?) to avoid any misunderstanding later on. The restaurant with rooms is a different sort of establishment all together. It may be a gastronomic restaurant or a very simple one but the emphasis will always be on the cuisine, however luxurious the rooms may be. And of course there is the small two-star or unlisted hotel without restaurant which provides breakfast only or sometimes light snacks for guests.

On the whole meal times in France are earlier than in England particularly outside main cities: 12–2pm is the accepted rule for lunch, the French starting their day early. It is an important point to remember when travelling through France, as in small restaurants especially, the cheap, good *plat du jour* (dish of the day) will have disappeared by 1 o'clock.

On the subject of restaurants perhaps it is worthwhile remembering that on the whole waiters do not like to be called *Garçon*. Raising one's hand to catch his attention and a simple *S'il vous plaît* brings about a far greater readiness to notice one's presence! Opening times of hotels and restaurants may vary and are not always obtainable. It is wise to check in advance.

Shopping Hours and Holidays

Most shops and banks close over lunchtime, 12–2pm. So do plan ahead when shopping for a picnic lunch. Banks are usually open until 4pm and post offices until 7pm, while shops generally remain open until 7.30pm. But this can vary from region to region, particularly in the South, where shops tend to remain closed until 3pm in the summer, because of the heat, and are therefore open later.

Public holidays

The main public holidays are as follows: 1 January, Easter, 1 May, 8 May, Witsun, 14 July, 15 August, 1 November, 11 November, Christmas Day.

Dates of festivals and fairs can be obtained from the French Tourist Office in London or at the local Office de Tourisme on the spot.

On the Motorway

Every car is required to carry a red triangle in case of emergency and a spare set of bulbs. Headlights must be adjusted to driving on the right. Seat belts are compulsory.

In case of breakdown on the motorway you must display your red triangle, having pulled in on the hard shoulder if you are unable to get to a service or rest area. Every 2Km emergency telephones are directly connected with the nearest police station, which will call a garage to help repair or tow it away. In the case of an accident the police will send an ambulance.

Service areas offer drinks, snacks, telephones and shops. Larger ones have restaurants, information offices and a hotel reservation service.

Rest areas provide picnic areas with tables and benches, drinking water and toilet.

Some tolls are operated automatically. It saves time to have the right change available.

Apart from the usual motorway restaurant, a chain of restaurants called *Courte-Paille* offers a very good service all day every day. For 50F a standard menu gives a choice of four starters, several main dishes and a sweet or cheese. They can be found at: Dunkerque, Lille, Nemours, Auxerre-Nord, Dijon, Pouilly-en-Auxois, Mâcon Sud, Lyon Pierre Bénite, Valence, Montélimar-Nord, Avignon-Sud, Nimes-Ouest, Montpellier-Sud, Toulouse, Bordeaux-Artigues, Tours-Sud, Orléans-Ouest and Orléans-Est.

Autoroute du Nord
Dunkerque–Lille (A25) Calais–Arras (A26) Lille–Paris (A1)

The Autoroute du Nord plunges through the heart of northern France, providing plenty of opportunities for the traveller to sample the varied charms of an area rich in interest. The section running south-east from Dunkerque to Lille is the A25, while the A26 takes a parallel course some 40Km further south, joining the main north-south route (the A1, Lille–Paris) at Arras.

The A25 runs through French **Flanders.** Along the coast the **Blooteland**, the bare country of flatlands or **Moeres** (marshes) was drained in the 17th century by the Flemish engineer Coebergher. Using dykes, canals and windmills he created a very fertile polder area producing sugar beet, wheat and flax, and dotted with prosperous farms on which horses and cattle are bred.

Inland the **Houtland** (wooded country), a landscape of rivers and canals which is punctuated by magnificent trees strikes a contrast with the bareness of the coast. Proudly upright poplars are aligned along dead straight roads or stand as sentinels around the low white-walled Flemish farms with their red roofs and open courtyards. Willows bend low over canals and rivers where pike, tench and bream abound, and regal elms accentuate the vast low landscape of the Flemish plain. The only high points on the horizon are the Monts de Flandres, whose chain of rounded hills continues into Belgium. The Houtland is as fertile as the Moeres and bears rich harvests of cereals, hops for the region's celebrated beer, flax for the textile factories of Lille and Roubaix, tobacco, sugar beet and many other crops, as well as delicious fresh vegetables from the Watergangs of St-Omer sent all over France.

Once on the main north-south route, the traveller passes through the rich country of **Picardie**, with its undulating country divided into large holdings and yielding abundant crops of wheat and sugar beet. Towards Compiègne, orchards and pastures appear among the wheat and beet fields, heralding the **Ile de France** with its market gardens, orchards and magnificent forests. The Forest of Compiègne is one of the most beautiful in France, while the towns of Chantilly and Senlis nestle in a picturesque setting of lakes, ponds, rivers, deep woods on sandy soils and varied crops.

Paris lies at the centre of the giant bowl of the Ile de France, stretching its tentacles far into the adjacent countryside, yet still surrounded by a crown of woody hills unspoilt enough to produce game of all sorts and mushrooms and berries for the local markets.

For centuries the northern corner of France has been the battlefield of

11

Europe. For a long time it was trampled as the southern approach to the Netherlands; then it suffered as the northern defence wall of France. Names such as Bouvines, Agincourt, Lens, Hondschoote and Dunkerque are linked with sombre memories of the dark times of war from the Middle Ages onwards. But then, as in our own century, the people of the north started all over again, building, sowing and planting as soon as the ravages of war were over. Dunkerque, Bailleul, Bergues, Arras and many other towns are living proof of this indomitable spirit. The French historian Michelet wrote in the last century that 'Flanders was created so to speak, against Nature. It is the creation of human labour', but it was certainly also created against man's own destructiveness. No wonder this forever sorrowing part of France has seen many of its sons attain high rank and honours in the French army. General de Gaulle himself was born at Lille.

Military fortifications are everywhere, from medieval castles with towers and dungeons to the classical 17th century ramparts of Vauban at Bergues. More poignantly near our time military memorials and cemeteries are places of pilgrimage for soldiers from many countries once united in a common cause.

The **beffroi** (belfry) is the characteristic landmark of the area. The buildings were used as watch towers and housed bells to raise the alarm at the approach of the enemy. They were valued symbols of civic freedom and when destroyed were always rebuilt. Their peals now proclaim more peaceful tidings.

Gothic architecture, although born in the Ile de France, developed to great heights of virtuosity in the far north and Picardie. Cathedrals and churches lavishly endowed by the local guilds and burghers, as well as more princely gifts, are telling reminders of the profound and vibrant faith of the Middle Ages as well as of the legitimate if slightly ostentatious desire to advertise the wealth of a city.

Traditions remain very strong in the far north of France and festivals, carnivals and village fairs provide opportunities for revelry and ritual banquets all the year round. (Dates and places can be obtained from the local *Office de Tourisme*, and will be found under the name of the town in this guide.)

The Ile de France became the centre of the first kingdom of France when Clovis, King of the Francs, made Paris his official capital in 508. The Ile de France has been intimately linked with French history through-out the centuries, and thereby with English history. (The marriage of the future Henry II of England to the ex-wife of Louis VII of France, Eleanor of Aquitaine, in 1152, brought about a struggle between the two countries which lasted for centuries, for she had as her dowry about one third of France.) From 1420 until 1436 the English occupied Paris. However the city, whose motto is *Fluctuat Nec Mergitur* (tossed but not sunk) and whose crest shows a freighted ship on a sea argent, survived this assault just as it was to survive subsequent ones in the 19th and 20th centuries. By 1453 the only English possession in the realm of France was Calais.

In 1469 the first French printing press was set up at the Sorbonne, long famed for the quality of its teaching. The development of the French Renaissance, following Italian literary and artistic precepts, was under way. The Ile de France bears witness in its châteaux to the high level of sophistication, during this period, of the French aristocracy, which was enjoying a more luxurious way of life and making the humanism of Italy its own. The 17th and 18th centuries saw the climax of artistic achievement in the Ile de France. Place-names such as Vaux-le-Vicomte, Versailles and Compiègne evoke the period's three styles of architecture and design, admired and imitated all over Europe: Louis XIV, full of pomp and grandeur; Louis XV, delicate and frivolous, with its emphasis on rococo curves; and Louis XVI, classical and elegant.

GASTRONOMY
Flanders and the Far North
The sun may not shine all the time in the north, but there is always warmth and brightness in the welcome given to strangers. In Flanders and throughout the region, the friendliness of innkeepers and restaurateurs is matched by the food, which is often simple and homely but of a high quality.

There are many specialities based on traditional country cooking, including: *Lapin au Pruneaux* (rabbit with prunes); *Flamiche aux Poireaux* (or *au Maroilles*) (open flan with leeks or maroilles, a strong local cheese); *Carbonnade de Boeuf* (beef stew with beer, onions and spices); *Anguille au Vert* (eel in a wine and herb sauce); *Coq à la Bière* (capon cooked in beer); *Maquereaux au Vin Blanc* (mackerel marinated in white wine with onions and spices); *Potche Vlees* (Flemish speciality of rabbit, chicken and veal pieces served in aspic).

Other dishes are more delicate in taste: *Gigot de Pré Salé* (leg of lamb from animals grazed on land that is covered by sea water at high tide, which gives a subtle flavour to the meat); *Sole* (or *Turbot*) *Sauce Mousseline* (sole or turbot with a light butter sauce). *Andouillette* (large sausage made with pork) is much appreciated by the connoisseurs, and even has its own fan club. It is generally eaten grilled.

The **cheeses** of the region are strong and can be rather smelly but are delicious all the same. The main ones to watch for are: *Maroilles* (soft and gold, dipped in beer); *Mimolette* (orange and ball shaped); *Boulette d'Avesnes* (a cone sprinkled with paprika); *Fromage du Mont des Cats* (less strong in flavour).

Every town has its own special **sweet** or **cake**: Dunkerque has its *Babeluttes*; Lille its *Petits Quinquins*; Douai its *Gayantines*; Cambrai its *Bêtises*. Try them all!

Picardie

In Picardie tender young vegetables (*primeurs*) are used in many soups, and there are *flamiches* (open flans) using leeks, onions and marrows. Frogs from the many ponds are used in *Potage de Grenouilles*. *Pâté de Canard en Croûte* (duck pâté in pastry) has been cooked at Amiens since the 17th century. *Rissoles de Viande* (or *de Poisson*) (deep-fried pasties filled with a meat or fish mixture) were popular in the Middle Ages. Another speciality is *Ficelle Picarde* (ham pancake with béchamel sauce and mushrooms).

Game such as *Bécassines* (snipe) and *Vanneaux* (plover) abounds and features on many menus, as do *Truite* (trout), *Anguilles* (eels), *Carpe* (carp) and *Brochet* (pike).

Beer has been produced in France since early times. The Franks drank it under the name of *Cervoise*, from that of the goddess of the fields and harvest, Ceres. Northern France, where oats and barley are grown, is the centre of French brewing and accounts for nearly a quarter of the country's output. It was monks from Picardie who went to Westphalia in the Middle Ages to teach the brewing of beer to the Germans! Light lager-type beers are produced, but so also are darker, stronger tasting brews more like the English 'bitter'. *Genièvre* is a strong local brandy made from juniper berries.

The Ile de France

The Ile de France produces some of the best fresh produce in France, be it young vegetables (*primeurs*), fruit, meat cut to perfection or fresh-water fish from the numerous ponds and rivers. Paris itself is, of course, a gastronomic centre of international repute: many a famous *maître cuisinier* has left to posterity some culinary *chef-d'œvre* elaborated in the kitchens of a Parisian restaurant. The Ile de France does not offer regional specialities in the way other regions of France do, but can boast a cuisine of great refinement and sophistication, thanks to the quality, variety and abundance of the produce available, the taste, care and artistry of its chefs, and the critical appreciation of the clientele for which it is destined.

The cuisine of the Ile de France reflects the varied moods of the capital. It can be elegant and frivolous, like *Paris–Brest* (a rich sweet created to commemorate the bicycle race of the same name), bourgeois and comforting like *Potage aux Primeurs* (spring vegetable soup) or *Entrecôte Bercy* (steak with white wine sauce), or earthy and full of high spirit like *Gibelotte de Lapin* (rabbit stew) or *Boeuf Mironton* (beef stew).

Cheeses produced in the region include *Brie*, already famous in the 15th century when Charles of Orléans, father of Louis XII, used to send it as a present to his friends. A *Coulommiers* is a small Brie. The Ile de France has no vineyards to speak of, although the grape harvest still takes place every October in the famous vineyard of Montmartre.

Dunkerque–Lille (A25)

BERGUES
Bergues/Dunkerque Centre exit, D916, 2.5Km
From Dunkerque, N225 to autoroute, then D916
Inhabitants: 4,824
Office de Tourisme: in the beffroi, Place de la République, 1 July–15 September, closed Friday

Only 11Km from Dunkerque, Bergues is the ideal overnight stop before or after taking the ferry. The approach from the D916 crosses several canals by way of small bridges brilliantly decorated with flower boxes, the whole reflecting the prettiness, orderliness and warm welcome of a typical Flemish small town. With its quiet streets, its large squares surrounded by imposing buildings and the peaceful atmosphere created by the numerous canals and orderly quays, Bergues lies sleepily behind its ramparts dreaming of a glorious past as a rich wool town, but is now content to be a mini Bruges in a farming area. The fortifications, visible from the D916, date back in parts to the Middle Ages. In the 17th century Vauban diverted the **Colme canal** into deep moats around fortified walls to the north of the city, creating a star-shaped defence system called the **Crown d'Hondschoote.**

Much of the town was destroyed during the last war, yet the restoration and rebuilding have been carried out judiciously and have not disturbed the harmony of its squares, streets and buildings. The highest point of the town is the **Groenberg**, a promontory on which stand the tower and ruins of the 11th century Benedictine **Abbey of St Winoc**, built by Beaudoin le Barbu, Count of Flanders. Benedictine monks, the original founders of Bergues, chose this high point, which offers natural defences as well as a wonderful view over the lower part of the town and the surrounding flat countryside. It is now reached by the Rue des Annonciades from the Place de la République where the *beffroi* stands. A garden obviously built within the ancient abbey precinct invites rest and meditation.

Returning to the centre, the **beffroi**, rebuilt after the last war in a simplified modern Flemish style, boasts a *carillon* of fifty bells. Concerts take place every Monday at 11am and on the eve of certain feast days.

The happy sound of bells playing tunes is one of the most delightful of Flemish customs. Even on a rainy day under a grey sky, it brings a joyous, festive note. Opposite the *beffroi*, the **town hall** dates from the 17th century and is built in an Italianate Renaissance style. Behind the church of St-Martin (restored) stands the **Mont-de-Piété** (pawn shop), an elegant building and a small masterpiece of Flemish baroque art. It is now a museum housing a collection of 16th and 17th century Flemish paintings by such masters as Breughel, Massys and Van Dyck, and a Rubens sketch, as well as an important work by George de la Tour (French 17th century), 'The Hurdy-gurdy Player', and a collection of 16th and 17th century drawings. On the second floor there is a natural history museum which particularly features birds and butterflies. (Open 10–12am and 2–5pm, closed Friday and 1 January, 1 May, 14 July, 1 November, Christmas Day.)

Hotels and Restaurants

Tonnelier (Near the church, opposite the Mont-de-Piété's gardens.) Small, cosy family-run hotel (and restaurant) offering a warm welcome as well as homely Flemish food in its panelled dining-room, with specialities such as *Soupe de Poissons* (fish soup), *Potche Vlees* (rabbit, chicken and veal pieces in aspic) and *Tarte Flamande* (custard flan with raisins soaked in rum). 59380, Bergues, Nord. Tel: (28) 68.70.05. 12 rooms, 55–140F. Meals 35–110F. Closed Friday and 19 August–13 September.

12.5Km from Bergues, in the small village of Bollezeele (1,328 inhabitants), the **Hostellerie St-Louis** offers delicious food and the peace and quiet of its lovely gardens. The very comfortable rooms, all looking out on the gardens, make it a stopping place to linger at and enjoy fully. Specialities: *Foie Gras Maison* (liver), *Truite Farcie* (stuffed trout), *Magret de Canard à la Sauge* (duck breasts cooked with sage), *Sorbet Hostellerie* (sorbet). 47 Rue de l'Eglise, 59470, Bollezeele, Nord. Tel: (20) 68.81.83. 15 rooms, 120–150F. Meals 85–150F. Closed Sunday night and Monday. To reach Bollezeele coming from Dunkerque by the N225, turn right on to the D916 just before the beginning of the *autoroute*, then take the D928 in the direction of St-Omer and turn off on to the D226 to Bollezeele. Coming from Lille take the Bergues/Dunkerque Centre exit and then continue as above.

Festivals, Fairs and Sporting Events

15 August: **Archery**, a tradition dating back many centuries in this part of France.

Garages

Peugeot/Talbot: Esquelbecq. Tel: (28) 65.61.44.

Renault: Wormhout. Tel: (28) 65.62.72.
Volvo: Socx. Tel: (28) 68.61.44.

CASSEL
From Dunkerque, Steenvoorde/Ypres exit, D948, 6Km
From Lille, Steenvoorde exit, D948, 6Km
Inhabitants: 2,492

Former capital of the Blooteland (coastal Flanders), Cassel is built on a hill 175m high which provides a fine panoramic view over the Flanders plain, as well as serving as a landmark for sailors. It is a perfect stop for a leisurely lunch at its fine restaurant and then a walk along its narrow picturesque streets up to the belvedere to admire the view over (so it is traditionally said) five kingdoms: France, Belgium, Holland, England and, in the sky above, the Kingdom of God.

With its low whitewashed houses built on terraces, its vast, roughly paved **Grand' Place** spread out on the hillside, its attractive town houses (*hôtels*) dating from the 17th and 18th centuries, Cassel is full of typical Flemish charm. For some it might strike a sombre chord, with memories of the last war, for the British army suffered heavy casualties here. By 1914, because of its strategic position, Cassel was the headquarters of Maréchal Foch. He stayed at the **Hôtel de Schoebecque**, 32 Rue du Maréchal Foch, just off the Grand' Place. In May 1940 a brigade from the British Expeditionary Force lost 2,000 dead and 1,000 prisoners in a fierce battle against a Panzer division.

Arriving from the D948 walk up the Rue du Maréchal Foch to reach the Grand' Place. Admire on your left the **Hôtel d'Halluin** with its Louis XVI façade, then the **Hôtel de la Noble Cour**, formerly the seat of the Flemish law courts. The stone façade, very rare in the north, has elegant lines which are Renaissance in style, as are such details as the windows with their alternating triangular and curved pediments and the doorway surrounded by grey marble columns with an ornate decorative frieze above. The high mansard roof is typically northern. The building now houses a museum exhibiting 17th and 18th century artefacts and furniture and Flemish faience and porcelain, as well as the desk and personal mementoes of Maréchal Foch. (Open 2–6pm July and August, and Sunday June–September.)

Climb up to the gardens, through the **Porte du Château** (1621). They are laid out on the site of a medieval castle. The equestrian **statue of Maréchal Foch** stands on the spot from where he used to observe the movements of the troops through field glasses. Enjoy the picturesque array of roofs tumbling down the hill and the vast panoramic view as far as Dunkerque and Ghent. The wooden **windmill**, dating from the 18th century, was brought from Arneke and placed here on the site of the mill belonging to the château. (Open 1May–31 October.)

On the way back from the gardens stop at the collegiate **Church of Notre Dame**, of Flemish Gothic style with its three high façades, three naves and square bell tower. In the dark hours of the war, Maréchal Foch used to come here to pray and meditate. Nearby the old **Jesuit chapel** has an elegant 17th century stone and brick façade.

Restaurant
Le Sauvage Specialities according to the time of the year. Home-made bread. 600 different wines. Enjoy a delicious meal in an old Flemish house, in summer in its panoramic restaurant, in winter by the fireplace in its cosy dining room. 38 Grand' Place, 59670, Cassel, Nord. Tel: (28) 42.40.88. Meals 87–133F. Closed Sunday night and Wednesday, and 1 February–1 March.

Festivals, Fairs and Sporting Events
February, last Sunday: **Carnival of the Giant Reuze-Papa.**
Easter Sunday and Monday: **Carnival of the Giants Reuze-Papa and Reuze-Maman.**
June, third Sunday: **Fair.**

BAILLEUL/MONT NOIR
From Dunkerque, Meteren/Bailleul exit, D933, 3Km to Bailleul, 7.5Km to Mont Noir
From Lille, Bailleul exit, D23 and D223, 2.5Km to Bailleul, 7.5Km to Mont Noir
Inhabitants: 13,483

A quiet, industrious city, Bailleul has a very good restaurant with fish specialities on the way to the Mont Noir, which is an ideal place for a walk and picnic or a leisurely excellent meal in the Hôtel-Restaurant du Mont Noir on top of the hill.

Bailleul was badly damaged during the last war and the **beffroi** over the 13th century Gothic hall was rebuilt in yellow brick in Flemish Gothic style. The **Musée Benoît de Puydt** on the Grand' Place has a fascinating collection of Chinese and Japanese porcelain as well as French faience, together with a display of Flemish furniture, tapestries from the 18th century and a typical Flemish kitchen. (Open Saturday and Sunday 2.30–5.30pm, closed feast days.)

From Bailleul, take the road for Ypres (D23), then turn left on to the D223 and just before reaching the Belgian frontier turn left again on to the D318 to the Mont Noir. The Mont Noir belongs to the only range of hills in Flanders, the Monts de Flandres, which carry their low curves on into Belgium. The Mont Noir itself stands 131m high and is thickly covered with the remnants of the thick dark forest of the Houtland (the wooded country), still surviving despite the onslaughts of man, from Roman times to our own century. The thick undergrowth harbours game, mushrooms and wild berries, a treasure trove for the kitchen. Weather permitting, a picnic and a walk under the tall trees would make a very pleasant halt. There is a fine view from the top of the hill, a panorama taking in Belgium and Mont Kemmel to the north-east. To the west the Mont des Cats is easily recognised by the neo-Gothic Trappist abbey sitting at the top (not open to the public).

To the north-west a glimpse of **Boeschepe Windmill** can be caught. Built of wood provided by the forest before the Houtland was transformed into agricultural land, it is one of the rare survivors of the 1,316 windmills counted in this region only a century ago. Used to extract oil from colza as much as to grind flour, the windmills, with their characteristic outline, stretched their arms towards the grey sky as if in anguish. Perhaps they knew the fate that the modern world held for them. From being the heart of activity in the village and the surrounding countryside, beating rhythmically to the breath of the wind, they now stand forlorn and silent, lonely reminders of a lost way of life. However, in the last decade, the Association Régionale des Amis des Moulins (Regional Association of the Friends of Windmills) has done much work to restore and bring back some life to the abandoned structures, and the Windmill of Boeschepe is now a centre for local festivals.

Hotels and Restaurants

A la Pomme d'Or Specialities: *Homard à l'Américaine* (lobster with tomato sauce), *Ecrevisses à la Nage* (or *au Gratin*) (fresh-water crayfish in their own juices or with béchamel cheese sauce), all other fish according to season. 27 Rue d'Ypres, 59270, Bailleul Nord. Tel: (28) 43.11.01. Meals 59–98F. Closed Sunday night and Monday. Credit cards: DC, EC, VISA.

Hotel Restaurant du Mont Noir Enjoy a first-class meal in the panoramic restaurant overlooking Belgium. Specialities: *Waterzooi de St Jacques* (Flemish speciality of scallops in a fish soup), *Gigue de Chevreuil Sauce Grand Veneur* (venison in a wine sauce), *Aiguillettes de Canard au Genièvre de Wambrechies* (duck breast cooked with juniper brandy), *Crêpes Flambées* (pancakes flamed in liqueur). Boeschepe, 59270, Bailleul Nord. Tel: (28) 42.51.33. Meals 55–110F. Closed Friday and February. The 7 rooms (55–105F) offer a peaceful night in quiet surroundings. Credit card: VISA.

Festivals, Fairs and Sporting Events

Shrove Tuesday and the preceding Sunday: **Bailleul Carnival** with the Giant Gargantua and Doctor Piccolissimo.

From the Steenvoorde exit

Take the D916 to **Hazebrouck** 10Km from the exit, then the D946 to **La Motte au Bois**, 5Km. In the middle of the Forest of Nieppe, a country inn offers peace and comfort as well as *haute cuisine* such as: *Chevreuil* (venison), *Filets de Sole à la Fine Champagne* (sole fillets cooked in brandy), *Contrefilet Poêlé Marchand de Vin* (steak with a red wine and shallot sauce), *Sabayon à la Mandarine Napoléon* (mousse with mandarin liqueur). **Auberge de la Forêt**, 59190, La Motte au Bois Nord. Tel: (28) 41.80.90. 15 rooms, 50–130F. Meals from 72F. Closed Sunday night and Thursday, and February. Credit card: VISA.

Another 7Km down the D946, at **Merville**, the **Auberge du Gros Chêne**, offers lunch and Saturday night dinner. Specialities: *Langoustines au Poivre Vert* (crayfish with green peppercorns), *Andouillette Flambée au Calvados* (sausage flamed in calvados), *Carbonnade Flamande* (beef stew with beer, onions and spices). Route d'Hazebrouck-Merville Nord. Tel: (28) 42.82.83. Meals 67–95F. Closed Monday.

4Km from Hazebrouck on the D916 at **Steenbecque** the **Auberge de la Belle Siska** offers the comfort of a (Michelin) two-star hotel in a peaceful country setting, as well as menus ranging from the *menu touristique* to the *menu gastronomique*. Specialities: *Flamiche au Maroilles* (open flan with Maroilles cheese), *Brochettes de Coquilles St Jacques aux Herbes* (scallops with herbs, grilled on a skewer), *Onglet à l'Echalote* (fillet of beef with a shallot sauce). 59189, Steenbecque Nord. Tel: (28) 42.61.77. Meals 38.50–81F. Closed Sunday night and Monday.

Calais–Arras (A26)

ARDRES

From Calais, N43, 17Km
Inhabitants: 3,165

Fifteen minutes away from Calais, Ardres is a small provincial town offering the comforts of a (Michelin) three-star hotel with high-quality food, as well as the attractions of a large lake well-equipped for tourism and water sports. Built between the coastal lands and the hills of Artois, Ardres has kept part of its fortifications, which date from a time when it held more importance. The **Field of the Cloth of Gold**, the historic meeting between Henry VIII of England and François I of France in 1520, took place between Ardres and Guines. A painting at Hampton Court by a contemporary artist records the week of feasting and jousting when each king tried to outshine the other with displays of splendour and magnificence. Ardres itself still has some fine old houses around its oddly shaped triangular **Grand' Place** (or **Place d'Armes**). They make a pictur-esque scene with their pointed roofs, surrounding the church, which dates from the end of the 14th century, and the **Carmelite chapel** (17th century).

Go sailing, rowing or fishing on the Lac d'Ardres, and then repair to the Grand Hôtel Clément for a truly delicious meal prepared by the owner and his son. Spend the night and enjoy the peace and comfort of a family-run hotel with its own garden.

Hotels and Restaurants
Grand Hôtel Clément Specialities: *Goujonnette de Sole au Citron* (fillet of sole with lemon sauce), *Noisettes d'Agneau et la Sauce Aigre-Doux au Genièvre* (tender pieces of lamb with a sweet-and-sour juniper brandy sauce). Place Maréchal Leclerc, 62610, Ardres, Pas-de-Calais. Tel: (21) 35.40.66. 18 rooms, 115–185F. Meals 100–220F. Closed 15 January–15 February, and Monday and Tuesday lunch-time 1 October–1 March. Credit cards: EC, VISA.
La Chaumière Small hotel without restaurant. 62610, Ardres, Pas-de-Calais. Tel: (21) 35.41.24. 12 rooms, 75–190F. Open all year.

Garages
Citroën: Tel: (21) 35.42.16.

ST-OMER
From Calais, N43, 40Km
From Arras, St-Omer exit, N42, 6.5Km
Inhabitants: 17,988
Office de Tourisme: Hôtel de Ville, Place du Maréchal Foch. Closed Saturday morning during season, and Sunday afternoon.

St-Omer has varied attractions to delight the traveller. It is well worth stopping overnight to explore the nature reserve of the Watergangs, built from the marshes during ten centuries of relentless effort. Perhaps take a boat trip, have a picnic while bird-watching or do some fishing.

The town itself offers many treasures between the **Cathedral of Notre Dame** and the ruins of the **Abbey of St-Bertin** which was once a major cultural centre. A comfortable hotel with a quality restaurant near the abbey is the ideal base from which to conduct one's visit.

A religious centre since the 7th century, St-Omer owes its unusual setting and its prosperity to the Benedictine and Cistercian monks (including St-Omer himself), who drained the marshes, educated the locals and made of this boggy area one of the first wool centres in Flanders, as well as a wealthy agricultural and industrial centre. Situated at the frontier between Flanders and Artois it became part of France in

1678, after which time it developed further. Many 17th and 18th century houses still line the quiet aristocratic streets around the cathedral, while along the river Aa, the low Flemish houses make a picturesque contrast.

Coming from Calais by the N42, follow the Boulevard des Alliés and Boulevard Vauban to the cathedral, the Basilica of Notre Dame. It is the finest and most imposing Gothic religious building in the area, and was erected between the 13th and 16th century. It is also the only important monument in St-Omer that was not destroyed by the Emperor Charles V in the 16th century. Its interior, of vast proportions, houses many works of art, among them 'Le Grand Dieu de Thérouanne' which comes from the façade of the cathedral of Thérouanne destroyed by Charles V. Admire the 'Last Judgement' on the tympanum of the south portal, and the 14th century Virgin on the centre pillar.

Take the Rue des Tribunaux and view the former **Bishop's palace** dating from the 17th century, now the law courts. Carry on down Rue Carnot to the **Hôtel Sandelin**, an 18th century town house, now a museum, surrounded by a garden. It counts among its treasures the famous 12th century Mosan (ie from the Moselle area) enamelled cross pedestal called the Pied de Croix de St-Bertin, as well as Dutch and Flemish paintings (by Steen, Ter Borch, de Keyser), ceramics from the St-Omer factory, 750 Delft pieces, and 18th century French paintings (Greuze, Prud'hon). (Open 10–12am and 2–6pm, closed Tuesday and 1 January, 1 May, 1 November, Christmas Day.)

Go down Rue Carnot to Rue St-Denis (second right) to have a look at the **Church of St-Denis** (13th century with 18th century restoration), then cross over to Rue St-Bertin to admire the former **Jesuit chapel**, now part of a school. Finished in 1639, it is a good example of the emerging Jesuit style. It is a handsome building of imposing proportions and with a striking façade of brick decorated with white stones and sculptures.

From the school chapel carry on to the **library** (*Bibliothèque*) in Rue Gambetta. It has on permanent display some 350,000 volumes, among them 1,600 precious manuscripts dating from the 9th to the 16th centuries and more than 200 early (before 1500) printed books. The famous Bible Mazarine is one of the latter. The old wood panelling from the Abbey of St-Bertin makes a fitting setting for such a splendid collection. (Open 1–5pm, closed Sunday, Monday and public holidays.)

Going back towards Notre Dame take the Rue Henri Dupuis and visit the **museum** in an 18th century house. A typical Flemish kitchen of the period with its Delft tiles, pewters and furniture, can be viewed, as well as a bird and shell collection. (Open 10–12am and 2–6pm, closed Tuesday and 1 January, 1 May, 1 November, Christmas Day.)

The **public gardens** beyond the Boulevard Vauban have been laid out on the site of the fortifications and are some of the most beautiful in France, as much because of their position, which gives a very fine view, as of their design, which combines the French and English styles. To the south an open-air public swimming pool has been built into one of the former moats.

The **Watergangs** are a unique complex of lakes, 100Km of rivers and 16Km of canals, covering altogether nearly 3,400Ha. This ancient marsh was first drained ten centuries ago by monks, to create a polder area. The only form of transport then as now was the flat-bottomed boats called *Escutes* or *Bacoves*. Part of the marshes is used for growing tender young vegetables (*primeurs*), particularly cauliflowers and chicory, sold all over France. Other parts are a nature reserve, where the flora and fauna are protected and encouraged, the migratory birds here being of particular note, while other areas are given to fishing and shooting. The Watergangs are open to the public, boats can be hired to explore them, and fishing permits can be obtained. Fish include pike, tench, bream and, especially, eel. (These used to grace the table of the monks of St-Bertin and Clairmarais.)

The **Forest of Clairmarais** is a very ancient one. Charlemagne used to hunt here in the 7th century. Covering a large area, it has been adapted to tourism, with the provision of car parks, picnic areas with tables and benches and a silent area around the **Etang d'Harchelles**, a 12th century lake used for fish farming by the Cistercian monks. It is now a very romantic spot with the lake nestling at the bottom of a deeply wooded valley. (All enquiries about fishing and boat hire should be addressed to the Office de Tourisme.)

Hotels and Restaurants

Le Bretagne A very comfortable hotel with a homely atmosphere and a high-quality restaurant with a woman chef of great distinction. She is a member of the Association des Restauratrices Cuisinières (Association of Women Chefs of France). Try the *Saumon Cru aux Passe-Pierres* (a French version of *Gravad Lax*, raw salmon marinated with spices), *Suprême de Turbotin aux Poireaux* (fillets of turbot with leeks) and delicious *Pâtisserie Maison* (cakes and pastries). 2 Place du Vainquai, 62500, St-Omer, Pas-de-Calais. Tel: (21) 38.25.78. 33 rooms, 87–200F. Meals 180–200F. Closed 13–29 August, 2–17 January, and evenings on Saturday, Sunday and public holidays. (A cheaper alternative to the restaurant is available at the Grill Maeva where the chef's husband offers quick-service simpler food. Closed 24 December–2 January, and lunch-times Monday and Saturday.) Credit cards: DC, VISA.

St Louis Comfortable, simple hotel without restaurant. 25 Rue Arras, 62500, St-Omer, Pas-de-Calais. Tel: (21) 38.35.21. 20 rooms, 65–120F. Closed 25 December–2 January. Credit cards: EC, VISA.

At **Tilques**, 3.5Km on the N43, is the **Hostellerie du Vert Mesnil.** A very comfortable hotel, with restaurant, in a 19th century château with its own park, garden and tennis court. A place to unwind in grand surroundings. 62500, Tilques par St-Omer, Pas-de-Calais. Tel: (21) 98.28.99. 40 rooms, 160–190F. Meals 60–120F. Open all year.

At **Lumbres**, 12Km on the N42, is the **Auberge du Moulin de Mombreux**, territory of one of France's *Maîtres Cuisiniers.* In the quiet setting of an old mill, with lovely gardens, it is a place to indulge oneself and spend a night after having dinner. Try the *Bar au Cresson Sauvage* (sea bass in a watercress sauce), the *Ris de Veau aux Girolles* (sweetbreads with chanterelles) or the *Tournedos Belle Hélène* (tournedos on a bed of artichokes, with *béarnaise sauce*). Route de Bayenghem, 62380, Lumbres, Pas-de-Calais. Tel: (21) 39.62.44. 6 rooms, 60–110F. Meals 100–145F. Closed Sunday night, Monday, and 20 December–1 February. Credit card: DC.

Festivals, Fairs and Sporting Events
May, last Sunday, and first Sunday of June: **Festival of the Green Hats** (from the famous French novel *Ces Dames aux Chapeaux Verts* which is set in St-Omer.) Written by Germaine Acremant.

Garages
Citroën: 33 Rue de Strasbourg. Tel: (21) 38.20.88; (night) (21) 98.42.13.
Peugeot: Rue St-Adrien. Tel: (21) 98.04.44; (night) (21) 98.49.10.
Renault: Route d'Arques. Tel: (21) 38.25.77.
Talbot: 201 Rue de Dunkerque. Tel: (21) 38.27.66.

ARRAS
From Calais, Arras Nord exit, N17, 6Km
From Paris, Arras Est exit, N39, 7Km
From Lille, Fresnes/Arras exit, N50, 13Km
Inhabitants: 50,386
Office de Tourisme: 11bis Rue Gambetta, closed Saturday afternoon and Sunday except in July and August.

Arras, the ancient capital of the Artois region, lies at the junction of two autoroutes: the A1 (Paris–Lille) and the A26 (Calais–Reims–Dijon), so that it is still a European crossroad, just as it has been since the Middle Ages. Its size should not deter the traveller. It was one of the first cities in France to introduce pedestrian precincts, and the many treasures of old Arras can be explored at leisure. Travel back in time and combine a visit to its buildings and monuments, some dating back to the 15th century, with a stay in a comfortable hotel and a delicious meal, which must include the famous *Andouillette*, Arras's speciality.

Arras developed in the 11th century, around the Abbey of St-Vaast, as a rich market town for wool and grains. Very soon it became an artistic centre as well, with rich bankers and burghers as the patrons. From 1384 a new lustre was added through the patronage of the Duke of Burgundy. The Arras tapestries became famous and were sought after all over Europe, to the extent that the Italian term for old tapestries is *Arazzi*. In 1434 Burgundy signed at Arras a treaty of reconciliation with France, and in 1659 the Artois became part of France. Robespierre, the famous revolutionary, was born here and started his career as a lawyer in Arras.

Aim for the *Centre Ville* (town centre) and the **Grand' Place** which, with the **Petite Place** (or **Place des Heros**) and the **Rue de la Taillerie** which links them both, constitutes a unique ensemble of Flemish architecture of the 17th and 18th centuries. Tall houses in brick or stone are aligned without interruption around the two *places* and along the Rue de la Taillerie. They are harmoniously welded into a whole by the stone cornice running continuously under the high pitched roofs, decorated with volutes, and by the ground floor of sandstone arcades where merchants used to shelter to discuss the price of grain or wool. The Grand' Place alone numbers 155 houses, the oldest one dating from the 15th century, and rests on 345 columns. Behind the columns deep cellars used to house merchandise. Every Saturday an open market is held on the two *places*.

Behind the Place des Héros the **Hôtel de Ville** with its 75m high *beffroi* was badly damaged during World War I and has been rebuilt in a Flamboyant Gothic style. Inside some curious frescoes by Hoffbauer, in the Salle des Fêtes upstairs, dating from 1932, portray the life of the people of Arras in the 16th century. (Open 8–12am and 2–5pm, closed Sunday afternoon, Monday morning and public holidays.) Surrounded by gardens, the **Cathedral** and the Abbey of St-Vaast display an 18th century classical symmetry and grandeur in contrast to the earlier buildings. The cathedral was built in the 18th century according to the plans of the architect of the Madeleine church in Paris. Its classical proportions and space give an impression of serene majesty further enhanced on the main façade by monumental steps and inside by the great line of tall Corinthian columns. Notice inside the wooden head of the Christ of Sorrows (15th century) and the gigantic statues of saints (19th century) which come from the Panthéon in Paris.

Adjacent to the cathedral stands the old **Abbey of St-Vaast** founded in the 7th century to receive the relics of St-Vaast, first bishop of Arras. Rebuilt in the 18th century by Cardinal de Rohan, the building, of noble proportions and symmetrical design, now houses a museum in its main wing. This museum is a gem as much because of its architectural setting as of its collections. Reach it via the Rue Paul Doumer or the Place de la Madeleine through the Cour d'Honneur. The cloisters, the refectory with its monumental marble fireplace and the Salle des Mays de Notre Dame contain many treasures. Some remarkable Romanesque and Gothic statuary and outstanding wood sculptures from the 15th and 16th centuries, notably a young woman's funeral mask, are worthy of note, as well as an important collection of Flemish paintings (by Fabritius, Jordaens, Brill and Breughel) and French works (by Lebrun, Philippe de Champaigne, Delacroix and Corot). A tapestry from Arras dating from the 15th century, and a gallery of porcelain from Arras and Tournai, illustrate the local artistic production. (Open 10–12am and 2–5.30pm, closed Tuesday and 1 January, 1 May, 14 July, 1 November, 11 November and Christmas Day.) Of more poignant connotations, a **memorial to the British army** commemorating the many dead British soldiers of World War I, stands outside the main centre off the Boulevard Général de Gaulle. Entrance through Avenue Newcastle.

Hotels and Restaurants

Le Chanzy A high-quality restaurant with a magnificent cellar of more than 100,000 bottles of all ages, some nearly a hundred years old! An opportunity for a real treat. Try some of the regional specialities such as: *Terrine de Porc aux Pruneaux* (pork pâté with prunes), the *Andouillette* (sausage) and the *Coq à la Bière* (*capon cooked in beer*). 8 Rue Chanzy, 62000, Arras, Pas-de-Calais. Tel: (21) 21.02.02. 22 rooms, 60–120F. Meals 55–100F. Open all year. Credit cards: AE, DC, EC, VISA.

Univers A very comfortable hotel, with restaurant, in a quiet setting. 3 Place Croix Rouge, 62000, Arras, Pas-de-Calais. Tel: (21) 21.34.01. 38 rooms, 110–190F. Meals 50–100F. Open all year.

Ambassadeur (Buffet de la Gare) An excellent restaurant with a large menu and unusual regional dishes such as *Harengs à la Flamande* (herrings Flemish style), *Pâté de Foie aux Pruneaux* (liver pâté with prunes), *Jambonneau aux Poireaux* (ham with leeks), as well as *Escargots en Bouchée* (snails in puff pastry) and *Sorbet au Genièvre* (sorbet with juniper brandy). Place Foch. Tel: (21) 23.29.80. Meals 65–100F. Closed Sunday night. Credit cards: AE, DC, EC, VISA.

There are two good, reasonably priced restaurants in a most attractive setting on the Grand' Place.

La Rapière 44 Grand' Place, 62000, Arras, Pas-de-Calais. Tel: (21) 55.09.92. Meals 40–65F. Closed 14 August–5 September, and 24 December–3 January, and Sunday (8 September–4 April). Credit cards: AE, DC, VISA.

Grandes Arcades 8 Grand' Place, 62000, Arras, Pas-de-Calais. Tel: (21) 23.30.89. Meals 40–105F. Open all year. Credit cards: EC, VISA.

Festivals, Fairs and Sporting Events

A June Sunday: **Rose Festival**
14 July, 15 July, 21 and 22 September: **jousting on water**

Garages
Austin/Morris/Triumph: 38 Boulevard Strasbourg, Tel: (21) 21.62.33.
BMW: 84 Avenue Lobedez. Tel: (21) 21.12.20.
Datsun: 22 Avenue Kennedy. Tel: (21) 21.65.79.
Fiat: 6 Avenue Michonneau. Tel: (21) 55.37.51.
Ford: 16 Avenue Michonneau. Tel: (21) 55.42.42.

Lille–Paris (A1)

DOUAI
From Lille, Henin Est/Douai exit, N43, 9Km
From Paris, Fresnes/Douai exit, N50, 14Km
Inhabitants: 47,570
Office de Tourisme: in the 18th century Maison du Dauphin, 70 Place d'Armes, closed Saturday

Douai is an old university town with many links with Britain. Stop for lunch or coffee in one of the many brasseries and restaurants on the Place d'Armes and soak up the typically northern atmosphere of this aristo-cratic city while waiting for the sixty-two bells of the *carillon* in the *beffroi* to chime a Scottish tune on the hour.

Situated on the River Scarpe, Douai was rebuilt in the 18th century and retains an air of grandeur despite the damage suffered during the two World Wars. The British connection dates from the 16th century when Roman Catholics came to Douai to escape religious persecution. Mary Queen of Scots founded the **Seminary of St Andrew of Scotland** at Douai and bequeathed it her last Book of Hours. Both unfortunately were destroyed during the last war. To this day however, one Roman Catholic version of the Bible is called the Douay Bible (the old French 17th century spelling for Douai). Published in 1609 by the English College of Douai through the efforts of Cardinal Allen, it translated the old Latin version into contemporary English with scholarly references to the Greek and Hebrew texts.

Driving from the N43 one crosses over the canal and the River Scarpe, lined by handsome old houses, and reaches the heart and soul of the city, the **Grand' Place** (or **Place d'Armes**). Greatly damaged during the last two wars it has been rebuilt and is now an airy place to stroll and relax with its fountains and flower-beds, its shops, brasseries and restaurants. The Maison du Dauphin at number 70 is the Office de Tourisme and one of the few 18th century houses still surviving.

The **beffroi** stands just off the Place d'Armes. It is one of the most famous in the whole of northern France, praised by Victor Hugo the poet, and immortalised by the painter Corot (both 19th century). It dates back to the late 14th and early 15th centuries. Its square Gothic tower ornamented with turrets, pinnacles and weathercocks dominates the whole city. The bells, on the fourth floor, are modern and replace the famous old *carillon* destroyed in 1917. Since the 14th century the chiming of bells has celebrated the passing of time all over Europe. At Douai bells still beat the quiet rhythm of simple provincial life, with a Scottish tune on the hour, a barcarole (gondolier's song) on the half hour and a local tune for the other quarters. Concerts are given on Saturdays and feast days at 10.45am, and there are further recitals at 9pm on Mondays in June, July and August.

Douai is truly the centre of bell-ringing in France. Since 1971 the Ecole Française de Carillon, situated at the **Hôtel de Ville** (part of the *beffroi*) has dispensed tuition and the title of *maître carillonneur*. The *beffroi* and the *Hôtel de Ville* are open weekdays 1 April–31 August 10–12am and 2.30–5.30pm, Sundays 2.30–5.30pm and in July and August 10–12am. From the *Hôtel de Ville* walk along the Rue de l'Université past the **Mont de Piété** (pawn shop), a 17th century building, and the **theatre** (18th century). Carry on to the Rue de la Comédie and admire the grand 17th century French baroque façade of the **Hôtel d'Aoust**. The **church of St-Pierre**, Rue St-Christophe, is an old collegiate church built from the 16th to the 18th centuries.

Further afield, crossing back over the River Scarpe, and off the Rue de la République, stands the **Old Chartreuse**. This is well worth a visit, allowing time for its fascinating mixture of buildings dating from the 16th, 17th and 18th centuries, and the extensive museum richly endowed with old masters not only from Flanders (including works by the Master de Flemalle, Mabuse, Breughel, Cuyp and Van Dyck), but also from Italy (Veronese and Annibale Carracci) as well as French masters of old and modern times (Nattier, David, Delacroix, Courbet, Corot, Renoir). Do not miss the extraordinary relief map of Douai made in the 18th century, and if you are lucky enough to meet the assistant curator, a dedicated Anglophile, you will be given a free 'guided tour' of the 18th century city and a fascinating insight into the old Douai by a man whose family has been here for generations and who loves and admires his native town. (Open 10–12am and 2–5pm, closed Tuesday and 1 January, 1 May, Ascension Day, 14 July, 1 November, 11 November, Christmas Day.)

Hotels and Restaurants
La Terrasse Behind the Church of St-Pierre. Quality restaurant with rooms. The emphasis here is on the food which is of very high standard with a welcome spirit of innovation. Try the *Escalope de Saumon à la Mousse de Homard* (salmon steak with lobster mousse), *Noisettes d'Agneau à la Menthe Fraîche* (tender pieces of lamb cooked with fresh

mint), *Poires Pochées et Caramélisées aux Fraises* (poached pears with strawberries and caramel sauce). 8 Terrasse St-Pierre, 59500, Douai, Nord. Tel: (27) 88.70.04. Rooms, 40–100F. Meals 36–200F. Open all year.

Grand Cerf Simple hotel, with restaurant, situated nearly opposite La Terrasse. 46 Rue St-Jacques, 59500, Douai, Nord. Tel: (27) 88.79.60. 38 rooms, 80–170F. Meals 42–80F. Restaurant closed August, and Sunday night and Saturday.

Festivals, Fairs and Sporting Events

The Sunday, Monday, and Tuesday after 5 July: **Fête des Gayants** celebrating the anniversary of Douai's becoming part of France in 1667. Five giants dressed in medieval costumes are paraded through the town to music and much revelry. After the giants have gone home for another year, there is an evening procession with music, dancing, carrying of torches and Chinese lanterns.

Week preceding 5 July: **Festival recitals of bell-ringing and organ; folk dancing, ballet and concerts.**

14 July: **Regatta, fireworks and military display.**

Garages

Renault: Route de Cambrai. Tel: (27) 87.29.72.
Citroën: 884 Rue de la République. Tel: (27) 87.36.22.
Fiat: 124 Avenue R. Salengro, Sin-le-Noble. Tel: (27) 88.82.28.
Ford: N17, Le Raquet, Lambres. Tel: (27) 87.30.63.

COMPIÈGNE

From Lille or Paris, Arsy/Compiègne exit, N31, 9Km
Inhabitants: 40,720
Office de Tourisme: Place de l'Hôtel de Ville

Compiègne, with its quiet, winding streets lined with old houses looking on to walled gardens, its outstanding historical monuments, its setting in one of the most beautiful forests in France, is well worth a visit for a leisurely lunch in an inn in the forest, or an overnight stop to enjoy fully its provincial charm and varied attractions.

Whatever the jaded traveller's interest Compiègne has an answer for it. For the art lover, the wealth of its architecture, with styles ranging from the Middle Ages to the 19th century, should satisfy the most demanding taste. For the historian the association of Compiègne with some of the most crucial events in French history and the long-standing royal connection should ensure plenty of interest.

In May 1430 Joan of Arc, captured by the English troops after being betrayed by John of Luxembourg, set off from the **Tour de Beauregard** (or **Tour Jeanne d'Arc**), close to the Hôtel de Ville. In 1918 the armistice between France and Germany was signed in the Forest of Compiègne at the **Clairière de l'Armistice** where a convenient rail track enabled Maréchal Foch's special carriage to be used as the meeting place. In 1940 the same train carriage was used again for the second armistice. Since the 6th century when a royal villa was built near the Church of St-Germain, Compiègne has been a royal city. Successive French kings have left their mark here, from Charles the Bold who built the first palace of the present site in 843 to Louis XIV and Napoléon III.

For the sportsman, the opportunities in Compiègne are just as numerous and varied: horse racing on the race course at the edge of the forest, golf on one of the oldest courses in France (eighteen holes), tennis on the courts nearby, rowing on the River Oise, swimming in the adjacent swimming pools both open-air and covered. Or one can explore the forest, discovering its villages and many-faceted beauty on horseback from the local *Haras* (stables) at the corner of the Boulevard Victor Hugo and the Rue St-Lazare, or by bicycle (hired from the Office de Tourisme) or by simply rambling along the hunting paths worn by the kings as they indulged in this king of sports and sport of kings.

Starting from the **Place de l'Hôtel de Ville**, where a flower market is held every Saturday, admire the **town hall** (*hôtel de ville*) itself, built of St-Leu d'Esserent stone, the finest in France. Built between 1499 and 1509 its late Gothic style heralds the Renaissance. The equestrian statue of Louis XII is surrounded by the figures of St-Denis, King Louis IX (St-Louis), Charles the Bold, Joan of Arc, Cardinal Pierre d'Ailly (native of the city) and Charlemagne. The *beffroi* still boasts the oldest existing bell dating from 1303, christened *La Bancloque*. Wait for the time to be struck by the 16th century figures called *Picantins*, which move every quarter hour.

Next to the town hall, the **Musée de la Figurine Historique** housing 85,000 tin soldiers, is a remarkable record of military costume throughout the ages. (Open every day 9–12am and 2–6pm.) Going along the Rue St-Corneille, see **St-Corneille**, the cloisters of the old abbey. Continuing down Rue Jeanne-d'Arc and then Rue St-Nicholas, admire the 13th century **Hôtel-Dieu** (hospital) founded by St-Louis. Cross over the Rue d'Austerlitz to reach the **Musée Vivenel.** This museum holds the best collection of Greek vases in France apart from the Louvre, as well as Egyptian and Roman antiquities. (Open every day 9–12am and 2–6pm, closed Tuesday and 1 January, Easter Monday, 1 May, Ascension Day, 14 July, 11 November, Christmas Day.)

The **Church of St-Antoine** at the corner of the Rue d'Austerlitz and the Rue St-Antoine has an elegant Flamboyant ornate façade and choir from the 16th century on a basic structure from the 13th century. The stained glass windows are 19th century. Take the Rue des Cordeliers up to the **Church of St Jacques** where Joan of Arc took communion the day before her capture, now a building of mixed styles from the 13th, 16th and 18th centuries.

Carry on up the Rue du Dahomey to reach the **Place du Palais** (now called **Place Charles de Gaulle**). From the right the vista provided by the **Parc du Palais**, which is 5Km long and reaches all the way down to the **Beaux Monts**, was created by Napoléon I in 1810 to remind his wife Marie-Louise of Austria of Schönbrunn. The full impact of the severely classical façade of the **Palace** can be experienced from the *place* before entering it on the right.

Louis XIV used to say: 'At Versailles I am housed like a king, at Fontainebleau like a prince, at Compiègne like a peasant', (a rather superior type of peasant!) The Sun King did not appreciate the limited comfort of Charles V's 14th century palace and ordered new apartments facing the forest. This turning towards nature, the park and the forest is the characteristic charm of Compiègne and one which subsequent additions carried even further. It was planned as a summer palace, airy and full of light. This explains the special place it always occupied in the hearts of French monarchs. Louis XV had it rebuilt in 1751 by Jacques-Ange Gabriel who used the awkwardly-levelled triangular site in a masterly fashion by placing the state appartments on the first floor facing the *cour d'honneur* but leading directly out on to the garden on the side of the park. From Louis XVI onwards Compiègne had a special romantic appeal to French sovereigns. Here Louis XVI met his queen, Marie-Antoinette of Austria, for the first time, when as a shy young prince he hardly dared glance at her. Here Marie-Antoinette's niece, Marie Louise of Austria, was bowled over by the impetuousness of her future husband, Napoléon I. Here Napoléon's nephew, Napoléon III, fell in love with the glamorous Spanish aristocrat, Eugénie de Montijo, who became his wife and for eighteen years presided at Compiègne over a brilliant court, giving a very exclusive kind of house party called the *Séries de Compiègne*, which were renowned for their stylish and lavish entertainment as well as for the personalities invited (aristocrats but also Pasteur, Verdi, Gounod, Flaubert and Viollet-le-Duc, the archeologist–architect).

The succession of rooms inside the palace offers a rich picture of the changes in style and taste in French interior decoration during the 18th and 19th centuries. Across the *cour d'honneur*, the **Musée du Second Empire** presents a faithful evocation of life at court and in the army in the 19th century with paintings, sculptures, *objets d'art* and personal mementoes of the imperial family. In another wing of the palace is the **Musée de la Voiture**, created in 1927 by the Touring Club de France. It has over 150 vehicles on display tracing the evolution of the car from the horse-drawn *hippomobiles* of the 18th century to the *De Dieu-Bouton* of

1899 which first broke the 100Km per hour record. The park, with its three avenues leading to the forest, is divided into the Small Park, with 18th century gardens altered by Napoléon I, and the Great Park, which he wanted 'to merge into the forest'. Palace and museums open every day 9.45–12am and 1.30–5.30pm, (4.30pm 1 November–1 March), closed Tuesday. Park open every day from dawn to dusk.

The **Forest of Compiègne** is one of the most beautiful in France and covers 15,000 Ha (about 38,000 acres). The main attractions are its magnificent woods of tall beech trees, its regal avenues and vistas cut through the forest by successive French kings from Clovis to Philip Augustes, François I to Louis XIV and Louis XV to Napoléon III, who all enjoyed the *chasse à courre* (stag hunting) here, as well as the various fascinating places to explore. These include:

The Clairière de l'Armistice (19Km from Compiègne by the Avenue Royale or 6Km on the D66) Visit the railway carriage in the spot where the two armistices were signed (it is not the original one but dates from the same period). The actual objects used by the signatories are exhibited in an outside building.

Les Beaux Monts (5Km by the Avenue des Beaux Monts) Magnificent oaks 500 years old and a wonderful view from the top make it a worthwhile excursion.

The Vieux-Moulin (10Km by the D332 and D973) Lovely village in woody setting at the foot of the Mont St-Marc. Wonderful views over the forest and the valley of the River Aisne.

Pierrefonds (16Km by the D332 and D85, 1,723 inhabitants) This lovely small city and its lake are dominated by the imposing Château de Pierrefonds, built in the 12th century and given to Louis d'Orléans by Charles VI, then destroyed in the 16th century and restored in the 19th by Viollet-le-Duc under Napoléon III's orders.

Morienval (15Km by the D332 and D163, 742 inhabitants) The Abbey of Morienval, one of the most beautiful Romanesque churches in the Ile de France, has in the ambulatory one of the earliest Gothic vaults. Before paying a visit to this lovely spot in its valley go and enjoy a meal at the Auberge du Bon Accueil.

Hotels and Restaurants

Résidence de la Forêt A very quiet, lovely private house (supposed to have belonged to the air pilot Georges Guynemer) converted into a very comfortable hotel, with restaurant, facing the golf and race courses. 112

Rue St-Lazare, 60200, Compiègne, Oise. Tel: (4) 420.22.86. 20 rooms, 70–150F. Meals 60–80F. Closed Sunday and Monday evenings and 15 January–15 February.

Hostellerie du Royal-Lieu (2Km on D932) A quality restaurant, with rooms. Enjoy a delicious meal in the cosy dining-room looking out on the forest before or after a refreshing brisk walk under the wonderful trees. Try some of the specialities: *Noisettes de Porcelet au Cidre* (tender pieces of suckling pig cooked in cider), *Gâteau de Coquilles St-Jacques au Beurre Rouge* (scallop mousse with red butter sauce), *Filets de Canard au Cidre* (duck breasts cooked in cider). 9 Rue de Sentis, 60200, Compiègne, Oise. Tel: (4) 420.10.24 (10Km from Compiègne). 20 rooms, 160–220F. Meals 80–150F. Open all year. Credit cards: AE, DC, VISA.

Auberge du Bon Accueil 10Km from Morienval, by the D332. Relax in the dining-room looking out on a lovely garden and be prepared for a gastronomic experience from the chef who has just been given the title of *Meilleur Ouvrier de L'Oise* (best chef in the county). Try the game dishes in season and the delicious *Morilles* (spring mushrooms from the forest), or the *Feuilleté de Petit Gris au Gingembre* (snails in pastry with ginger). Carrefour Morienval–Vaudrampont, 60127, Morienval, Oise. Tel: (4) 442.84.04. Meals 95–155F. Closed Monday evenings, Tuesday and February.

Festivals, Fairs and Sporting Events

October–15 April, Wednesdays and Saturdays: **stag hunting**
1 May: **Festival of the Lily of the Valley**
July, beginning: **horse racing grand prix**
September: **horse racing and horse show**
September: **antique fair**
Throughout the summer: **Séries de Compiègne** (various shows and exhibitions). Enquire at the Office de Tourisme.

Garages

Alfa Romeo: 2b Rue du Chevreuil. Tel: (4) 420.29.94.
BMW/Opel: 20 Rue de Clermont. Tel: (4) 483.27.17.
Citröen: Venette. Tel: (4) 83.28.28; night (4) 483.28.84.
Fiat: 24 Rue du Bataillon de France. Tel: (4) 440.12.90.
Ford: 186 Avenue O. Butin, Margny. Tel: (4) 483.32.32.
Peugeot: Rue Cl. Bayard. Tel: (4) 420.19.63.
Renault: Avenue Général Weigand. Tel: (4) 420.32.57.

Camping

SENLIS
From Lille, Senlis/Meaux exit, N324, 1.5Km

From Paris, Senlis exit, N324, 1.5Km
Inhabitants: 14,387
Office de Tourisme: Place du Parvis de Notre Dame, closed 1 December–
1 March, Tuesday and mornings.

Senlis is an ancient town built on a hill on the right bank of the River Nonette. In the midst of deep forests, just 44Km from Paris, it has all the charm of a cathedral city and the peace and quiet of the provinces. Spend the night here or have lunch before attempting the journey around Paris on your way to the south. It will be a rewarding experience, for the whole city is classified a Historical Monument.

Park your car and walk the **Rue Vieille de Paris**, climbing steeply towards the cathedral, and try to recapture the medieval past of Senlis. The Rue Vieille de Paris starts at the medieval ramparts now mostly large airy boulevards. The Merovingian and Carolingian kings (8th and 9th centuries) used to stay here in a fortified castle on the site of the first Roman fortifications. The last king to stay in the **château** was Henri II in the 16th century before Compiègne and Fontainebleau replaced Senlis in the French monarchs' affections and as their hunting-ground.

Before reaching the Rue du Châtel turn right into the Rue du Haubergier where the **Musée Haubergier** houses a museum of the archaeology of Senlis and the region in a lovely stone and brick Renaissance building. Carry on down the Rue du Châtel, which used to be the main street of Senlis, admiring the many fine old houses on the way to the Place du Parvis. Pause in front of the west façade of the **Cathedral of Notre Dame.**

Partly destroyed by fire in the early 16th century, it combines the sobriety of the 12th century (it was built ten years before Notre Dame de Paris in 1153), to the more richly decorated Flamboyant style of the late Gothic in the 16th century. The façade is wholly 12th century and there is a remarkable naturalism and freedom of treatment in its sculptures of the life of the Virgin and, on the tympanum, Her coronation. It is one of the earliest examples of the devotion shown to Mary by the Gothic sculptors. Enter through the south door to appreciate the majestic dimensions of the nave, with its rhythm of pillars and columns climaxing in the magnificent soaring effect of the choir. This cathedral is one of the greatest Gothic monuments in France.

Having paused to take in the atmosphere of silent prayer locked in the very stones of the building, explore the surrounding streets. Walk through the small garden to the east of the cathedral where the deconsecrated **Church of St-Pierre** is now a covered market place. Admire the west front in Flamboyant Gothic style bearing the date 1516 and perhaps designed by the great master of the Flamboyant style, the architect Martin Chambiges, while he was restoring the cathedral. Return to the Place du

Parvis and pass to the west of the cathedral to visit the **royal castle (Castel du Roi)**. A square keep and a few Romanesque and Gothic remains containing the bedchamber of the king and the oratory of St-Louis (King Louis IX) constitute a picturesque ensemble. (Open 10–12am and 2–6pm, closed Tuesday, Wednesday morning, Christmas Day, 1 January.)

In the park of the *château*, which is bordered by the Gallo-Roman fortifications, a priory, founded by St-Louis and rebuilt in the 18th century, houses the only **museum of hunting (Musée de la Vénerie)** in France. For those interested in the sport of kings, there are exhibits ranging from hunting costumes to hunting knives and *cors de chasse* (French horns), together with pictures and engravings. (Opening hours as for the *château*.)

To the west of the town a Roman amphitheatre was discovered in 1863. It dates from the 1st century AD and could seat 10,000 spectators. (Enter from the Place de Creil.)

Hotels and Restaurants

Hostellerie de la Port Bellon Simple, quiet and comfortable hotel with restaurant. 51 Rue Bellon, 60300, Senlis, Oise. Tel: 453.03.05. 19 rooms, 50–150F. Meals 58–110F. Credit card: VISA.

Rôtisserie de Formanoir An excellent restaurant just by the cathedral in the 16th century buildings of a former convent. A beautiful dining-room with old beams makes a fitting setting for a delectable lunch which could include: *Huîtres Chaudes en Coquille* (hot oysters in sauce) or *Ecrevisses aux Petits Légumes* (fresh-water crayfish with vegetables). 17 Rue du Châtel, 60300, Senlis, Oise. Tel: (4) 453.04.39. Meals 95–140F. Open all year.

Hôtel St-Eloi A modern, comfortable hotel on the non-motorway road to Paris (the N17). No restaurant. 40 Faubourg St-Martin, 60300, Senlis, Oise. Tel: (4) 453.02.93. 20 rooms 61–175F. Closed Sunday. Credit cards: AE, DC.

Festivals, Fairs and Sporting Events

May, second fortnight: **Salon des Arts et Métiers** (display of arts and crafts) in the Church of St-Pierre.

September (every second year): **Rendez-vous de Septembre.** For two days the whole city is closed off to cars. Musicians, singers, dancers and acrobats take over the streets and bring back to Senlis the medieval *joie de vivre* while hearty rustic banquets and buffets of medieval proportions sustain spectators and participants alike. This is, moreover, a unique opportunity to discover the hidden treasures of Senlis, as the owners of the beautiful old private houses, normally hidden away behind their walled gardens, open their doors to the visitors for these two days.

Garages
Citroën: 51 Faubourg St-Martin. Tel: (4) 453.12.42.
Peugeot: 56 Avenue de Creil. Tel: (4) 453.16.46.
Renault: 64 Avenue du Général de Gaulle. Tel: (4) 453.08.18.

CHANTILLY
From Lille, Senlis/Meaux exit, N324 to Senlis then D924, 11.5Km
From Paris, Senlis exit, N324 to Senlis then D924, 11.5Km
Inhabitants: 10,684
Office de Tourisme: Avenue du Maréchal Joffre, 1 March–15 November,
closed Tuesday

Depending on the traveller's interests, the name of Chantilly evokes either an elegant race course where the equivalent of the Derby and the Oaks take place every year, a château with royal connections and outstanding collections of paintings and *objets d'art* or simply a forest 42Km from Paris, where *chasse à courre* (stag hunting) still exists and where ramblers and riders can enjoy the natural beauty of its copses, groves and lakes by way of the old hunting paths. A golf course of eighteen holes at Lys Chantilly in the forest, is an added attraction to the sportsman, while several excellent inns and restaurants in the town and the forest make Chantilly an ideal stop near Paris, a place and experience to remember.

Coming from Senlis by the D924, turn left on the Grand Canal, a channelled tributary of the River Nonette. Before the Rue du Connétable turn left again under the Porte St-Denis. The best approach, however, is from the Chapelle St-Serval, by the D924 through the forest. Approaching Chantilly by this route, one gets the full impact of the château, as it lies below in its setting of lakes, canals, lawns and majestic trees.

Chantilly has featured in the history of France for the last 2,000 years. Five châteaux have been built on this spot on the River Nonette. Anne de Montmorency, Constable of France in the 16th century, a man of war as well as an enlightened patron of the arts, was the first of several impressive figures to own, transform and embellish Chantilly. Royal visitors such as Charles V, the Hapsburg emperor, admired the splendour of the new Renaissance château (only the **Petit Château** still exists). Henry IV (nicknamed the *Vert Galant*, the 'old buck') stayed here often while pursuing amorous adventures.

When the Grand Condé in the 17th century brought the gardener Le Nôtre to design the **park** and **forest**, the fountains became the most talked about in the whole of France. (Versailles would have to do better!) 'Chantilly was his (Condé's) delight', wrote Saint-Simon. All men and women of importance in the arts, politics or high society visited Chantilly: Bossuet, La Bruyère, Molière, Boileau, La Fontaine, Madame de

Sévigné. Louis XIV of course came to stay, with a retinue of 5,000. It was here at Chantilly that the faithful steward Vatel died by his own sword, when after twelve sleepless nights spent preparing the great repast for the king, there was no roast at two of the tables.

A great grandson of Condé, Monsieur le Duc, a man of great taste and refinement, gave to Chantilly the famous stables, which were described as 'ridiculously grand and beautiful'. Built by Jean Aubert in the 18th century, they were a masterpiece of monumental architecture of the time. The Revolution took its toll: only the Petit Château escaped destruction. The Duc d'Aumale, son of Louis Philippe, inherited Chantilly from his great uncle. It is to him that we owe the structure of the château as we now know it. The fifth **château**, of Renaissance style, was built between 1875 and 1881, and was a suitable setting for the remarkable collection which the Duc d'Aumale gathered, mostly while in exile in England from 1848 to 1870, when he lived in Twickenham at Orleans House and in Worcestershire at the Manor of Woodworton.

The château is now a **museum** and well worth a visit for the impeccable taste which went into the making of this collection, which is of very high quality and amazing diversity. From tapestries to paintings (including Sassetta, Raphael, Memling and Van Dyck) to a rare collection of the work of Clouet (French 16th century), the choice is vast. The **library** houses 12,500 books, each chosen for its rarity, binding or origin, as well as 1,493 manuscripts, among which the *Très Riches Heures du Duc de Berry* is the most outstanding being a priceless illustration of medieval life exquisitely executed and displayed for our delight. It was the duke's most prized possession, and he used to handle it only when wearing white kid gloves!

The **stables (Ecuries)**, on the right of the Porte St-Denis, turn their sumptuous façade towards the **race course** where the first race took place in 1833 between a guest at the château, Prince Labanoff, who had arrived from Russia to hunt stags, and his friends. As they were returning to the stables, the air was crisp, the turf inviting, the horses spirited, 'and the thundering hooves that morning heralded what was going to become one of the most famous race courses in the world', wrote Princesse Thérèse de Caraman-Chimay. Inside the immense hall where carriages are now displayed, 240 horses and a total of 420 hounds for stag, wild-boar and deer hunting, as well as the attendant staff, could be housed.

The **forest**, covering 6,300Ha has been developed over five centuries of careful and patient tending by aristocratic hunting enthusiasts. It is a place to explore with the same love and respect for nature. Motorists can use the main arteries which criss-cross the woods, while hunting paths offer ideal tracks by which ramblers and riders can discover the beauty of the groves of oaks, pines and silver birches, the lakes like the **Etangs de Commelles** (reached via the D924, in the direction of Paris from

Chantilly) or its picturesque follies, such as the **Château de la Reine Blanche**, near the *Etangs* and built as a *rendez-vous de chasse* (hunting lodge) in 1826 on the site of an old 14th century castle belonging to Queen Blanche of Navarre.

Hotels and Restaurants

Relais du Coq Chantant An excellent inn with delicious specialities such as: *Emincés de Ris de Veau aux Cèpes Crus* (sweetbreads with raw wild mushrooms, in season only), *Pigeonneau de Grain aux Poires Fraîches* (farm pigeon with fresh pears) and a well-stocked cellar. 21 Rue de Creil, 60500, Chantilly, Oise. Tel: (4) 457.01.28. Meals, 65–200F. Closed February. Credit cards: AE, DC.

Relais Condé At the edge of the forest, this restaurant, in a deconsecrated chapel, offers such delights as *Saumon Frais aux Pâtes Fraîches* (fresh salmon with fresh pasta) and *Tarte fine Chaude aux Pommes* (warm light apple tart), cooked by a former employee of the Tour d'Argent, and enjoyed on an open terrace in the garden. 42 Avenue du Maréchal Joffre, 60500, Chantilly, Oise. Tel: (4) 457.05.75. Meals 80–100F. Closed Monday, Tuesday and July. Credit cards: DC, VISA.

Les Quatre Saisons de Chantilly A good simple restaurant with a garden and terrace where the inclusive menu consists of a starter and a main course for a fixed price, for example *Saumon Frais à l'Aneth* (fresh salmon with dill) followed by *Andouillette à la Ciboulette Parfumée au Chablis* (sausage with chives and Chablis). 9 Avenue du Général Leclerc, 60500, Chantilly, Oise. Tel: (4) 457.04.65. Meals 48F.

Restaurant du Château Just opposite the stables a simple restaurant, with rooms, offering very honest cuisine in a garden with terrace. 22 Rue du Connétable, 60500, Chantilly, Oise. Tel: (4) 457.02.25. 8 rooms, 80–110F. Meals 70–100F. Credit cards: AE, VISA. Closed 5–26 November, 5–19 February, and Tuesday nights and Wednesday.

At **Lamorlaye** 7Km on the N16, is the **Hostellerie du Lys**, a very comfortable and quiet hotel in its own park with swimming pool and tennis court nearby. It has an excellent grill restaurant. Rond Point de la Reine, Lys Chantilly, 60260, Lamorlaye, Oise. Tel: (4) 421.26.19. 36 rooms, 160–220F. Meals 95–110F. Closed 19 December–4 January.

At **Toutevoie** 6.5Km by the D909 to Gouvieux, then the D162, is the **Pavillon St-Hubert**, a very quiet hotel, with restaurant, in an attractive site with a terrace overlooking the River Oise. 60270, Gouvieux, Oise. Tel: (4) 457.07.04. 19 rooms, 80–105F. Meals 85–125F.

Festivals, Fairs and Sporting Events

June: **horse racing** (*Prix du Jockey Club*)
June, second or third Sunday: **horse racing** (*Prix de Diane*)

July (end) and September: **horse show**
September, three first Sundays: **horse racing**

Garages
Citroën: Gouvieux. Tel: (4) 457.02.98.
Fiat/Lancia: 29 Avenue du Maréchal Joffre. Tel: (4) 457.13.83.
Opel: 33 Avenue du Maréchal Joffre. Tel: (4) 457.05.09.
Renault: 37 Avenue du Maréchal Joffre. Tel: (4) 457.01.59.

ERMENONVILLE
From Lille, Senlis/Meaux exit, N330, 13Km
From Paris, Senlis exit, N330, 13Km
Inhabitants: 604

Situated south of Senlis, Ermenonville is a small village, with a camping site, well worth a visit for the beauty of its setting at the edge of the **Forest of Ermenonville** and an ideal place for a family outing and picnic.

The **Jean-Jacques Rousseau Park**, just off the N330, was created by the Marquis de Girardin in the 18th century in emulation of the English-style gardens which he had admired at Blenheim and Stowe. He was also a great admirer of Jean-Jacques Rousseau, the 18th century philosopher, whose theory of the 'happy savage', and advocacy of a return to nature to improve Man's moral status, influenced the marquis's garden as much as its English antecedents. He was rewarded for his adulation of the philosopher when the latter came to stay at the **château** in May 1778. He remained there until his death in July 1778 and was buried in the **Ile des Peupliers** (the Island of Poplars) where a mausoleum in the shape of an ancient altar was erected bearing the words 'Here lies a Man of Truth and Nature' and 'Consecrate your Life to Truth' in Latin. (Rousseau's remains were moved to the Panthéon in Paris after the Revolution.) As in all the forests of the Ile de France it is in the autumn that the melancholy atmosphere most enhances the charm of the setting. Walk along the banks of the lake from the **Autel de la Rêverie** (the altar of meditation), where Rousseau loved to sit, to the Temple of Philosophy, a symbolic building in classical style, erected in honour of the world's greatest thinkers, and try to recapture the romantic mood of the 19th century writer Gérard de Nerval, hovering between the stuff of dreams and reality in works like *Sylvie*, set in this part of France. The park is open 9am–7pm. The château, built in the Middle Ages and much altered in the 17th and 18th centuries, is not open to the public.

After visiting Ermenonville's park, go back on to the N330 towards Senlis and drive for half a kilometre to the **Abbey of Chaalis.** The abbey was founded in 1136 by Louis XI. The monks lived in this idyllic spot a life of typical Cistercian austerity, reflected in the surviving ruins of the north transept. The abbot's private chapel, dating from the 13th century but much restored in the 19th, contains, on the vaulted ceiling, 16th century paintings often ascribed to the Italian Primaticcio, who worked at Fontainebleau. They date from the time of the abbot Cardinal de Ferrara, son of Lucrezia Borgia and Alfonso d'Este, and builder of the Villa d'Este at Tivoli.

The **gardens** were laid out then too, but the 18th century saw the destruction of most of the abbey. The domain which inspired Romantic poets and painters (a pupil of Ingres restored the 16th century paintings) changed hands several times before being finally owned by a remarkable woman, Madama Jacquemart-André, who in 1912 bequeathed the château (as it was by then) to the Institut de France. Built in the 18th century by the same architect as the stables at Chantilly, Jean Aubert, the **château** is now a **museum** containing Madame Jacquemart-André's wide-ranging collection of Roman and oriental antiquities, medieval sculpture and *objets d'art*, and Italian Renaissance painting, sculpture and furniture. Last but not least, there is a truly magnificent collection of 18th century furniture in recreated interiors. It is indeed, as she herself said, 'a place of beauty and rest'. (Open 2–5.30pm, Sundays, Mondays, Wednesdays, Saturdays and public holidays, first Sunday of March to 1 November. Gardens open 10am–7pm, every day May–November.)

Natural beauty is very much in evidence too, and the landscape around the two lakes, where the monks used to breed fish for their table, is full of charm, while the **Mer de Sable** (the sandy sea), directly opposite on the other side of the N330, is a natural curiosity of great attraction. A deep bank of sand had surfaced following the deforestation of this particular spot at the end of the 18th century. Since then no vegetation has grown back, and the *Mer de Sable* now looks like a white lunar landscape of dunes, surprising in the midst of the forest.

A small train leading to a village peopled by clockwork figures crosses the *Mer de Sable* and an amusement park of 30Ha makes it a perfect stop for the whole family to enjoy after a picnic in the forest. Combine this visit with a walk in the **Desert**, the wildest part of Ermenonville's park, 1.5Km down the N330, where the heath, lake and trees conjure up the spirit of Jean-Jacques Rousseau's 'happy savage', back to primeval nature. He used to love wandering along its paths, immersing himself in its unspoilt atmosphere. We too can gain much pleasure and serenity from its untamed quality. Or else go to Ermenonville's **zoo and safari park** which boasts a wide selection of animals from dolphins to lions and orang-outangs. Access is indicated from the N330, opposite the Desert's lake, about 1Km down the lane.

Hotels and Restaurants

Croix d'Or Quiet, simple, comfortable hotel, with restaurant. Place de l'Eglise, 60440, Nanteuil-le-Haudoin, Oise. Tel: (4) 454.00.04. 11 rooms, 72–110F. Meals 66F. Closed Friday and 15 December–1 March.

Auberge de Fontaine Excellent restaurant with rooms. Fontaine Chaalis, 60300, Senlis, Oise. Tel: (4) 454.20.22. 7 rooms, 125–145F. Meals 88–110F.

Camping

Autoroute du Soleil
Paris–Lyon (A6)

The A6 leaves the **Ile de France** soon after **Nemours** having passed through **Fontainebleau** and its forest of tall trees and picturesque sand-stone formations. From then onwards it runs through the varied part of France called **Bourgogne (Burgundy).**

Between Nemours and **Auxerre** the A6 crosses the **Gâtinais**, a country of heathland, lakes and pine trees, a land for fishing and shooting, rich in game of all sorts. From Auxerre to **Avallon** the **Puisaye** displays the same characteristics but the more fertile land allows cattle breeding and the famous Charolais cattle can be spotted, creamy white in the fresh green fields behind the high hedges. The **Auxois**, around **Semur-en-Auxois**, a rich land, concentrates entirely on cattle breeding: the white Charolais for meat, and the spotted breed from Montbeliard for milk and robust beasts of burden. On top of some of the rocky promontories old fortified cities such as Semur stand as sentinels at the crossroads of routes going north and south, east and west.

To the south-west of the Auxois, the **Morvan** with its poorer soils is characterised by a thick blanket of forests which covers its high hills, and by lakes and clear rivers. From the 16th century to the beginning of our own, logs felled from the forest used to be floated all the way down to Paris to furnish the capital's fireplaces. On a given day the dams would be opened and carry away the logs piled up by the woodcutters on the river banks. The **Lac des Settons** was created for this particular purpose. Very wild and sparsely populated, the Morvan is a very beautiful nature reserve which modern life has hardly touched.

To the south, next to the Morvan, the **Charollais** with its wide undulating countryside of rich fields raises the renowned breed of white cattle which are fattened for thirty months on the thick, rich grass. Between **Beaune** and **Dijon**, the **Côte d'Or** is the very heart of Burgundy. The composition of the soil, the south-westerly orientation of the slopes, the climate and the particular kind of grapes, the *Pinot Noir*, all combine to produce the liquid gold, the great wine of Burgundy. The higher ground is occupied by varied crops, woods and fields, while 37,500Ha of the southern slopes are thickly covered with the famous vineyards, the names of which ring like a luscious hymn to Bacchus, so sensuously evocative are they of the unique quality of the great Burgundy wines.

The **Côte de Nuits**, south of Dijon, is a narrow band of low hills with a dozen villages along its **Route des Grands Crus** (Great Wines Route). It is the home of world-famous red wines, such as **Gevrey-Chambertin, Clos**

de-Vougeot, Vosne-Romanée and **Nuits-St-Georges.**

The **Côte de Beaune**, south of Beaune, is characterised by its grand red wines like **Pommard, Corton** and **Volnay** and some prestigious whites such as **Mersault** and **Montrachet.**

The **Hautes Côtes**, the higher part of both the Côte de Nuits and Côte de Beaune, produce a **Bourgogne Aligoté**, a white wine of fruity taste which when mixed with **Crème de Cassis** (blackcurrant liqueur from Dijon), constitutes that favourite Burgundian aperitive **Kir** (from the name of Canon Kir, mayor of Dijon).

Around **Mâcon**, a range of hills prolongs the Côte d'Or. The **Mâconnais** produces a great white wine, the **Pouilly-Fuissé**. In the plain it is a rich country of poultry breeding and a range of crops. The **Côte de Beaujolais** overlooks the valley of the **River Saône** and its sunny slopes cover an area about 60Km long and 12Km wide. By geographical position and tradition, the Beaujolais region belongs more to the **Lyonnais** than to Burgundy.

Burgundy is a very old part of France where successive civilisations have left their imprint over thousands of years. Four thousand years ago a race of men which had attained enough sophistication to practise the art of drawing lived in the **grottoes** at **Arcy-Sur-Cure**. The famous Arcy horse is a visual record of this nebulous past. During the Bronze Age, Burgundy used to trade in tin originating in Britain, exporting it to Greece and Italy. The famous bronze **Vix vase** in the **Châtillon Museum** and the gold diadem found in a tomb date from this period.

Burgundy had already achieved a high level of civilisation by Roman times. It was at **Alesia** on top of **Mont Auxois** that the independence of the country of Gaul was relinquished by a battle against the Romans and the defeat of Vercingétorix. At the collapse of the Roman Empire, the most civilised of the barbarian tribes, the *Burgondes*, invaded the country and gave their name to their new territory. Burgundia became Burgundy.

By the 5th century AD, Christianity was spreading throughout Burgundy. In the 9th century Charlemagne established the basis of Burgundy as we know it by splitting his empire between his three sons. The River Saône became a frontier, its right bank being the heart of the Duchy of Burgundy, owing reluctant allegiance to the King of France. From the 11th to the 14th centuries Burgundy was at the forefront of Christian expansion, and its spiritual, intellectual and artistic centre. In the 11th century, **Cluny**, the great Benedictine abbey was more important than Rome. 'You are the light of the world', the Pope told St Hugh, Cluny's abbot. The line of aristocratic abbots ensured the importance of Cluny in the affairs of the time; they were the counsellors of kings and popes alike. The abbey was rich and powerful, and its influence radiated all over Europe. The abbey church itself remained the largest church in Christendom until the building of St Peter's in Rome in the 16th century.

However, against the comparatively ostentatious display of wealth found at Cluny, in the 12th century, the voice of St-Bernard was preaching a return to austerity and poverty. The monks of the **Order of Cîteaux** at **Clairvaux** vied for power with the Cluniac order and St-Bernard played an active if reluctant part in the politics of Europe as a whole.

Many abbeys and churches of this period are witnesses to this period of rapid development for Christianity. The 'white mantle of the new churches' is woven with names such as **Tournus, Vézelay** and **Autun.** During the 14th and 15th centuries the court of the **Valois, Dukes of Burgundy** was a place of luxurious, refined living and the centre of an artistic activity which, attracting artists from Flanders, Spain, Germany, France and Italy, created a Burgundian School of architecture and sculpture. At the same time painting, while owing much to northern realism and treatment of light, developed here a warmth all its own.

The towns were proud and prosperous, the churches magnificently endowed, and the Dukes were extending their possessions to the northern territories of **Flanders, Luxembourg** and for a time the **Duchy of Lorraine.** The power and magnificence of Burgundy were at their zenith. Such a wealth of natural, artistic and intellectual riches made it an attractive prey for its immediate neighbours, and in 1476 Louis XI of France occupied Burgundy, on the death of the last of the Valois Dukes, **Charles le Téméraire**, who dreamt of being a new Alexander. In 1601 the duchy formally became part of France.

The memories of past glories however still live on in such jewels of the Burgundian crown as Dijon, the old capital, Beaune, with its famous *hôtel-Dieu* (hospital), and such lesser known fortified towns as Avallon and Semur-en-Auxois. All bear witness of the grandeur which was once Burgundy, in which so many buildings, whether simple fortified farms, rustic and homely, or princely palaces exquisitely adorned, are fashioned with the unmistakable hallmark of good taste developed by centuries of civilised life. That same grandeur is alive today in the incomparable bouquet of Burgundy's great wines.

GASTRONOMY

Burgundy has indeed been blessed by the benevolent gods who dispense the pleasures of the table. The combination of a favourable geographical position and climate, and the ingenuity and creativity of man have produced remarkable achievements in the culinary arts. **Dijon**, with its annual gastronomic fair, preserves the traditional Burgundian virtues of good drinking and good eating. Even in Roman times Dijon was recognised as a home of good food (some Latin inscriptions on stone fragments in the archaeological museum tell us as much!)

The first vineyards were introduced by the Romans, but more significant is the labour of the monks of the Middle Ages, particularly the

Cistercians, which transformed the lands given to the religious communities into vineyards, by deforestation and careful tending of the soil. All the great names such as **Chablis, Pommard, Meursault, Clos de Vougeot** etc were created in the 12th century or after. The techniques and traditions themselves have carried on more or less unchanged. The monks, who started their work for the greater glory of God and sold their wines in order to provide for the needy, have handed down a tradition, which remains intact, of devotion to quality in the making of the great Burgundy wines.

In the 14th century the wines of Burgundy acquired a fame which has never faltered since. In 1477 Louis XI, having occupied Burgundy, ordered for his own consumption the total output of the **Clos des Ducs** vineyard at **Volnay**, an action which marks him out as a connoisseur! In the 18th century the time, care and devotion which goes into the making of a great wine was more widely recognised. At **Beaune** first, then at **Dijon**, the first dealers started exporting their wines all over Europe. Nowadays the great wines are beyond the reach of all but the best-lined wallets, as quality is always given precedence over quantity. However the humbler Burgundies, made not from the noble **Pinot Noir** grape which produces all the prestigious names, but from the humbler **Gamay** are very good. In ordering wine look out for **Bourgogne Ordinaire** (*Gamay*) and **Bourgogne Passetoutgrain** (*Gamay* and *Pinot Noir* mixed). Tasting of both the great and lesser names is available in countless *caves* at the villages concerned.

As for **brandy**, try the *Marc de Bourgogne*, distilled from grapes after the last pressing. *Crème de Cassis* is a sweet blackcurrant liqueur made at Dijon, while *Prunella* (sloe) and *Anisette* (aniseed) contain less sugar. The remarkable variety of fresh products available in Burgundy make it a paradise for the gourmet, quite apart from the wine. Blessed with the unequalled Charolais beef, game from the Gâtinais, poultry from Bresse, and fresh-water fish from the Loire (pike etc), and the mountain rivers of the Morvan (trout, fresh-water crayfish), Burgundy offers as well many varieties of mushrooms from its forests and delectable fruit (cherries, blackcurrants, etc) from its orchards, without mentioning its *escargots* (snails) of world fame.

Brillat-Savarin, the 18th century lawyer, but more famous for his culinary writings, was a Burgundian and claimed that the pleasures of the table were to be enjoyed only by *les hommes d'esprit* (people of wit and taste). He recorded in detail the banquets held at the time of the *vendanges* (grape harvest), with their plentiful fare fit for both gourmet and gourmand! Then as now the menu would include many wine-based sauces: the *Meurettes* used for fish (carp, tench, eel), sweetbreads, eggs and beef. Notable dishes using a wine sauce include: *Oeufs en Meurettes* (poached eggs, with a red wine sauce) and *Boeuf Bourguignon* (beef stew with red wine sauce). Cream is part of many dishes too, such as *Jambon à la Crème* (ham with a cream sauce). *Saupiquet* is a piquant cream sauce used to accompany ham. Other specialities include: *Jambon Persillé* (ham in aspic with parsley), *Coq au Vin* (capon in a wine sauce) and *Pochouse* (fish stew with wine, similar to *Matelote* and usually using a fresh-water fish such as eel).

The **cheeses** of Burgundy are delicious on their own but also complement the wine beautifully. The main cheeses are *Bleu de Bresse* (mild blue cheese), *Epoisses* (soft with orange surface), *Chaource* (creamy, best in summer and autumn), *Amour de Nuits* (very similar to *Chaource* but even more subtle in taste) and *Chevroton de Mâcon* (goat cheese with nutty taste and bluish surface).

The region's **sweets** include: *Nonette* and *Pain d'Epice* (spiced honey cake, the first in the shape of a small scone, the second in a loaf) from Dijon, *Massepain* (small marzipan cakes) from Arnay-le-Duc, and the traditional biscuits of Avallon and Chablis.

FONTAINEBLEAU
From Paris, Fontainebleau exit, N37 and N7, 16Km
From Lyon, Fontainebleau exit, N7, 14Km
Inhabitants: 19,595
Office de Tourisme: 38 Rue Grande, closed Saturday afternoon

Fontainebleau is a must for anyone remotely interested in history. There, as Napoléon said, is 'the house of centuries, the true dwelling of kings'. The château therefore is the focal point of any visit. However the château only came into existence because of the French kings' passion for hunting and the surrounding forest harbouring game such as stags, wild boars, herons and kites, all highly prized catches. The forest is the strangest, most spectacular and fascinating in the Ile de France, well worth a visit to ramble, ride or have a picnic, to discover its particular atmosphere and charm. Famous inns and restaurants provide fare fit for a king. Sport is well catered for at Fontainebleau. Two **race courses**, the **Hippodrome de la Solle** in the forest and the **Hippodrome of the Grand Parquet**, are venues for race meetings and horse shows. A **golf course** of eighteen holes, off the N51, spreads by the Gorge du Loup, while tennis, riding, stag hunting (in the winter) and swimming in the open-air and covered pools are also available.

Since the 12th century French kings, St-Louis for example, have loved to come and hunt at Fontainebleau, the name coming from a spring, Fontaine Bliaud, still in the garden. The town itself remained a hamlet until the 19th century when the taste for country resorts in the peace and quiet of the forest developed. The true creator of Fontainebleau was

François I in the 16th century. He brought Italian artists such as Rosso and Primaticcio and not only made of the medieval hunting lodge an actively creative artistic centre from which Renaissance concepts and decorative schemes spread all over France and Europe, but also gave to his **château** the lustre and appeal which it retained for all subsequent French kings down to Napoléon I, Louis Philippe and Napoléon III. It was the home of the Valois dynasty before Versailles was built, and it reassumed this place in the hearts of French monarchs after the fall of the Bourbons. François I used to say 'Let us go home', when he spoke of Fontainebleau, ideally situated between his palaces in Paris and those of the Loire Valley.

This royal devotion to Fontainebleau explains the enormous diversity in style and decoration, as each successive generation added its own contribution to the favourite family seat. François I gave it the **Cour du Cheval Blanc** (known since Napoléon I as the **Cour des Adieux**, as it is here that he bade farewell to the Imperial Guard in 1814 after his abdication) and the **Cour de l'Ovale**, the two being linked by the famous **Galérie François Premier** from which the European Renaissance took its inspiration, as well as the **Porte d'Orée** (from the French word *orée*, verge of the forest) of Italianate design.

Henri II carried on his father's work and the **Salle de Bal** (ballroom) displays his cipher, 'H', with that of his wife, 'C' for Catherine of Medici. However they are linked together to form a double 'D' cipher–for Diane de Poitiers, the king's mistress! This was the sort of *double-entendre* the Renaissance courts loved.

Henri IV devoted much time to Fontainebleau. His wife Marie of Medici gave birth to his son and heir Louis XIII at the château in 1601. The **Cour des Offices** and the **Cour des Princes**, together with the **Galerie de Diane**, are his achievement.

Louis XIII endowed Fontainebleau with the magnificent horseshoe staircase in the **Cour du Cheval Blanc** and the two sumptuous ceilings in the **Salle du Trône** (throne room) and the **Chambre de la Reine.**

In the reign of Louis XIV, a passionate hunter, the entire court moved to Fontainebleau every autumn for four or five weeks of hunting. This move used to be referred to as *le voyage de Fontainebleau*. In 1684 Louis XIV married Madame de Maintenon here.

Louis XV and Louis XVI both redecorated the suite of royal apartments. Marie-Antoinette's **boudoir**, executed between 1785 and 1786, is a perfect example of the exquisite taste and craftsmanship of French 18th century art. All silver and gold it epitomises the ethos of an era, a height of refinement which has never been reached again.

Napoléon I brought to the **Petits Appartements** his 'passionate interest in detail' and ordered every fitting himself. His nephew Napoléon III entertained here on a grand scale. The imperial family enjoyed at

Fontainebleau their last happy days together before the turmoil which brought to an end the royal and imperial regimes of France.

The gardens have been as much the subject of alterations over the centuries as the château itself. The **Jardin de Diane** dates from the Middle Ages, while the **Grotte de la Tour des Pins** by the Italian architect Serlio (near the **Etang des Carpes**) dates from François I. The Etang des Carpes (carp pond) was created in the days of Henri II and stocked up with enormous fish which were hunted by specially trained cormorants in a sort of aquatic falconry, a sport of Chinese invention. The **Fontaine Bliaud** (or **Bleau**) stands in the centre of the **Jardin Anglais**, laid out in the 19th century. The **formal parterre** was designed by the famous 17th century gardener Le Nôtre. (Château and gardens open 10–12am and 2–6pm, closed Tuesday.)

The **forest** which covers nearly 20,000Ha of sandy wasteland punctuated by sandstone rocks which pile up in vast and chaotic picturesque landscapes ('our delightful deserts of Fontainebleau' as François I used to call them) is best explored from the **Route Ronde** (D301), a circular road taking in all the historical spots in the forest as well as some of the rock formations. The trees in the forest are mostly oaks, beeches and silver birches; pines were only introduced in the 19th century reforestation. To get on to the *Route Ronde*, coming from Paris by the N7, turn right at the **Carrefour du Grand Veneur.** After 2.5Km leave the car to explore on foot the **Gorges de Franchard** at the **Carrefour de la Croix de Franchard.** The rocky gorges are a wonderful sight from the **Grand Point de Vue**, a plateau reached via the house next to the chapel in the clearing known as the **Ermitage de Franchard**, a 13th century pilgrimage spot centred around a weeping rock shedding, supposedly, miraculously healing water. The panorama over the forest, the gorges and the distant plain is well worth the climb.

Returning to the D301 or *Route Ronde*, turn right to reach the **Carrefour de Recloses** where, in the 16th century, the Emperor Charles V of Austria was entertained by François I with festivities and jousting lasting for days. Another 2.5Km and the **Croix de St Herem** marks the place where Napoléon I contrived in 1804 to meet Pope Pius VII, whom he had summoned to crown him Emperor, apparently while hunting wild boar. A further 4Km, at the **Croix du Grand Maître**, turn left on to the D148 to reach the avenue leading to the château.

Hotels and Restaurants

L'Aigle Noir A truly palatial hotel with luxuriously furnished rooms overlooking the gardens of the château, all in period style either Louis XVI, Empire or Restoration. The restaurant offers superb cuisine, striking just the right note between hallowed tradition and an awareness of the modern taste for lighter food. Prices are high but a glimpse at the menu, including *Rouget en Salade avec une Vinaigrette au Jus de Truffe* (red mullet with a salad garnish and a truffle sauce), *Emincé d'Agneau aux Légumes Confits* small pieces of lamb with vegetables), and the superb wine list will justify the cost of a wonderful meal cooked with creativity and an expertise originating in the best teaching grounds (the chef was at Maxim's and the Tour d'Argent) and served with style in a luxurious Empire interior. 27 Place Napoléon-Bonaparte, 77300, Fontainebleau, Seine-et-Marne. Tel: (6) 422.32.65. 29 rooms, 295–440F. 4 suites, 530F. Meals 115–230F. Open all year. Credit cards: AE, DC, EC, VISA.

Le Bistrot St-Antoine An offshoot of the Aigle Noir, just round the corner, this restaurant offers very good simple food at a fraction of the price of its more prestigious parent. 20 Rue de France, 77300, Fontainebleau, Seine-et-Marne. Tel: (6) 422.15.33. Meals 70F. Closed 2–23 August, 8–15 February, and Sunday evening and Monday. Credit cards: AE, DC, EC, VISA.

Ile de France In a lovely 1830 house set in a pretty garden, a Hong Kong chef is seducing his French customers with such specialities as *Canard Laqué Pékinois* (Peking Duck) and *Cuisses de Grenouilles en Papillotes* (frogs' legs in foil). 128 Rue de France, 77300, Fontainebleau, Seine-et-Marne. Tel: (6) 422.85.15. Meals 29.50–100F. Open all year. Credit cards: DC, EC, VISA.

Chez Arrighi Family restaurant with homely dishes such as *Lapin à la Moutarde* (roast rabbit with mustard sauce) served in a comfortable dining-room. 53 Rue de France, 77300, Fontainebleau, Seine-et-Marne. Tel: (6) 422.29.43. Meals 49–180F. Closed Monday, and Tuesday lunch-time. Credit cards: AE, DC, EC, VISA.

Toulouse Small, comfortable hotel without restaurant. 183 Rue Grande, 77300, Fontainebleau, Seine-et-Marne. Tel: (6) 422.22.73. 18 rooms, 74–178F.

At **Recloses** in the forest, 7Km by the N7 and the D63E, heading south, is the **Casa del Sol** a very quiet small comfortable hotel, with restaurant, in the forest of Fontainebleau. 77116, Ury-par-Recloses, Seine-et-Marne. Tel: (6) 424.20.35. 8 rooms, 150–190F. Meals 85–105F. Closed November–March, and Monday night and Tuesday. Credit cards: AE, DC.

Festivals, Fairs and Sporting Events
April to September: **horse shows**
Mid June: **horse show** at the Hippodrome du Grand Parquet
August, first three weeks: **theatrical performances** in the Salle des Colonnes at the château.
September, Wednesday of the third week: **horse racing** (Grand Prix) at the Hippodrome de la Solle.

October, second week: **horse shows** (French championships)
November–April: **stag hunting** in the forest.

Garages

Alfa Romeo/Lada: 86 Rue de France. Tel: (6) 422.31.59.
Austin/Jaguar/Morris/Rover/Triumph: 111 Rue de France. Tel: (6)
422.31.88.
Fiat: 44 Rue du Château. Tel: (6) 422.24.19.
Ford: 9 Rue de la Chancellerie. Tel: (6) 422.15.08.
Renault: 74 Rue de France. Tel: (6) 422.24.52.
Volvo: 9 Rue de la République. Tel: (6) 422.17.15.

BARBIZON

From Paris, Fontainebleau exit, N37 and D64, 7Km
From Lyon, Cély exit, N372, N37 and D64, 7Km
Inhabitants: 1,189

Barbizon is a small village the very ordinariness of which made it a cheap place to live for the 19th century Realist artists who came here – among them Rousseau, Daubigny and Millet. In this forest hamlet they could be part of the simple rural life of country people. Nowadays the village consists of a long main street lined with hotels, restaurants and a few private villas, and the name Barbizon has become synonymous with luxury hotels and inns serving high-quality food. The surrounding forest, though, has changed very little since the 19th century, and is an ever-lasting source of pleasure in natural beauty.

For the artists of the **Barbizon School**, moving away from Paris to the countryside was a means of retreat from the artificial and conventional world of the Academy's *Salons* (yearly exhibitions) whose hanging committees were repeatedly selecting anaemic, backward-looking paintings and consistently refusing theirs. They felt that in order to be true to their artistic vocation and to put across their social message they had to live the life they depicted in their works.

Millet was actually of peasant stock, from Normandy, and doubtless felt more at home in the rural environment of Barbizon than in a Parisian studio. 'Peasant I am, peasant I shall die. I have to tell things as I have seen them.' The woman depicted in the celebrated 'Angélus', Adèle Moscher, lived at Barbizon and to the end of her days was called *La Mère Angélus*. Some of the houses where the artists used to live can be visited. **Millet's house** is the first house on the left in the Grand' Rue, coming from Fontainebleau. (Open 10am–6pm, closed Tuesday.) **Théodore Rousseau's house** is on the same side of the street, behind the war memorial. (Open 10am–6pm, 1 November–Easter. Also open 11am–5pm, 2 November–Easter.)

The inn where the artists used to eat very cheaply (55 sous, including unlimited wine), the **Vielle Auberge du Père Ganne**, can be visited also. On the walls and furniture are paintings by the artists. (Open 10am–6pm, Easter–1 November, closed Tuesday. Also open 2 November–Easter, 11.30am–4pm, Wednesday, Friday, Sunday.)

It is ironical to see the humble surroundings of the artists, and to contrast the dire penury they knew with Barbizon's current celebrity, which it owes to the glory they have assumed posthumously, and to its reputation for exclusive cuisine provided for a wealthy clientele.

From Barbizon an excursion through the forest can include a visit to the rocky **Gorges d'Apremont**. Follow the Grand' Rue and leave Barbizon, by the Route Forestière which continues it. At the **Carrefour du Bas Bréau** turn right into the Route de Sully. The **Chaos d'Apremont** and the gorges are on either side of the road and are best explored on foot. Climb up the path to the left of the cottage by the Carrefour. Follow the signs to the top of the picturesque rocky promontory, to enjoy a panoramic view over the gorges and the valley.

Hotels and Restaurants

Hôtellerie du Bas Bréau A luxuriously appointed hotel in an historic inn opened in 1867 as the Auberge de l'Exposition by an owner who used to exhibit paintings by Corot, Millet, Diaz etc on his walls. Napoléon III and the Empress Eugénie were visitors, while Robert Louis Stevenson was a regular guest. There is still an atmosphere of elegance and refinement characteristic of a more leisurely age, and the tone of the welcome is to make one feel a privileged guest in a private home. The restaurant is truly magnificent and one can enjoy in the beautiful setting of the garden specialities such as: *Grouse d'Ecosse aux Epinards et Foie Gras* (grouse with spinach and foie gras), *Le Suprême de Turbot au Pamplemousse Rose* (turbot fillet with pink grapefruit), and the *Soufflé chaud aux pralines* (hot praline soufflé). Rue Grande, 77630, Barbizon, Seine-et-Marne. Tel: (6) 066.40.05. 12 rooms, 500–550F. 7 suites. Meals 170–230F. Closed 1 January–15 February. Credit cards: AE, VISA.

Les Charmettes Lovely, comfortable, old hotel, with restaurant, in a pretty garden. 40 Rue Grande, 77630, Barbizon, Seine-et-Marne. Tel: (6) 066.40.21. 40 rooms and suites, 80–360F.

Hostellerie de la Clé d'Or The oldest hotel in Barbizon opposite the Vieille Auberge du Père Ganne, with comfortable rooms giving out on to the garden. With restaurant. 76 Rue Grande, 77630, Barbizon, Seine-et-Marne. Tel: (6) 066.40.96. 13 rooms, 130–200F. Closed Sunday night, Monday, and 15 November–15 December. Credit cards: AE, EC, VISA.

La Flambée Small country inn offering an all-inclusive menu with excellent grilled steaks as the main course, plus a starter, cheese, a desert, wine and coffee for 60F. Very good value. 26 Grande Rue, 77630, Barbizon,

Seine-et-Marne. Tel: (6) 066.40.78. Closed evening Monday–Thursday.
Le Relais Simple restaurant with a small garden, serving traditional French food such as *Pied de Veau Ravigote* (calf's foot in a piquant white sauce) or *Caneton aux Fruits de la Saison* (duckling with fruit). 2, Avenue Charles de Gaulle, 77630, Barbizon (Seine et Marne). Tel: (6) 06.40.28. 4 rooms, 60F. Meals 70–120F. Closed Tuesday, Wednesday, and 16 August–10 September and Christmas.
Au Grand Veneur, on the N7, 1.5Km in the direction of Fontainebleau. Traditional restaurant of well-established reputation specialising in game (in season) and offering an elegant and well-thought-out cuisine in a vast dining room decorated with hunting trophies. 77630, Barbizon, Seine-et-Marne. Tel: (6) 066.40.44. Meals 200F. Credit cards: AE, DC.

Festivals, Fairs and Sporting Events
November: **painting exhibition and competition.**

MILLY-LA-FORÊT
From Paris, Fontainebleau exit, N37 and D372, 7.5Km
From Lyon, Cély exit, D372, 7.5Km
Inhabitants: 3,492

Milly is a very old small market town gathered around its handsome 15th century **Halles** (covered market), which has kept its rural atmosphere while becoming something of a fashionable resort for Parisians in search of peace and quiet. An outstanding restaurant with a 12th century vaulted dining-room, part of a former convent, makes it a pleasant halt for the traveller.

The history of Milly goes back a long time. There is even a standing stone at a nearby farm, and archaeological excavations have brought up a wealth of objects, from sarcophagi to Roman jewellery. The **forest** around the town provided the people with readily available game and food. The **château** was built in the Middle Ages. Only two of the gate-house towers survive, above the River Ecole. The Seigneur de Granville, the lord of Milly, refurbished it in the 15th century and built the *Halles* by royal licence, granted by Louis XI in 1479. Built of oak and chestnut timber which has become very hard over the centuries, its beams are of impressive dimensions and support a high, pitched roof.

The **church** (11th and 12th centuries) has retained its elegant tower. The choir stalls with their misericords date from the same period. Milly has been a centre for the cultivation of medicinal herbs since the 12th century, when a religious community set up a Maladerie (infirmary) de St-Blaise to tend the lepers. The *simples* (medicinal herbs) are still cultivated in the pollution-free environment of the forest and sent all over

France, seasonal workers from Brittany being hired every year to gather them.

The **Chapel of St-Blaise des Simples**, restored in 1958 and decorated in 1959 by Jean Cocteau, writer, dramatist, poet and artist, was part of the 12th century hospital. Around the chapel, in a small botanical garden, are grown the most commonly used herbs. The inside of the chapel is entirely covered with frescoes and line drawings showing the Crowning with Thorns and the Resurrection as well as medicinal herbs – mint, aconite and belladona – all depicted in the typically graphic style and subdued colours of Cocteau. Jean Cocteau lived at Milly-la-Forêt in one of the former gatehouse towers of the old château in the Rue de Lau, while Christian Dior converted the **water mill** into a weekend cottage. (Chapel open 10–12am and 2–6pm, closed Tuesday.)

Hotels and Restaurants

Le Moustier Exquisite and subtly refined cuisine in a 12th century vaulted dining-room belonging to a former convent and very atmospheric. The menu reads like a poem and tastes like a dream: *Mousseline d'Huîtres aux Herbes* (oyster mousse with herbs), *Filets de Sole à la Vapeur de Tilleul* (sole fillets cooked in lime-blossom steam), *Soupe de Melon et d'Asperges aux Fruits de la Passion* (melon and asparagus soup with passion fruit). The harmonious combination of delectable food, refined décor and excellent service is a delight. 41bis Rue Langlois, 91490, Milly-la-Forêt, Essonne. Tel: (6) 498.92.52. Meals 110–260F. Closed Monday night and Tuesday. Credit card: VISA.

Garages

Peugeot: 5 Rue du Lau. Tel: (6) 498.80.12.

NEMOURS

From Paris or Lyon, Nemours exit, N375, 2Km
Inhabitants: 11,233
Office de Tourisme: 17 Rue des Tanneurs, closed every morning except Saturday and Sunday during the summer

Nemours is an old Roman city on the **River Loing** which subsequently became the seat of a duchy. Nowadays it is a pleasant market town and a favourite weekend and holiday resort for Parisians (Paris is only 79Km away), because of its attractive setting and the sporting activities it offers. Go rambling in the surrounding woods and the **Valley of the River Loing** and discover the many picturesque strangely shaped rocks on heathlike plateaus among the groves of tall trees. Rowing is available on the River Loing, as is swimming, while tennis and clay-pigeon shooting are alternatives. An excellent inn, a very comfortable hotel and a camping site together cater for all tastes and purses.

Approaching from the autoroute by the N375, the best view of the old town with the 12th century church and the château is from the **bridge** (the Grand Pont). The château now consists only of one wing, four towers and a dungeon. A small **museum** inside exhibits documents related to local history as well as paintings and sculpture. (Open 10–12am and 2–5.30pm, Saturday, Sunday and Monday.)

The **Prehistoric Museum** formerly housed here is now situated on the Route de Sens (Rue Montgagnant, the D225), with access from the Rue des Tanneurs right by the bridge. The evolution of prehistoric man is traced through his artefacts and a reconstituted environment. (Open 10–12am and 2–6pm, closed Tuesday.)

The **church** was built at the end of the 12th century to house the relics of St-John the Baptist, brought back from the Second Crusade. Much of this building has disappeared and the existing church dates from the 16th century. Follow the Rue Gauthier Premier to the tributary of the River Loing, the Rivière des Petits Fossés, cross the bridge to Place Victor Hugo and another bridge over the **Canal du Loing** to reach the Avenue de la Mairie and the entrance, in front of the **Church of St-Pierre**, to a very attractive park which has rocks of extraordinary shape, one of them known as the Tortoise (*la tortue*). A fine view can be enjoyed of the town itself and the surrounding countryside.

There are many more excursions to see strangely shaped rocks in unusual settings to be made from Nemours. One place of particular interest is **Larchant**, 8Km from Nemours on the D16. It is a small village of 505 inhabitants, at the edge of the **Bois de la Commanderie**, perched on the upper ridge of an old geological depression. The ridge of semi-circular shape is covered with rocks and woods, while the bottom of this natural amphitheatre can be very marshy, altogether creating a landscape of weird atmosphere.

Larchant itself is the native town of St-Mathurin (born in 3AD). The village church stands on the site of a famous pilgrimage centre where the Kings of France used to come. The present church is a mixture of styles from the 12th to the 17th centuries. At a distance of 2Km from Larchant the hamlet of **Bonnevault** extracts white sands of great chemical purity that are exported worldwide to all famous glass factories.

Hotels and Restaurants

L'Ecu de France Comfortable old inn with a chef who is a *Maître Cuisinier de France*. Try such specialities as *Turbot Grillé Béarnaise* (grilled turbot with *béarnaise* sauce) or *Noisettes d'Agneau à l'Estragon* (tender lamb with tarragon) in a cosy homely decor. 3 Rue de Paris, 77140, Nemours, Seine-et-Marne. Tel: (6) 428.11.54. 28 rooms, 56–130F. Meals 55–160F.

Open all year. Credit cards: AE, DC, EC.

St-Pierre Comfortable small hotel without restaurant. 12 Rue Carnot, 77140, Nemours, Seine-et-Marne. Tel: (6) 428.01.57. 25 rooms, 45–145F. Closed 1–15 March and 25 September–5 October.

For travellers in a hurry, a very comfortable motel at the Nemours service station just beyond the Nemours exit, coming from Paris (before it, coming from Lyon), offers large pleasant rooms, air conditioned and soundproof with a restaurant nearby.

Eurotel, Autoroute (A6). Tel: (6) 428.10.32. 103 rooms 181–227F. Open all year. Credit cards: AE, DC, EC.

Garages
Citroën: Avenue J.F. Kennedy. Tel: (6) 428.11.17.
Peugeot: 18 Avenue J.F. Kennedy. Tel: (6) 428.03.27.
Talbot: 16 Avenue du Général de Gaulle. Tel: (6) 428.00.27.

Camping

JOIGNY
From Paris, Joigny/Toucy exit, D943, 13Km
From Lyon, Auxerre-Nord/Joigny exit, N6, 22Km
Inhabitants: 11,925
Office de Tourisme: Gare Routière (station) Quai H. Ragobert, closed Sunday except morning in summer.

Joigny is a small town at the edge of Burgundy, built on the River Yonne. Its old streets and houses cascade down the slope of the Côte St-Jacques on the right bank. The effect is of an amphitheatre, crowned by the dark woods of the **Forêt d'Othe**. Joigny is a fitting gateway to the gastronomic pleasures of Burgundy and boasts several gourmet restaurants as well as superbly comfortable hotels. Only 148Km from Paris Joigny is the ideal overnight stop before continuing south.

The old town is reached by the D943 across the 18th century bridge over the very wide River Yonne. The quays along the river are lined by lime trees, forming the pleasant **Promenade du Mail.** In less than an hour the traveller can discover the old town and its monuments by following the Rue Gabriel Cortel and the Rue Montant-au-Palais. On the left coming from the bridge the **Church of St Thibault** of Gothic and Renaissance style, has a 17th century square tower. Inside, there are works of art worth noting: several paintings from the Low Countries and a medieval sculpture of a 'Smiling Virgin'. Turning right into the Rue Montant-au-Palais one reaches the **Church of St-Jean** in Renaissance style. Inside take a look at the tomb of the Countess of Joigny and the early 18th century panelling and furniture, from the abbey at Vézelay, in the sacristy. The streets around these two churches have many medieval and Renaissance houses, while the **Porte du Bois** with its round towers, at the end of the Rue Porte du Bois, is all that is left of the 12th century castle.

There is a lovely view from the top of the **Côte St-Jacques**, which runs for about 1.5Km beyond the Porte du Bois on the D20. Stop at the **Croix Guemard** and look down on Joigny and the Yonne valley with its rolling hills of fields and the first vineyards of Burgundy.

Hotel and Restaurants

A la Côte St-Jacques A good restaurant with a few luxurious rooms in an 18th century house. The cuisine is in the Burgundian high tradition with notable innovations such as *Homard aux Légumes* (lobster with vegetables) and *Salade de Pigeonneau au Foie Gras* (pigeon salad with *foie gras*). An absolute must for an overnight stay. Refinement and artistry are the hallmarks of the house, in the surroundings, the cuisine and the wine list. Heated swimming pool. 14 Faubourg de Paris, 89300, Joigny, Yonne. Tel: (86) 62.09.70. 18 rooms, 190–300F. Meals 140–350F. Closed Monday night, Tuesday and January. Credit cards: AE, DC, VISA.

Modern' Hôtel, Le Maillet d'Or A very comfortable hotel near the station, with a pretty garden, soundproof rooms, a heated swimming pool and a quality restaurant tended by generations of the Godard family, who produce delights such as *Cassolette d'Escargots* (snails, the Burgundian speciality), *Saupiquet de Saumon Fumé* (smoked salmon in a piquant sauce), *Caille Fourrée en Tablier de Choux* (stuffed quail wrapped in a cabbage leaf). Excellent cellar. 17 Avenue Robert Petit, 89300, Joigny, Yonne. Tel: (86) 62.16.28 or 62.14.53. 22 rooms, 180–240F. Meals 120–250F. Closed Monday, and 27 November–15 December. Credit cards: AE, DC, EC, VISA.

Le Relais de l'Escargot Small family hotel without restaurant. 1 Avenue Roger-Varrey, 89300, Joigny, Yonne. Tel: (86) 62.10.38. 10 rooms, 50–60F. Credit cards: AE, DC, EC, VISA.

8Km from the autoroute by the D943 and the D194, at **La Celle St-Cyr** (the Joigny/Toucy exit from Paris, and the Auxerre-Nord/Joigny exit from Lyon) is the **Auberge de la Fontaine aux Muses.** Comfortable, small, very quiet hotel, with restaurant, in a park with a lake, swimming pool and tennis court. The rooms have direct access to the garden. Musical evenings, exhibitions and other events are organised. 11 rooms, 130–185F. Meals 85–125F. Closed Monday.

Garages
Opel: 6 Faubourg de Paris. Tel: (86) 62.05.02.

Peugeot/Talbot: 24 Faubourg de Paris. Tel: (86) 62.12.25.
Renault: Route de Migennes. Tel: (86) 62.22.00.

AUXERRE
From Paris, Auxerre-Nord exit, N6, 7Km
From Lyon, Auxerre-Sud exit, N65 and N6, 7Km
Inhabitants: 39,481
Office de Tourisme: 2 Quai de la République, closed Sunday out of season

Auxerre, the capital of Lower Burgundy, is harmoniously built on the slope of a hill overlooking the **River Yonne.** It is the centre of a vine-growing area the most famous product of which is the wine of Chablis (19Km away by the D965). The nearby hills produce pleasant reds and rosés such as **Irancy** and **Coulanges la Vineuse.** Auxerre with its historical monuments, boating activities (a marina has been built in a sheltered spot on the banks of the Yonne) and its hotels and restaurants, is a very pleasant halt at the portals of Burgundy.

The best way to arrive at Auxerre is from the right bank of the river. The two bridges give a panoramic view of the city, with the chevets of its four churches rising out of the picturesque array of roofs, creating a glorious skyline of Gothic splendour. Coming from the N6 from Paris drive across the river to the right bank, and then along the quay to cross again at the Pont Paul Bert. From Lyon the N6 reaches the town at the bridge itself, giving an immediate view.

It is best to explore the city on foot as the streets are narrow and steep, full of the nooks and crannies characteristic of the Middle Ages. Climb up to the **Cathedral of St-Etienne** from the Quai de la Marine. The cathedral dominates the whole city with its superb Gothic outline. Built from the 13th to the 16th centuries it stands on the site of an earlier Romanesque cathedral, of which only the crypt, displaying unique medieval frescoes of Christ in Glory riding a white horse surrounded by four mounted angels, still exists. The main building has a late Gothic façade in soft white stone much damaged by the weather and the religious wars. The main portal depicts Christ in Glory and the Last Judgement. The two lateral portals are dedicated respectively to St-Etienne and St-Germain, patron saint of Auxerre. Inside, the choir and ambulatory have elegant proportions. The most outstanding feature of the interior is the set of 13th century stained-glass windows which rank in quality with those of Chartres and the Sainte Chapelle in Paris.

From the cathedral take the Rue Cochois down to the Benedictine **Abbey of St-Germain**, founded in the 6th century on the spot where the saint was buried. St-Germain was a wealthy Gallo-Roman lawyer who was converted by St-Amâtre, the founder of the cathedral, whom he succeeded as bishop. He went to England to preach Christianity and died at the imperial court at Ravenna in 445. His embalmed body was brought back to Auxerre to be buried with great pomp and reverence at the expense of the emperor. The Gothic church was built between the 13th and 15th centuries and is dominated by a Romanesque bell tower of Burgundian style. The crypt constitutes a subterranean church (9th century) with two superimposed sets of arcades and three naves. The upper part is decorated with magnificent frescoes, also 9th century, and among the oldest in France. They depict the life and death of St-Etienne together with an Adoration of the Magi and a peacock spreading its tail (the peacock is the symbol of Christ, its flesh supposedly being incorruptible). The lower part of the crypt, where the body of St-Germain was buried, contains a vault painted with sun motifs, recalling the Ravenna mosaics where the saint died.

Returning via the quays to the Rue du Pont, opposite the Pont Paul Bert, look at the **Church of St-Pierre** and its 16th and 17th century classical façade. Carry on down the Rue des Boucheries to the Place Surugue where the **Church of St-Eusèbe** (12th–15th century) has on show a magnificent 9th century Byzantine cloth, traditionally known as the **shroud of St-Germain**. Nearby, in the Rue d'Egleny (Number 9bis), the **Leblanc-Duvernois Museum** has a splendid collection of 18th century Beauvais tapestries as well as faience and paintings of the French School. (Open 1.30–5.30pm, 21 June–16 September. Otherwise 2pm–5pm. Closed Tuesday, 1 January, 1 May, 14 July, Christmas Day.)

The **surrounding countryside** is most attractive with small old villages scattered over the hills. The spring brings out glorious blossom, mostly cherry, in the numerous orchards, dotted among the vineyards, which gives a white ethereal look to the vast rolling landscape.

Leave Auxerre by the N6. Take the D956 and 4.5Km from Auxerre on the left visit **St-Bris-le-Vineux** (896 inhabitants). A pretty village in the midst of vineyards, it has a Gothic church dating from the 13th century with Renaissance additions and some 14th and 15th century houses. Carry on for another 1.5Km and then turn right on to the D38. This is a picturesque road leading to **Irancy** (387 inhabitants), nestling in a valley among orchards. Irancy produces the most famous red and rosé wines in the Auxerre region.

Having tasted the Irancy wine continue on the D38 to the N6, which crosses the River Yonne at Vincelottes. Turn right on the N6 back to Auxerre and the D163, stopping *en route* at Vaux for a gourmet lunch at **La Petite Auberge.**

Hotels and Restaurants

Le Jardin Gourmand Delicious food in a lovely setting, and a warm welcome. A hint of the *cuisine nouvelle* in the *Sorbet de Carottes à la*

Sauce au Poivre Vert (carrot sorbet with green pepper sauce), *Mousse d'Asperges et d'Huîtres* (asparagus and oyster mousse) and *Bar à la Mousseline d'Estragon* (sea bass with tarragon mousse). 56 Boulevard Vauban, 89000, Auxerre, Yonne. Tel: (86) 51.53.52. Meals 70–150F. Closed Tuesday night, Wednesday, and 1–15 May, and 15–31 October. Credit card: VISA.

La Grilladerie Traditional French food treated with care. Try the *Andouillette* (sausage) and *Tête de Veau* (calf's head). 45bis Boulevard Vauban, 89000, Auxerre, Yonne. Tel: (86) 46.95.70. Meals 52–120F. Closed Sunday. Credit cards: AE, VISA.

La Fontaine A charming, comfortable family hotel, without restaurant, in the centre of Auxerre. 12 Place Charles-Lepère, 89000, Auxerre, Yonne. Tel: (86) 52.40.80. 33 rooms 50–220F. Closed 15 December–15 January. Credit cards: AE, DC, EC, VISA.

La Petite Auberge Very small restaurant offering subtle dishes like *Salade de Truite au Coulis de Tomatoes* (trout salad with tomato sauce), *Langoustines au Sauternes* (Dublin Bay prawns with a Sauternes wine sauce) and *Gratin de Fruits* (Fruit pudding). 2 Place du Passeur, Vaux, 89290, Champs-sur-Yonne, Yonne. Tel: (86) 53.80.08. Meals 70–180F. Closed Sunday night, Monday, public holidays, and 18 February–2 March, and 1–15 July. Credit card: VISA.

Festivals, Fairs and Sporting Events
The Sunday closest to 11 November: Auxerre **wine festival at St-Bris-le-Vineux**. (The local wine society at St-Bris-le-Vineux is the *Chevaliers des Trois Ceps*.)

Garages
Alfa-Romeo/Fiat 14 Rue J. Ferry. Tel: (86) 52.53.08.
Citroën: 18 Boulevard Vaulabelle. Tel: (86) 51.59.33.
Datsun/Volvo: 34 Avenue Charles de Gaulle. Tel: (86) 52.43.20.
Ford: 45 Boulevard Vauban. Tel: (86) 49.90.23.
Renault: 2 Avenue Jean Mermoz. Tel: (86) 52.75.45.

CHABLIS/TONNERRE
*From Paris, Auxerre-Sud exit, D965, 12Km to Chablis, 29Km to Tonnerre
From Lyon, Nitry exit, 24Km to Tonnerre by the D944, 17Km to Chablis
by the D91*

Turn off the autoroute at Auxerre-Sud, take the D965 to Chablis, taste the lovely fresh and tangy white wine in one of the *caves* and carry on to Tonnerre, an attractive small old town with a wonderfully comfortable hotel and an excellent restaurant in a 10th century former abbey.

CHABLIS
Inhabitants: 2,408
Office de Tourisme: 9 Avenue Oberwesel.

Chablis, the 'golden gateway' to Burgundy, is the wine capital of Lower Burgundy. Dating back to the Middle Ages, Chablis vineyards produce a dry white wine of great bouquet and a subtle fragrance which develops a few months after the *vendange* and holds well for a long time. Made from Chardonnay grapes or *Beaunois*, the great names are **Vaudesir, Valmur, Blanchot, Grenouille, Les Clos, Les Preuses** and **Bougros.** Chablis is the perfect wine to drink with shellfish and *charcuterie.*

This small town on the **River Serein** was once a place of pilgrimage in honour of St-Martin de Tours and the old **Collegiate Church of St-Martin** was built to shelter the relics of St-Martin by the Canons of St-Martin de Tours, fleeing Norman invaders.

From the D965 take the Boulevard Dr Tacussel and turn right into the Rue J. Rathier to reach the **Caveau Chablisien**, situated in the former chapel of the 13th century *hôtel-Dieu* (hospital) in a garden, and taste the fragrant wine of Chablis. Return to the Place Lafayette to get back to the bridge and the D965, which will take you on to Tonnerre.

The **Promenade de Patis** beside the River Serein is a peaceful walk, with trees centuries old, and gives a lovely view of the town and the river.

Garages
Citroën: Tel: (86) 42.40.22.
Renault: Tel: (86) 53.11.55.

Festivals, Fairs and Sporting Events
August, first Sunday: **Fête de la Vigne (wine festival)**
November, last Sunday: Exhibition of the Chablis wines (the local wine society is the *Piliers Chablisiens.*)

TONNERRE
Inhabitants: 6,517
Office de Tourisme: Rue du Collège, closed Tuesday and 1 October–1 April.

Tonnerre is an attractive town leaning against a hill overlooking the River Armançon and surrounded by vineyards and woods. It was destroyed by fire in the 16th century but its old hospital (13th century) survives with a very moving sculpture of the entombment of Christ, dating from the 15th century, in one of its chapels.

The **Old Hospital** is reached via the D965 down the Rue Vaucorbe and the Rue de l'Hôpital. It is a handsome building in the Burgundian tradition, topped by a vast high roof of 4,500 square metres. Built in 1293 by Marguerite de Bourgogne, widow of Charles d'Anjou, King of Sicily and Naples and brother of Louis IX, the hospital still possesses its **Hall of the Sick**, an oak-panelled room 101m long designed to hold forty patients in wooden alcoves along the walls. The foot of each bed is turned towards the altar of a chapel at the end of the room, so that the patients could watch Mass from their beds. Beaune, 150 years later, would adopt the same plan. This chapel holds the tomb of Marguerite de Bourgogne, the foundress.

Near the main altar a small door gives access to the **Revestière Chapel** which contains the hospital's most precious possession – the **Entombment** donated in 1454 by a rich burgher of the town. The seven mourning figures around the dead body of Christ are a masterpiece of pathos and spirituality in the tradition of Claus Sluter, sculptor at Dijon.

The **Tomb of Louvois** in the side chapel dates from the 17th century and was brought here from a Paris Capuchin convent.

Near the hospital, in the Rue des Fontenilles, the **Hôtel d'Uzes**, a lovely Renaissance building, has the dubious glory of being the native house of the Chevalier d'Eon, the famous 18th century transvestite who pursued a high-flying military, diplomatic and social career. He died in London in 1810 and was buried at St-Pancras. (The question of his sex is still debated.)

From the **Church of St-Pierre**, situated on a rocky promontory, there is a panoramic view over the town and its surroundings, including the Old Hospital, its roof looking like the hull of an immense overturned boat. The Church of St-Pierre itself was rebuilt in 1566 after the fire. Nearby the **Fosse Dionne** is a natural curiosity worth a visit. A spring of turquoise-coloured water fills a basin around which is a 16th century washhouse.

Time permitting, the **Château de Tanlay**, 9Km from Tonnerre by the D965, is well worth a detour. If one arrives from the D965, there is a superb view of the handsome building, surrounded by a moat in the green setting of its park. It is a magnificent example of fully developed French Renaissance architecture, with two distinct sections: the *Petit Château*, with elegant lines, built in 1569 by François de Coligny d'Andelot; and the main château, built in 1642 by Michael Ponticelli, Minister of Finance under Mazarin. The Château de Tanlay belonged to the Huguenot family of Coligny, and was the scene of many meetings between Huguenot conspirators during the Wars of Religion. On the top floor a 16th century frescoed ceiling depicts in allegorical form the most important characters in the Catholic and Protestant movements.

Hotels and Restaurants

L'Abbaye St-Michel Joan of Arc spent time in this 10th century abbey, on a spiritual retreat. It is now a very comfortable hotel with a lovely garden and a tennis court. The restaurant is luxurious and specialities to try are *Escargots à la Mode de Chablis* (snails cooked with Chablis), *Daube Bourguignonne* (stew with red wine) and *Poularde Truffée au Persil* (chicken with parsley stuffing). Montée de St-Michel, 89700, Tonnerre, Yonne. Tel: (86) 55.05.99. 10 rooms and suites, 270–440F. Meals 140–190F. Closed Monday (October–May) and 20 December–31 January. Credit cards: AE, DC.

Hôtel du Centre Quiet simple hotel with restaurant. Very good value. 63 Rue de l'Hôpital, 89700, Tonnerre, Yonne. Tel: (86) 55.10.56. 30 rooms, 39–100F. Meals 30–75F. Closed 24 December–25 January.

Garages

Citröen: Route de Paris. Tel: (86) 55.08.12.
Opel: Rue G. Pompidou. Tel: (86) 55.08.80.
Peugeot: 86 Rue G. Pomidou. Tel: (86) 55.14.11.
Renault: Route de Paris. Tel: (86) 55.15.89.

AVALLON

From Paris, Avallon/Saulieu exit, N146 and N6, 8Km
From Lyon, Avallon exit, N146 and N6, 8Km
Inhabitants: 9,255
Office de Tourisme: 24 Place Vauban, closed Monday out of season and Sunday

Avallon with its lovely position on a granite promontory overlooking the ravine in which the River Cousin flows, its camping site, numerous hotels and restaurants ranging from the luxurious to the simple, is the perfect centre to stay at and from which to explore the picturesque Cousin Valley and the nearby wild and fascinating region of the **Morvan** with its lakes and rivers, providing for fishing, sailing, rowing and windsurfing.

Avallon is situated on a very ancient site; its name comes from the Gallic *Aballo.* Its position dominating several valleys made the town an important fortified outpost, the northern gate of the Morvan, from the 9th century onward. With its fortifications, gardens and narrow cobbled streets lined with fine old houses, it is now an attractive market town. On Saturday mornings, the market takes over the centre of the city, in a more northerly version of the markets of Provence, with the garlands of fat, pink garlic heads hanging over succulent fruit and vegetables.

Arriving by the N6, aim for the Place Vauban where stands the famous **Hostellerie de la Poste**, an old coaching inn. Napoléon I slept here on his way from Elba. Walk up the Rue Aristide Briand inside the city walls to the **Hôtel de Ville**, dating from the 18th century, and the **Hôtel de Conde.**

Carry on to the **Tour de l'Horloge** (in the Grande Rue), a 15th century watch tower with a bell tower from which the view extends for miles around. In a small street opposite, a 17th century college houses a **museum** of local mineralogy, geology and prehistory, as well as an important collection of Greco-Roman statues, and paintings of the French School (by Toulouse-Lautrec, Rouault and others). (Open 10–12am and 3–7pm, 15 June–10 September. Closed Monday, and 15–30 June, and Monday and Tuesday 15 June–10 September. Also closed 11 September–10 October. 11 October–14 June by appointment only. Tel: (86) 34.03.19.)

The Grande Rue leads on to the Place St-Lazare where the old **Collegiate Church of St-Lazare** was built in order to accommodate the pilgrims who flocked to venerate the skull of Lazarus, a relic given to the church in the year 1000 which had the power to ward off and cure leprosy. The floor follows the slope of the hill, the choir being 10ft lower than the west front. It is a remarkable example of Burgundian Romanesque, with a beautifully proportioned nave and two stunning portals (1150) richly decorated with exuberant carvings of a florid Romanesque style depicting the signs of the zodiac and the labours of the months, together with stylised vegetal forms and elegant small barley-sugar columns alternating with plain ones.

From the Church of St-Lazare walk down the **Promenade de la Petite Porte** admiring the panorama over the Cousin Valley and the Morvan from this terrace, lined with lime trees, on the ramparts. It is well worth walking all round the ramparts and recalling the medieval past of Avallon. The **Beurdelaine Tower**, the oldest, was built in 1404 by Jean Sans Peur, Duke of Burgundy. One can get a good view of the fortifications from the Rue des Minimes down in the ravine.

Further away (2Km), along the N6 (Rue de Lyon and Rue des Minimes, then Chemin de la Goulotte and Avenue du Parc), is the **Parc des Chaumes**, with tennis courts and swimming pools and a marvellous all-embracing view of Avallon with its gardens cascading down the ravine and its golden ramparts like a crown round the city.

From Avallon explore the **Valley of the River Cousin**, leaving Avallon by the D427 which is reached by following the Route de Cousin-le-Pont. The road follows the river in a woody gorge. Old mills and houses have been converted into very comfortable hotels in a lovely green setting on the banks of the River Cousin. A most relaxing place to spend a weekend away from it all.

Hotels and Restaurants

Hostellerie de la Poste An old coaching inn now a luxury hotel with a fine restaurant, the Hostellerie de la Poste has a lovely cobbled inner courtyard with a riot of flowers, on which the very comfortable rooms look out. The restaurant has long been famed but has paid tribute to the *nouvelle cuisine* without losing any of the refined artistry of the traditional Burgundian cuisine. *Soupe de Homard aux Artichauts* (lobster soup with artichokes), *Pigeonneau au Concombre* (young pigeon with cucumber) and the *Poularde de Bresse à la Vapeur* (corn-fed white-fleshed chicken from the Bresse area, steamed) are all delectable specialities. 13 Place Vauban, 89200, Avallon, Yonne. Tel: (86) 34.06.12. 29 rooms, 180–450F. Meals 140–350F. Closed December. Credit cards: AE, DC, VISA.

Le Morvan An excellent restaurant in its own garden which offers such delights as *Rougeot* (fillet of smoked wild duck), *Boudin de Fruits de Mer* (seafood in a sausage shape) and *Escalope de Veau Fumée à l'Oseille* (thin smoked veal steak with sorrel). 7 Route de Paris, 89200, Avallon, Yonne. Tel: (86) 34.18.20. Meals 95–160F. Closed February, Thursday and every night (except Saturday) except in season. Credit cards: AE, DC, VISA.

Les Capucins An excellent, very reasonably priced restaurant, with rooms, in a pretty house near the station. Try the *Pâté de Brochet* (pike mousse) or the *Jambonnette de Volaille au Chablis* (chicken leg cooked in Chablis wine). 6 Avenue Paul Doumer, 89200, Avallon, Yonne. Tel: (86) 34.06.52. 16 rooms, 45–75F. Meals 40–130F. Closed January and Wednesday. Credit card: VISA.

Le Manoir A very quiet simple family hotel, without restaurant, in its own garden. Friendly atmosphere. 8 Route de Vézelay, Avenue de Pepinster, 89200, Avallon. Tel: (86) 34.00.30. 15 rooms 80–140F. Open all year. Credit cards: AE, DC, VISA.

3.5Km from Avallon along the D427, is **Le Moulin des Ruats.** An old mill converted into a comfortable country inn with terraces and a restaurant overlooking the river. Delicious food. Vallée du Cousin, 89200, Avallon, Yonne. Tel: (86) 34.07.14. 21 rooms, 110–190F. Meals 90–180F. Closed November–March. Credit cards: AE, DC, EC, VISA.

5Km along the D957, at Pontaubert, is **Le Moulin des Templiers.** A very comfortable and friendly family hotel, with lovely rooms overlooking the quiet shady garden on the bank of the Cousin. No restaurant. Pontaubert, Vallée du Cousin, 89200, Avallon, Yonne. Tel: (86) 34.10.80. 14 rooms, 90–160F. Closed November–15 March.

Garages

Citroën: 10 Rue Carnot. Tel: (86) 34.01.23.
Ford: 15 Rue Carnot. Tel: (86) 34.06.17.
Renault: 30 Rue de Paris. Tel: (86) 34.19.27.

Camping

VÉZELAY/ST-PÈRE-SOUS-VÉZELAY

From Paris, Avallon/Saulieu exit, N6 and D957, 23Km (15Km from Avallon)
From Lyon, Avallon exit, N6 and D957, 23Km (15Km from Avallon)
Inhabitants: 543
Office de Tourisme: Place du Champ de Foire, open at Easter, and 1 July–15 September, closed Tuesday. Also at the Mairie *(town hall) closed Saturday and Sunday*

Vézelay, a small town centred round a basilica, is situated on the top of a hill overlooking the valley of the **River Cure** with its slopes covered with vineyards and woods. It is one of the most important religious and artistic centres of Burgundy and France as a whole.

A superb restaurant and very comfortable hotel make Vézelay an ideal stopping place, while the Morvan forests nearby are perfect for rambling. The River Cure provides rowing and fishing.

Vézelay owes its existence to Girart de Roussillon, Count of Burgundy, who founded a monastery on the site of the village of **St-Père** 2Km south-east of Vézelay on the D957. Norman raids destroyed the monastery and obliged the Benedictine monks to take refuge on the nearby hill. The **Abbey of Ste Madeleine** established an immediate reputation all over Christendom, as it held the relics of St-Mary Magdalen brought from Provence for protection from the Saracens. Moreover Vézelay was an important church on one of the four great roads to the centre of pilgrimage at Santiago de Compostella in Spain.

It may be difficult for the modern traveller visiting the little town, its quiet cobbled streets and houses with walled gardens tumbling down the sides of the hill, and the whole dominated by the imposing presence of the basilica, to imagine the thronging pilgrims and merchants it would have seen in the Middle Ages and the intense spiritual attraction it exercised. Here, in 1146, St-Bernard preached in favour of the Second Crusade, in front of the King of France and a lordly assembly. Here the French king, Philippe Auguste, met Richard the Lion Heart, King of England, before setting off on the Third Crusade in 1190. St-Francis of Assisi decided to create the first Fransciscan monastery in France here in 1217. Restored by Viollet-le-Duc between 1840 and 1859, after centuries of neglect, the basilica now once more attracts crowds of visitors in search of beauty and peace.

From the Place du Champ de Foire at the foot of the hill drive up the one-way street through the Porte du Barle to leave your car near the basilica. Better still, park on the Champ de Foire and walk up the Grande Rue, admiring on the way the fine old houses with their sculptures and mullioned windows. From the **Terrasse du Château** behind the basilica there is a wonderful view over the Morvan and the valley of the River

Cure. The **basilica** itself is one of the largest monastic churches in France with a Romanesque narthex and nave from the mid 12th century and a choir and transept in early Gothic style. The tympanum of the narthex portal is one of the most eloquently spiritual creations of Romanesque sculpture: Christ in Glory after the Resurrection is entrusting his apostles with their mission: 'Go ye into all the world and preach the Gospel to every creature' (St Mark). The nave is a wonderful sight, with its admirable proportions (it is 62m long) and the rhythmic arrangement of the barrel-vaulted bays, the polychrome blocks of limestone giving it an almost Moorish appearance, climaxing in a dazzlingly white choir. Light-golden but subdued by the subtle colour gradations of the stone – floods through, enhancing an atmosphere of deep spiritual peace. The capitals of the pillars in the nave are outstanding examples of Romanesque sculpture. Lyricism, drama, wit and a certain mischievousness are all used to depict, in an educational spirit (for that was the purpose of these sculptures) and with an impressive sense of composition and movement, biblical events, the lives of the saints or, in allegory, the vices and virtues. It was intended that, as the pilgrims moved along the nave to the choir, they should be edified and strengthened in their faith by the scenes represented.

Although heavily restored the Madeleine of Vézelay still exudes an aura of prayer and spiritual fervour that even the traveller without the absolute faith of the medieval pilgrim can experience and enjoy, as he takes in the sheer beauty of its proportions and the eloquence of its Romanesque carvings.

To return to the Place du Champ de Foire, follow the **Promenade des Fossés** with its seven round towers which were once part of the medieval ramparts.

Hotels and Restaurants

Poste et Lion d'Or A very comfortable hotel with a high-quality restaurant at the foot of Vézelay's hill. Specialities include: *Gâteau de Lapin à la Confiture d'Oignons* (rabbit with onion purée), *Saumon Farci aux Herbes* (fresh salmon with a herb stuffing). The dining-room is large and welcoming. Place du Champ de Foire, 89450, Vézelay, Yonne. Tel: (86) 33.21.23. 52 rooms, 90–390F. Meals 90–170F. Closed Tuesday, and Wednesday lunch-time.

Relais de Morvan An inexpensive restaurant, near the Poste et Lion d'Or, with simple rooms. Place du Champ de Foire, 89450, Vézelay, Yonne. Tel: (86) 33.25.33. 10 rooms, 45–100F. Meals 35–70F. Closed 1–15 June, 15–30 January, Sunday night and Monday.

Festivals, Fairs and Sporting Events
July 22: **Pilgrimage for the feast day of St Mary Magdalen.**
July–August: **Concerts.**

ST PÈRE-SOUS-VÉZELAY
2Km south-east of Vézelay on the D957 is St Père-sous-Vézelay (384 inhabitants).

Here you can have an outstanding meal in marvellous surroundings and spend the night in a converted mill nearby. It is a small village in a lovely spot on the River Cure at the foot of the Vézelay's hill. Its fine Gothic **Church of Notre Dame** shows the evolution of Gothic style between the 13th and 15th centuries. The most striking feature of the building is the effortlessly elegant spire with its four angels, at the corner of the second storey, sounding the trumpet for the Last Judgement which is depicted on the tympanum of the main portal. The interior has a simple plan and is a very good example of late Gothic style.

The **Regional Museum of Archaeology**, in the 17th century presbytery, contains Gallo-Roman artefacts discovered locally, together with Merovingian weapons and jewels found in tombs, and medieval sculptures. (Open 9–12.30am and 2.30–6.30pm, 1 March–23 December. Closed Wednesday except Easter–September.)

The site which yielded the Gallo-Roman antiquities in the museum can be visited (2Km away on the D958). The **Fontaines Salées (salt springs)** consist of Gallo-Roman baths and a 200BC Gallic temple with a sacred pond dedicated to the gods of springs and water. These salt springs were in use until the 17th century, when they were blocked by order of the Salt Tax Collector. They are now in use again as a remedy for arthritis.

L'Espérance is a fine restaurant in an old house in a garden with a stream. The old mill nearby has been coverted into a hotel. L'Espérance is a dream. Truly exceptional meals are served in its glass-fronted dining-room overlooking the garden. Specialities include: *Salmigondis de Pigeon* (pigeon stew), *Feuilleté de Fromage Chaud* (hot cheese vol-au-vent) and *Pintade Farcie en Cocote* (stuffed braised guinea fowl). The hotel has lovely rooms, very comfortable and furnished with antiques, looking out on to the garden. A marvellous place for a romantic week-end. St Père-sous-Vézelay, 89450, Vézelay, Yonne. Tel: (86) 33.20.45. 19 rooms, 130–350F. Meals 100–300F. Closed Tuesday and January. Credit card: VISA.

SEMUR-EN-AUXOIS
From Paris, Bierre-les-Semur exit, D980, 8Km
From Lyon, Bierre-les-Semur exit, D980, 8Km
Inhabitants: 5,371
Office de Tourisme: Place Gaveau, closed Saturday afternoon and Sunday out of season.

Semur, capital of the Auxois region, was called in the 18th century the 'Little Athens of Burgundy'. Clustered on the sides of a pink granite promontory with the River Armançon meandering at its foot, and crowned by the Gothic 'miniature cathedral', the Church of Notre Dame, it is a most attractive small town, ideal for an overnight stay. There are good restaurants, comfortable hotels, a camp site and a nearby lake with water sports and a quiet hotel at its edge.

The most impressive view on arrival is to be had coming from the *autoroute* before reaching the Pont Joly (1783) which crosses the river in a single daring span to the foot of the Tour de l'Orle d'Or, one of the town's main gates. Then the overall view of clambering small houses and scattered gardens, dominated by four large towers with red tile roofs and the elongated spire of Notre Dame can be taken in in a single sweeping glance.

Semur was one of the impregnable citadels of Burgundy. Only four great towers remain from the former ramparts (the **Tour de l'Orle d'Or**, the **Tour de la Gehenne**, the **Tour de la Prison** and the **Tour Margot**), the town having been savagely punished by Louis XI of France, in the 15th century, for its allegiance to the last Duke of Burgundy's daughter Mary.

A cramped medieval street leads to the small Place Notre-Dame, lined by fine old Burgundian houses. It is the heart of the town and has considerable charm. The **Church of Notre Dame** is one of the loveliest Burgundian Gothic churches. The north portal, the **Porte des Bleds** (corn door) has retained a splendid tympanum depicting the Doubt of St Thomas. Notice on the side columns two carved snails, symbols of the Burgundian love of good food even in the 13th century and characteristic of the medieval taste for realistic detail. Inside, the narrow nave emphasises the height of the vaulting and the fine columns. It is the only Burgundian church with an ambulatory which is not a pilgrimage church.

A fine 15th century coloured sculpture of the Entombment of Christ in the second chapel is noteworthy for its monumental proportions (akin to the Claus Sluter tradition). In the third chapel look at the beautiful 16th century stained-glass window illustrating the legend of St Barbe. The last two windows were donated by the local butchers' and drapers' guilds and depict scenes from the everyday work of the tradesmen.

In the Rue J.J. Collenot a small **museum and library** is housed in the former Jacobine convent. Local geological and archaeological collections are exhibited, together with manuscripts (one dating from the 10th century), Anne de Bretagne's missal and one of the earliest books printed by Gutenberg, the inventor of the printing press. Two rooms contain paintings and sculpture from the 13th to the 18th centuries. (Museum open 2.30–6.30pm, Wednesday and Friday, 15 June–30 September. Library open 2–6pm, all year round.)

The Tour de l'Orle d'Or, part of the ramparts, is now the headquarters of the Société des Sciences Historiques et Naturelles de Semur (Semur History and Natural History Society) and has a small **museum** attached to it with geological, archaeological and folk art collections. There is a fascinating view over the town and ramparts from the top rooms. (Open July and August. Enquiries to the Office de Tourisme.)

One can walk one section of the ramparts, from where is a pretty view of the valley of the River Armançon.

Outside Semur (3Km along the D103B), at the **Lac de Pont**, a man-made reservoir feeds the Canal de Bourgogne. The lake, 6Km long, offers a beach, a good hotel-restaurant and organised water sports such as sailing, wind-surfing etc in a lovely spot surrounded by rocks and woods.

Hotels and Restaurants

Hôtel des Gourmets A small welcoming family hotel with an inner court-yard and garden, in the heart of Semur. The restaurant offers regional specialities. Very good value. 4 Rue Varenne, 21140, Semur-en-Auxois, Côte d'Or. Tel: (80) 97.09.41. 15 rooms, 45–120F. Meals 45–100F. Closed 25 October–1 January, and Friday (1 January–1 July).

La Cambuse Excellent restaurant with a friendly welcome and specialities such as: *Coquilles St Jacques à la Nage* (scallops in wine stock) and *Pigeonneau au Raisins* (pigeon with grapes). 8 Rue Fevret, 21140, Semur-en-Auxois, Côte d'Or. Tel: (80) 97.06.78. Meals 60–150F. Closed Tuesday (September–May) and 15 November–15 March. Credit cards: DC, EC.

Hôtel du Lac A quiet friendly country inn with delicious food. Good value. Lac de Pont, 21140, Semur-en-Auxois, Côte d'Or. Tel: (80) 97.11.11. 23 rooms, 60–150F. Meals, 49–90F. Closed 15 December–1 February, and Sunday night and Monday except July and August.

Garages
Citroën: Tel: (80) 97.07.89.
Peugeot: Tel: (80) 97.13.43.
Renault: Tel: (80) 97.05.10.
Talbot: Tel: (80) 97.07.18.

Festivals, Fairs and Sporting Events
May 31: **the Course de la Bague** a horse-race from Villenotte to the

Promenade du Cours at Semur which replaced in 1643 an even older tradition of a foot-race in which the runners exposed themselves pointlessly to death and endangered their souls by indulging in sports reminiscent of pagan Antiquity.

Camping

SAULIEU/THE MORVAN
From Paris, Bierre-les-Semur exit, D980, 21Km
From Lyon, Bierre-les-Semur exit, D980, 21Km
Inhabitants: 3,156
Office de Tourisme: Rue Argentine, 1 June–30 September, closed Sunday afternoon

Saulieu has a reputation for good food going back to the 16th century when the writer Rabelais, a true connoisseur of fine cooking to judge from the descriptions of meals in his famous books *Pantagruel* and *Gargantua* – from the former of which comes the expression *un repas pantagruelique* (a pantagruelic meal, a lavish meal) – noted that 'one ate and drank well at Saulieu'. This fame was further reinforced in 1651 when the States of Burgundy decided to revive the old Roman road between Paris and Lyon as an important route. Saulieu became a busy staging-post and more inns developed to cater for the needs of hungry and thirsty travellers. Its reputation has not faltered to this day and many a traveller may feel sympathy for Madame de Sévigné who, in 1677, had to endow the Church of St Andoche with a statue of the Virgin in order to expiate her gastronomic excesses!

Saulieu is truly a place not to be missed, on the edge of the **Auxois** and the **Morvan**, with the wooded hills nearby (Christmas trees are a major export) offering the opportunity to work off the after-effects of too good a meal! The 768Ha of the **Forest of Saulieu** include picnic areas, paths for walking and riding, and beautiful lakes and streams with trout fishing.

The town itself still has the feel of a staging post, spread along the N6 with a dazzling array of wonderful restaurants, comfortable hotels and tempting food shops.

It is worth tearing oneself away from culinary delights to admire the **Basilica of St Andoche**, an example of Burgundian Romanesque. It has unfortunately suffered badly through the centuries, and the choir was burnt by the English in 1359 and rebuilt in 1704. The capitals of the pillars in the nave, with decorative motifs and scenes from the life of Christ, are the outstanding feature of the church. The tomb of St Andoche, martyred on the site, is in the second side chapel.

The **museum** in the nearby presbytery has Burgundian works of art, from Gallo-Roman tombstones found at Saulieu to religious statues dating from the 12th to the 18th centuries, together with documents relating to Saulieu's culinary traditions and works by the 20th century animal sculptor François Pompon, who was born at Saulieu in 1855. His tomb is in the **Church of St Saturnin**, off the Rue de Verdun, with one of his works, a condor, on top. A sculpture of a bull, one of his most powerful works, was erected in a square just off the N6 in 1948.

Hotels and Restaurants

La Borne Impériale A traditional *haute cuisine* restaurant, with rooms, with an emphasis on excellent sauces, in such dishes as *Jambonneau de Canard à la Sauce à l'Orange* (duck with orange sauce). Also delicious *pâtisserie*. 14 and 16 Rue d'Argentine, 21210, Saulieu, Côte d'Or. Tel: (80) 64.19.76. 7 rooms, 54–100F. Meals 60–160F. Closed Tuesday and 15 November–15 December. Credit cards: EC, VISA.

La Côte d'Or A world-famous restaurant with a delectably inventive menu, with some comfortable rooms in the former house of the legendary chef Alexandre Dumaine. Having a meal here is an unforgettable experience, from the *Bavaroise d'Artichauts à la Purée de Tomates Fraîches* (artichoke mousse with fresh tomato purée) to the *Aiguillettes de Canard aux Pêches Jaunes* (small duck fillet with yellow peaches) and the exquisite *Glace à la Vanille et aux Fraises des Bois* (vanilla and wild strawberry ice). 2 Rue d'Argentine, 21210, Saulieu, Côte d'Or. Tel: (80) 64.07.66. 17 rooms, 150–230F. Meals 120–300F. Open all year. Credit cards: AE, DC, VISA.

La Poste A 17th century staging-post with very comfortable cosy rooms overlooking a pretty inner courtyard. No restaurant. 1 Rue Grillot, 21210, Saulieu, Côte d'Or. Tel: (80) 64.05.67. 48 rooms, 65–185F. Open all year. Credit cards: AE, VISA.

Garages

Citroën: Tel: (80) 64.17.99.
Peugeot: Gare. Tel: (80) 64.00.87.
Renault: Tel: (80) 64.03.45.
Talbot: Tel: (80) 64.08.08.

Festivals, Fairs and Sporting Events

August: **Charolais Cattle Festival.**

THE MORVAN

From Saulieu take the D26 and D302 to the **Lac des Settons**, about 20Km away, stopping *en route* at **Alligny-en-Morvan** (11Km from Saulieu) for lunch at the **Auberge du Morvan**.

The Morvan (Celtic for 'black mountain') is a wild country of heath and woodland, Burgundy's only highland area. Isolated and poor (before the introduction of fertilisers) the Morvan could barely provide enough food for its population and seasonal workers used to migrate down to the richer plains and valleys to earn a living, while the women at home became wet-nurses to Parisian infants whose fashionable mothers (in the 19th century) declined to feed them themselves.

From the 16th century until the opening of the **Nivernais Canal**, the running of logs from the High Morvan to Paris by the **River Yonne** and the **Cure**, its tributary, provided the only export from this sterile land. Stacked on the river banks, the logs were carried away by an artificial spate created by the opening of sluices. The Lac des Settons, created in 1861, was one of the dammed reservoirs used to activate the flow of the River Cure. Now that the natural beauty of the Morvan has been recognised as a tourist attraction, the lake has been developed, so that it now offers beaches, marinas and paths for walking. Covering 359Ha and surrounded by fir and pine trees, it is a beautiful spot where one can fish and shoot in season, go sailing or windsurfing, or on pedalo and motor-boat trips. Its banks are dotted with small hotels and restaurants.

Hotels and Restaurants

Auberge du Morvan A rustic Morvandelle inn with excellent regional specialities and a few rooms in which a quiet night can be spent. Try the *Jambon au Saupiquet* (ham with piquant cream sauce) or the *Filet de Charolais en Croute* (Charolais beef fillet in pastry). Alligny-en-Morvan, 58230, Mont Sauche Nièvre. Tel: (86) 76.13.90. 6 rooms, 48–58F. Meals 35–100F.

La Morvandelle 25Km from Saulieu on the D977B before reaching the Lac des Settons. A comfortable hotel in the hills with an excellent restaurant. Specialities: *Ecrevisses au Whisky* (fresh-water crayfish with whisky sauce), *Côte de Boeuf à la Moutarde* (beef cutlet with mustard sauce). Good value. Lac des Settons, 58230, Montsauche Nièvre. Tel: (86) 84.50.62. 23 rooms, 58–150F. Meals 40–90F. Closed 11 November– 15 March.

Les Grillons Good regional specialities are offered by this restaurant with rooms, including *Civet de Porcelet Bourguignon* (suckling pig in a wine sauce), *Truite* (trout) and *Ecrevisses* (fresh-water crayfish). Good value. Lac des Settons, 58230, Montsauche Nièvre. Tel: (86) 84.51.43. 17 rooms, 55–120F. Meals 40–95F.

Garage
Citroën: Montsauche. Tel: (86) 84.52.26.

ARNAY-LE-DUC
From Paris, Pouilly-en-Auxois exit, N81, 17Km
From Dijon, Pouilly-en-Auxois exit, N81, 17Km
Inhabitants: 2,473

A quiet small old town built on a promontory over the valley of the **River Arroux**, Arnay-le-Duc is worth a visit for lunch at one of its good restaurants and a look at the **Maison Régionale des Arts de la Table** in the old **Hospice St-Pierre.** A better introduction to the culinary arts could not be found. An extensive survey of the art of the table from ancient to modern times is presented, together with some antique faience and a dish by the famed 16th century French potter Bernard Palissy, who used to burn his own furniture in order to fire his pots when too poor to afford wood! Of more contemporary interest, one can taste regional products, and an exhibition of the hotel industry in Burgundy completes the list of attractions of a museum dedicated to a typically French interest. (Open 10–12am and 2–6pm. Closed Monday.)

Arnay-le-Duc's name features in the annals of French history because of a rather sad episode – the capture by the Revolutionaries of the aunts of Louis XVI, Mesdames Adelaide and Victoire, as they were fleeing to safety in Italy.

The 15th and 16th century **Church of St Laurent** has an interesting coffered Renaissance ceiling. Behind the church the **Tour de la Motte-Forte** is the only remaining part of the medieval castle destroyed during the Wars of Religion.

Hotels and Restaurants
Hôtel de la Poste Small family hotel in the centre of Arnay-le-Duc. No restaurant. 20 Rue St-Jacques, 21230, Arnay-le-Duc, Côte d'Or. Tel: (80) 90.00.76. 14 rooms, 80–125F. Open only June–end September.
Chez Camille An old-established restaurant with a high reputation, shortly to reopen under expert new management. (Unfortunately it was still closed on our visit.) 1 Place E. Herriot, 21230, Arnay-le-Duc, Côte d'Or. Tel: (80) 90.01.38.

At **Jouey** 5Km north-west of Arnay-le-Duc, by the N6, is **La Crémaillère** a friendly simple restaurant serving excellent traditional specialities such as *Jambon à la Crème* (ham with cream sauce) and *Coq au Vin.* Good value. Jouey, 21230, Arnay-le-Duc, Côte d'Or. Tel: (80) 90.10.95. Meals 27–38F. Closed Sunday, public holidays and November. Lunch only.

Garages
Peugeot: Tel: (80) 90.05.16.
Renault: Tel: (80) 90.07.09.

Camping

DIJON
From Paris, Pouilly-en-Auxois exit, H6, 41Km
From Lyon, Beaune exit, A37, 38Km
Inhabitants: 156,787
Office de Tourisme: Place Darcy and Hôtel Chambellan, 34 Rue des Forges, closed Saturday afternoon and Sunday

Dijon, the old capital of Burgundy, is a must for anyone at all interested in good food, art or history. Dijon's two main culinary specialities, *Moutarde* (mustard) and *Pain d'Epices* (gingerbread) were introduced by foreigners. Mustard was brought over by the Romans. The *Moutarde à l'Ancienne* is still made according to an 18th century recipe. Gingerbread, invented by the Chinese, was introduced to Europe by the troops of Genghis Khan. Rheims was the main production centre but the bakers moved to Dijon during the Revolution and stayed there.

Despite its size the traveller will find a stay here a particularly serene experience. In a land which remains staunchly rural and agricultural, despite its abbeys and châteaux, Dijon the capital is a town of small, intimate streets and private courtyards. 'Dijon is one of those provincial towns where one can stroll agreeably', said the writer Huysmans at the end of last century. It is still true today. Life has a slow provincial rhythm, a feeling of timeless security, to be enjoyed with family and friends, as one savours the riches with which God has endowed Dijon and Burgundy as a whole.

An old Roman city, Dijon enjoyed a reputation for good food even then, as the Latin inscriptions, carved in stone, in the museum of archaeology, testify. The city was completely destroyed in the 12th century, then rebuilt, and reached its apogee in the 14th and 15th centuries under the reign of the Valois dukes, to whom it came as an apanage. Through brilliantly planned marriages, the Dukes of Burgundy expanded their territories and fortunes into Flanders, Holland, Belgium, Luxemburg, Alsace and Lorraine. Their taste for luxury, their pomp and magnificence and their extensive possessions and great wealth brought them the title of 'Grands Ducs d'Occident'. For 100 years they attracted artists from their foreign domains to their brilliant court and fostered a flourishing Burgundian style in the arts.

From whatever direction you arrive, leave your car at the edge of the *Centre Ville* (town centre) and walk to the Place de la Libération, as all the sights are within walking distance, linked by pedestrian precincts.

The **Place de la Libération** was designed by Jules-Hardouin Mansart, the architect of Versailles. The elegant lines of its semi-circular design, with rusticated lower arcading, are in keeping with the façade of the **Logis du Roi**, former palace of the Dukes of Burgundy, which became the

Palais des Etats in the 17th century, and is now the **Hôtel de Ville** and Musée des Beaux Arts (museum of fine arts). The palace was rebuilt in 1682 on Jules-Hardouin Mansart's plans.

Of the original medieval palace little is left except two towers, the guardroom, the old kitchen and some vaulted ground-floor rooms. As it is now, it displays all stages of French classical architecture from late 17th century baroque to late 18th century neo-classical, by way of rococo.

The **Musée des Beaux Arts**, founded in 1783, is one of the richest in France. On the ground floor visit the **museum of sculpture**, with works ranging from the Middle Ages (Claus Sluter) and the Renaissance (Hughes Sambin) to the 18th and 19th centuries with Rude (native of Dijon), Carpeaux and the 20th century sculptor Pompon whose *Ours Blanc* (polar bear) sits in the garden in Place Darcy.

On the first floor is the **museum of painting**. Paintings from the Italian Primitives of the 14th and 15th centuries are exhibited with works from the 17th and 18th century French School. On the second floor some modern works are on display, from the Impressionists (Manet, Monet, Boudin and Vuillard) to the more contemporary Nicholas de Staél.

The **Salle des Gardes** (guardroom) is the museum's most famous room. Built by Philippe le Bon in the 15th century, it was restored in the 16th. It has on display works of art from the Chartreuse of Champmol (Carthusian monastery). The Chartreuse was founded in 1383 by Philippe le Hardi to replace Cîteaux as the mausoleum of the Valois dukes. Philippe attracted the best artists to work at his court and the Chartreuse was adorned with numerous works of art.

The **tomb of Philippe le Hardi** was executed between 1385 and 1410 by Jean de Marville, Claus Sluter and his nephew. The most remarkable feature of this alabaster and marble tomb is the procession of mourners designed and realised by Claus Sluter who revolutionised tradition by imparting a realistic psychological individuality to each small figure, each one stands alone in the utter desolation of human sorrow depicted, despite the small scale, with a monumental breadth of design.

The second tomb, by Juan de la Huerta, repeats the same features. Two altarpieces commissioned for the Chartreuse dazzle with their brilliance and virtuosity. Carved by the sculptor Jacques de Baerze, they were gilded and painted by Melchior Broederlam and are masterpieces of the International Gothic, a style of courtly magnificence and the realistic depiction of details – flowers, jewellery, fabrics. The shutters of the Crucifixion altarpiece are famous examples of this particular style and depict scenes from Christ's life. (Museum open 9–12am and 2–6pm, closed 1 January, 25 December, and mornings of 1 May, 1 November, 11 November and Tuesday.)

Leave the museum by the north exit to reach the **Rue des Forges**, which is lined with some of the most beautiful houses of old Dijon: number 34,

Hôtel Chambellan in the 15th century Flamboyant style; number 38, the **Maison Milsand**, 16th century in the style of Hughes Sambin; number 40, the **Hôtel Aubriot**, a 13th century façade with a 17th century classical doorway.

From the Rue des Forges walk to the **Church of Notre Dame**, 'a jewel without a jewel-case' according to Vauban. It is true that the restricted space of the site tends to detract from the impact of the building. Yet the architect has accomplished a miracle of technical virtuosity and Notre Dame is a superb example of Burgundian Gothic, illustrating an original solution to the problem of a monumental façade. Here it consists of a flat wall stretched like a hanging between two corner turrets. Two superimposed galleries with two rows of false gargoyles animate the surface. At the south corner of the façade stands the **Jacquemart** clock, brought back from Courtrai in 1382 by Philippe le Hardi following his victory over the Flemish revolt. The pipe-smoking figure tolled the hour without failing until 1610 (when he forgot!) A wit then suggested that he might be lonely and a bride was given to him. In 1714, however, the poet Piron felt sorry for the couple, who seemed to have taken a vow of chastity, and a son, Jacquelinet, was added to strike the half-hours. In 1881 the family was completed by Jacquelinette, a daughter, who strikes the quarters.

The interior of the church of Notre Dame is very harmonious, with the delicate columns of the triforium and the wide lantern at the crossing in front of the surprising polygonal choir. In the right-hand chapel the wooden statue of the Virgin of Notre Dame de Bon Espoir has been the object of a special veneration since 1513 when the devout credited the deliverance of their city from the Swiss army to the miraculous intervention of the Virgin. The heady qualities of the Burgundy wines had a lot to do with the defeat according to the chroniclers!

Leave Notre Dame by the north entrance on the Rue de la Chouette, and touch the little owl carved in the wall. Generations of the inhabitants of Dijon have stroked it for good luck.

Carry on down the **Rue Verrerie**, in which numbers 8, 10 and 12 form a beautiful group of half-timbered houses. The projecting upper storeys rest on carved beams with delightful anecdotal scenes or traditional Burgundian symbols such as grapes and snails. Skirt the Musée des Beaux Arts and crossing the **Place du Théâtre** reach the **Rue des Bons Enfants** and the **Musée Magnin** where a collection of Old Masters from the 15th to the 19th centuries is exhibited in a handsome 17th century house. (Open 9–12am and 2–5pm, closed Tuesday, 1 January, 1 May morning, 1 November, Christmas Day.)

Continue down the Rue du Palais. The **Palais de Justice**, the former seat of the Parliament of Burgundy, was begun under François I. The carved oak doors are replicas of Hughes Sambin's originals, now in the museum. Sambin was the founder of a school of provincial architects in the Mannerist style who influenced even Parisian artists. (Open August 9.30–11.30am and 2.30–5.30pm except Saturday and Sunday. Otherwise 9–12am and 2–6pm except Sunday. Closed Easter Monday and Whitsun.)

Behind the Palais de Justice, the **Bibliothèque Municipale (library)** is housed in the 17th century chapel of a former Jesuit college. 250,000 volumes are kept here, including some rare and precious manuscripts from Citeaux, dating from the early 12th century.

Return to the Place du Théâtre, take the **Rue Vaillant** and admire the **Church of St Michel** (1499–1540), one of the most pleasing of France's Renaissance church fronts. Walk back to the Place de la Libération and along the Rue de la Liberté to have a look at the **Cathedral of St Benigne** off the Rue Dr Maret. St Benigne is a Gothic church built on the site of a 10th century Romanesque basilica, the crypt of which, under the present church, contains fascinating column-capitals.

To the north of the church, in a garden, the former monks' dormitory of the Benedictine Abbey of St Benigne is now a **museum of archaeology** exhibiting prehistoric, Gallo-Roman, medieval and Renaissance works in a beautiful 12th century vaulted room.

After your extensive tour return to the Rue de la Liberté and then carry on to the **Place Darcy.** Sit in the garden, the entrance to which is guarded by Pompon's polar bear. Or have a drink in the brasserie in the Place Darcy and enjoy its *belle époque* charm with mirrors, gilt columns and stucco.

The **Chartreuse of Champmol** was destroyed during the Revolution. Only a 15th century portal and the monument called the **Puits de Moïse** (Moses' well) escaped the iconoclasts. The portal is now the inner door of the chapel and has five admirable statues by Claus Sluter, a Flemish sculptor whose naturalism and monumental style influenced Burgundian carving. The statues represent the Duke Philippe le Hardi and his wife, together with their patron saints on either side of the Virgin and Child.

The Puits de Moïse is by Claus Sluter and his nephew Claus de Werve, his assistant and successor at the ducal court. The so-called 'well' is in fact the pedestal of a polychrome Calvary which used to stand in a pool at the centre of the great cloister. The symbolic theme of the monument was the Fountain of Life, stemming from the redeeming blood shed by Christ. The six figures, over life-size, which adorn the hexagonal base depict the prophets of the Old Testament who foretold the Passion with a striking realism and grandeur. Of these the statue of Moses, with his rippling beard and heavily draped figure, is the most impressive (hence the name given to the sculpture).

An asylum now stands on the site of the Chartreuse, but the chapel and the *Puits* are open to the public. The monastery is about ten minutes by car from the centre of Dijon and well worth a visit. Take the Avenue Albert Premier past the station, then take the N5. The entrance to the

Chartreuse is signposted on the left. (Open 8am–6pm. Ask at the porter's lodge.)

The other works of art from the Chartreuse are now in the guardroom in the museum, except for the head of Christ from the Calvary which is in the museum of archaeology near the Cathedral of St Benigne.

Hotels and Restaurants

Le Chapeau Rouge A very comfortable hotel in the centre of Dijon, with soundproof rooms and a good restaurant serving such delicacies as *Steak de Lotte à la Menthe* (monkfish with mint sauce) and *Blanc de Turbot Soufflé au Basilic* (turbot in basil sauce). A perfect stopping place in Dijon. 5 Rue Michelet, 21000, Dijon, Côte d'Or. Tel: (80) 30.28.10. 33 rooms, 185–325F. Meals 105–200F. Closed 20 December–10 January. Credit cards: AE, DC, EC, VISA.

Hôtel de la Cloche A luxurious hotel entirely refurbished and decorated in Napoléon III style with an excellent restaurant offering exquisite dishes such as *Morilles Farcies de Ris de Veau* (mushrooms stuffed with calves' sweetbreads) and *Beignets Légers de Queues d'Ecrevisses* (deep-fried fresh-water crayfish). A place for self-indulgence. 14 Place Darcy, 21000, Dijon, Côte d'Or. Tel: (80) 30.12.32. 80 rooms and suites, 280–800F. Meals 120–230F. Credit cards: AE, DC, EC, VISA.

Hôtel du Nord A small central hotel with an excellent restaurant serving Burgundian specialities as well as more adventurous dishes such as *Feuilleté de Turbot au Cerfeuil* (turbot in pastry with chervil) or *Filet Mignon de Porc aux Pruneaux* (fillet of pork with prunes). Place Darcy, 21000, Dijon, Côte d'Or. Tel: (80) 30.55.20. 26 rooms, 75–180F. Meals 70–150F. Closed 23 December–14 January. Credit cards: AE, DC, VISA.

Restaurant Thibert Gourmet restaurant in Old Dijon serving delicious food. Good value. Specialities include *Cassolette d'Escargots au Vin Rouge* (snails in red wine sauce) and *Magret de Canard à la Confiture de Cassis* (duck with blackcurrant jam). 23 Rue Crebillon, 21000, Dijon, Côte d'Or. Tel: (80) 30.52.34. Meals 55–160F. Closed Sunday, Monday lunch-time and 1–15 August. Credit card: VISA.

Le Vinarium A traditionally Burgundian restaurant in a 13th century crypt in a courtyard of the old Dijon. Good value. 23 Place Bossuet, 21000, Dijon, Côte d'Or. Tel: (80) 30.36.23. Meals 50–120F.

Garages

Citroën: Impasse Chanoine-Bardy. Tel: (80) 71.81.82.
Ford: 12 Rue Gagnereauz. Tel: (80) 74.41.11.
Peugeot: 42 Avenue Aristide Briand. Tel: (80) 71.47.23.
Renault: 139 Avenue J. Jaurès. Tel: (80) 52.51.34.

Volvo: 25 Rue du Transvaal. Tel: (80) 30.26.69.

Festivals, Fairs and Sporting Events

June, first weekend: **Grand Prix de France** Formula 1, Dijon–Prenois.
July–August: **summer festival** (ballet, films, concerts, plays).
September, first two weeks: **international folk festival** and **vendanges** (grape harvest) festivities.
November, first fortnight: **international gastronomic fair** (Dijon is the seat of the Etats Généraux de la Gastronomie Française.)

LA CÔTE D'OR – ROUTE DES GRANDS CRUS

From **Dijon** to **Beaune** take the *Route des Grands Crus* (the D122) and explore the small villages whose names are known all over the world as the names of the most prestigious of Burgundy wines. It is a journey back in time through one of the most prosperous areas in France. The small- or medium-sized villages and towns exude a feeling of comfortable security, which has its roots in the profitable business provided by the unbroken tradition of centuries of vine-growing and wine-making, handed down through the generations of a very stable peasant race. They are people with the refinement of connoisseurs when it comes to food and wine, the wisdom of philosophers (as befits a people close to nature) and the sharp critical wit of those who deal only with the best.

This innate taste is also apparent in the spacious old stone houses, usually built around a small courtyard with an outer staircase giving access to the living quarters on the first floor under a protective arcaded awning, while the ground floor is occupied by the *cuverie* (vat house) and a complex subterranean city of cellars. The particular beauty of these houses resides in the functional solidity of their construction, ensuring their survival as cherished ancestral homes as well as work places for, in some cases, over 600 years. History is therefore indissolubly linked with our wine-tasting pilgrimage along the ridge, with its patchwork of vineyards, stretching for some 70Km named the Côte d'Or.

CÔTE DE DIJON

Chenove (21,548 inhabitants, 3Km from Dijon) is now part of the suburbs of Dijon. The **Clos du Roy** (or **Clos du Chapitre**) vineyard evokes the memory of the former owners, the Dukes of Burgundy and the Canons of Autun. In the **Cuverie des Ducs de Bourgogne** two splendid wine presses dating from the 13th century can be admired. (Open 8–12am and 2–7pm.)

Marsannay-la-Côte (6,590 inhabitants, 7Km from Dijon) is the only village of the Côte de Dijon still producing wine in quantity. Its darkish rosé, obtained by a short vatting of the *Pinot Noir* grapes is called Bourgogne Rosé de Marsannay. It has a light fragrance but with a distinction all its own.

Hotels and Restaurants
Le Boucanier A grill-restaurant with fish specialities such as *Plateau de Fruit de Mer* (assorted seafood platter, in winter only), *Sole à la Bourguignonne* (sole in the Burgundy manner), and *Cuisses de Grenouilles à la Dijonnaise* (frog legs in mustard sauce). 16 Route de Dijon, 21300, Chenove, Côte d'Or. Tel: (80) 52.60.41. Meals 60–120F. Closed Monday in winter, Sunday in summer. Credit cards: AE, VISA.

Les Gourmets Fine restaurant in a beautiful house (with a garden where one can eat outside) offering traditional Burgundian fare as well as more innovative specialities such as *Foie de Veau à la Vapeur* (steamed calf's liver) or the *Terrine de Rascasse* (scorpion fish terrine) together with the *Jambon Persillé* (ham in aspic with parsley) and *Escargots* (snails). 8 Rue du Puits-de-Tet, 21160, Marsannay-la-Côte, Côte d'Or. Tel: (80) 52.16.32. Meals 75–170F. Closed Monday night, Tuesday and January. Credit cards: DC, VISA.

CÔTE DE NUITS
The famous Côte de Nuits begins at **Fixin** (817 inhabitants, 10Km from Dijon) whose own production is mostly **Côte de Nuits Village.** The Côte de Nuits wines, consisting mainly of great reds rich and full-bodied, need eight to ten years to mature. At Fixin the memory of Napoléon I is particularly revered, as a result of the devotion shown by one of the emperor's former grenadier captains, Claude Noisot, who had a house built as a replica of the fort on St Helena. This house, in a park, is now a **museum** containing mementoes of the imperial campaigns. The centrepiece of the parkland is a hill topped by a bronze statue of 'Napoléon Awakening to Immortality' by the Burgundian sculptor Rude, whose statue of the 'Marseillaise' adorns the Arc de Triomphe in Paris. Noisot's tomb stands nearby, so that he is watching over his emperor even in death.

Fittingly, after Fixin's tribute to the Emperor, the wine of **Gevrey-Chambertin** (3,000 inhabitants, 12Km from Dijon) owes its fame to Napoléon's patronage. The **Chambertin** (from *Champ de Bertin* – Bertin's field) is a full-bodied wine acquiring a strong bouquet with age and considered to be one of the greatest Burgundies.

The **château**, built on the highest point in the sleepy village, dates from the 10th century and was restored by the monks of Cluny in the 13th century. The medieval interior is worth a visit while the cellars are still used for storing wine. (Open 10–11.50am and 2–5.30pm, Sundays and holidays 11–11.50am and 2.15–6.30pm. Closed Thursday, Christmas, 1 January, Easter and 1 November.) The **church**, dating mostly from the 15th century, has a Romanesque portal and contains the tombstone of Claude Jobert de Chambertin, who died in 1768. The owner of the vineyard of the **Clos de Beze**, Claude Jobert de Chambertin was a clever administrator as well, and his role in spreading the fame of the Chambertin wine in the 18th century was a decisive one. His former house is situated in the **Rue du Chambertin.**

Hotels and Restaurants

Rôtisserie du Chambertin A woman chef reigns over this gastronomic paradise with the accent on the Burgundian *nouvelle cuisine*. Dishes include: *Saumon à la Mousse de Haddock* (fresh salmon with haddock mousse), *Raviolis aux Truffes* (ravioli with truffles) and *Bavarois aux Poires* (pear in custard jelly). An excellent selection of Burgundies completes this feast, in lovely surroundings. Rue du Chambertin, 21220, Gevrey-Chambertin, Côte d'Or. Tel: (80) 34.33.20. Meals 200–220F. Closed Sunday night, Monday and August.

Le Richebourg Excellent food in a farmhouse décor. Specialities include: *Emincé de Rognons à la Menthe* (thinly sliced kidneys cooked with mint), *Coffret de Fraises Tièdes au Coulis de Framboises* (warm strawberry tart with raspberry sauce). Good value. 18 Rue Richebourg, 21220, Gevrey-Chambertin, Côte d'Or. Tel: (80) 34.30.37. Meals 50–120F. Closed Sunday night, Monday and 21 December–31 January. Credit cards: EC, VISA.

Les Terroirs Small family hotel with a comfortable cosy atmosphere. No restaurant. Route de Dijon, 21220, Gevrey-Chambertin, Côte d'Or. Tel: (80) 34.30.76. 18 rooms, 80–160F. Closed 23 December–15 January. Credit cards: AE, DC.

Chambolle-Musigny (403 inhabitants). Musigny is another famous *cru* of the Côte de Nuits.

The small village of **Vougeot** (178 inhabitants, 17Km from Dijon) with its vineyard, **Clos de Vougeot** (50Ha) which belonged to the Cistercian monks from the 12th to the 18th century, has become a symbol of Burgundy throughout the world. According to the 19th century writer Stendhal the famous vineyard was even given a full military salute by the Regiment of Colonel Brisson on his return from Italy.

The folklore associated with the Renaissance château (restored in the 19th century), now owned by the **Confrérie des Chevaliers du Tastevin**, dates from 1934 when at a gathering at **Nuits-St Georges** a group of

Burgundian merchants and growers decided to promote 'the wines of France in general and those of Burgundy in particular'. For this purpose they founded the *Confrérie* and ten years later purchased the Château at Clos-de-Vougeot as the venue of their 'chapters', held several times a year, in the 12th century cellar. Five hundred guests from all over the world take part in the *Disnées* (dinners) designed to enhance the fame and prestige of Burgundian wine and gastronomy. The Grand Master and the Grand Chamberlain, clad in robes of scarlet and gold, enthrone new members according to a burlesque ritual taken from Molière's play *Le Malade Imaginaire*. It is a true Burgundian event where the seriousness of the approach to food and wine is matched by a spirit of wit and good humour. It provides the opportunity to savour much-prized wines in perfect circumstances as well as to participate in festivities which, in true Burgundian spirit, more often than not end up in hearty singing.

The first day of the **Trois Glorieuses** (the three glorious days), namely the third Saturday, Sunday and Monday of November, provides a similar opportunity. This first day is the **Journée des Vins de Nuits** and takes place at Vougeot. The second day sees the auctioning of the **Beaune Hospice** wines and the third the **Paulée de Meursault** when a banquet is held at **Meursault.**

The **château** at Vougeot is open to the public. See the *Grand Cellier* (12th century) where the Confrérie des Chevaliers du Tastevin meets, and the *cuverie* (13th century) with four gigantic medieval wine presses. (Open 9–11.30am and 2–5.30pm, 5 January–20 December.)

Garages
Peugeot: Tel: (80) 34.30.62.

Vosne-Romanée (613 inhabitants, 21Km from Dijon). 'If Chambertin is the king of wines, Romanée is the Queen', its delicate fragrance and its rarity (6,500 bottles a year) make it one of the most highly prized and sought-after Burgundies, 'mingling velvet and satin in a bottle' according to an epicurian Archbishop of Paris.

Nuits-St Georges (5,072 inhabitants, Nuits-St Georges exit on the A37, from Dijon, 25Km; from Beaune, 13Km). Capital of the Côte de Nuits, this is the internationally best-known vineyard. Its fame dates from the days of Louis XIV, whose doctor advised him to drink a few glasses of Nuits and Romanée with his meal, for medicinal purposes, a prescription many of us would like to follow!

The vineyards themselves are 1,000 years old. Gallo-Roman artefacts found locally are exhibited in the **museum of archaeology.** (Open 2–6pm, 1 July–15 September, and 2–6pm, Sundays and holidays only 1 May–30 June.)

15Km along the D8 from Nuits-St Georges amid the forests of the Saône valley, stands the **Monastery of Cîteaux**, founded in 1098 by monks from the Abbey of Molesme. In search of solitude they settled among the rushes or *cistels* of the local marshes. The Cistercians owe their fame and expansion to St Bernard, who joined the order in 1112 and made them the standard-bearers of the Church Militant.

Nothing remains of the original monastery, though the site, all of forest and water, which St Bernard imbued with his fervour and enthusiasm must have changed little. It is now a Trappist monastery (Reformed Cistercian Rule) and the routine of the monks' lives has not changed very much since St Bernard's days. Men only are allowed to visit, any afternoon except Sundays and holidays. The monks make a mild soft cheese which is well worth a try.

Hotels and Restaurants
La Côte d'Or Quality restaurant, with rooms, offering such specialities as *Tourte de Pigeon* (pigeon in a crusty pie) and *Navarin de Queues de Langoustines* (Dublin Bay prawn stew). 1 Rue Thurot, 21700, Nuits-St Georges, Côte d'Or. Tel: (80) 61.06.10. 10 rooms, 115–150F. Meals 75–180F. Closed Sunday night and August. Credit cards: DC, EC.

Garages
Citroën: Tel: (80) 61.02.40; (night) (80) 61.05.71.
Peugeot: Tel: (80) 61.02.23.
Renault: Tel: (80) 61.22.44 or (80) 61.06.31.
Talbot: Tel: (80) 61.10.43.

Festivals, Fairs, and Sporting Events
March/April, Palm Sunday: **Auction of the wines of Nuits-St Georges**

The small village of **Comblanchieu** (641 inhabitants) on the N74 is renowned for its beautiful white limestone, which resembles marble when polished. The Paris Opera is built of Comblanchieu stone.

CÔTE DE BEAUNE
The Côte de Beaune stretches from the north of **Aloxe-Corton** (218 inhabitants 5Km north of Beaune) to **Santenay** some 20Km beyond Beaune. It produces some great white wines, fruity and rich and some famous reds which mature earlier than the **Côte de Nuits**. Aloxe-Corton is an attractive sight with the typically Burgundian polychrome roof of its small 18th century château emerging from a mass of vegetation.

Aloxe-Corton has the characteristic of producing both a great red wine (the **Corton**, the only red *grand cru* of the Côte de Beaune, with a fine bouquet) and a great white wine (the **Corton-Charlemagne**, which is the only white *grand cru* beside Puligny-Montrachet).

Corton-Charlemagne's name comes from a tradition that Charlemagne, when rebuilding the **Abbey of Saulieu** in 775, endowed it with some of his vineyards at Aloxe. However the legendary white beard of the Emperor became stained by the crimson colour of his favourite Corton wine, and in order to please his wife, who nagged him on the subject, he had part of his vineyards replanted with white wines.

Although wine-tasting can be enjoyed in many *caves*, some of them are situated in historical surroundings and are especially worth a visit. The **Château de Corton-André**, dating from the 18th century, in its romantic setting of greenery and with its lovely polychrome roof in the Flemish style, has on show an exhibition on the art of Cooperage (vat making) as well as offering tasting of its best *crus*. (Open 9.30–12am and 2.30–6.30pm every day.)

On the other side of the hill of Corton lies **Savigny-les-Beaune** (6Km from Beaune), whose wines mature faster than any others in the Côte de Beaune. Light and scented, they have inspired the Cousins de Bourgogne, a Bacchic association on the lines of the Confrérie des Chevaliers du Tastevin, with some fine mottoes (*Toujours gentilshommes sont cousins* – the members of the Cousins are always gentlemen) and exhortations ('There are five reasons for drinking: the arrival of a guest, present thirst, thirst to come, the excellence of the wine and any other you can think of') written in Latin. A more eloquent proof that a cultivated mind goes together with a cultivated palate surely cannot be found!

Hotels and Restaurants

L'Ouvrée A small, comfortable family hotel, with restaurant, and lovely rooms looking out on an inner courtyard and a garden. The owner has some cellars at Corton and Savigny-les-Beaune which he is always pleased to show to visitors. Route de Bouilland, 21420, Savigny-les-Beaune, Côte d'Or. Tel: (80) 21.51.52. 22 rooms, 110–140F. Meals 50–110F. Closed 1 February–15 March.

At **Bouilland** (10Km from Savigny-les-Beaune on the D2, 16Km from Beaune) is the **Hostellerie du Vieux Moulin**. An old mill, in the heart of Burgundy, converted into a very comfortable quiet hotel with an excellent restaurant. Bouilland, 21420, Savigny-les-Beaune, Côte d'Or. Tel: (80) 21.51.16. 8 rooms, 120–180F. Meals 110–190F. Closed Wednesday, except in season, and 4–31 January. Credit cards: AE, DC, VISA.

Both on the N74:

L'Ermitage de Corton A fine restaurant with the most amazingly grand décor in a panelled dining-room with coffered ceiling and heavy curtains. The food is of the same ilk in both quality and quantity: Burgundian with panache. *Terrine de Grenouilles* (frog pâté), *Coquilles St Jacques aux Truffes* (scallops with truffles), *Canette à l'Infusion de Cassis* (duck cooked with blackcurrant tea). Route du Dijon, Chorey-les-Beaune, 21200, Beaune, Côte d'Or. Tel: (80) 22.05.28. Meals 85–220F. Closed Sunday night, Monday, and school holidays in February and 1–15 July. Credit cards: AE, DC, VISA.

Le Bareuzai An excellent restaurant serving traditional Burgundian dishes in a cosy Burgundian décor. Specialities: *Escargots* (snails), *Oeufs en Meurettes* (soft poached eggs on toast with a red wine sauce) and the classic *Coq au Vin*. Very good value. Route de Dijon, Chorey-les-Beaune, 21200, Beaune, Côte d'Or. Tel: (80) 22.02.90. Meals 36–130F.

Garages

Peugeot: Savigny-les-Beaune. Tel: (80) 21.52.06.

At **Chorey-les-Beaune** (4Km north-east of Beaune by the N74), between Aloxe-Corton and Beaune, the **Domaine Goud de Beaupuis**, a lovely house in a park sitting in the midst of its own vineyard offers tasting, in its vaulted cellars, of the best **Pommard, Beaune, Aloxe-Corton, Savigny** and **Chorey-les-Beaune** *crus*. A monolithic stone wine press weighing 7 tons and still in use can be viewed. (Open every day.)

Pommard (754 inhabitants, 3Km south of Beaune on the D973) is among the best known names of Burgundies (like Beaune and Nuits-St Georges) because of its sheer availability. The most full-bodied wine of the Côte de Beaune, its name comes from an ancient goddess of fruit and gardens: *Pomone*. It was particularly appreciated by connoisseurs such as Henry IV and Louis XV of France.

There is tasting at the historic **Château de Pommard**, founded in 1098 by Eudes, the first Duke of Burgundy. The present château is 18th century and the *caves* are adjacent. With its 20Ha of vineyards Pommard is the largest single domain in Burgundy. (Open 8.30am–7pm 26 March–22 November, 8.30am–2pm Sunday and holidays. In the winter visitors are received at the château.)

Volnay (464 inhabitants, 6Km south of Beaune of the D973) produces wine which is the most delicate and exquisitely scented of all Burgundies. The Dukes of Burgundy recognised it as such and had here one of their most prized vineyards as well as one of their favourite country seats. Louis XI, on his triumph over the last Duke of Burgundy, Charles le Téméraire, in 1477, celebrated by taking to his château of Plessis-les-Tours the entire vintage of that year for his own delight.

The wine of **Auxey-Duresses** (329 inhabitants, 8Km south of Beaune on the D973) was formerly sold as Pommard or Volnay before the law on the *Appellation d'Origine* laid down strict conditions for the use of the famous names. These red wines are still excellent value as their names do not allow them to command the inflated prices of their better-known neighbours. The local church has a magnificent 16th century triptych.

Hotels and Restaurants

La Crémaillère Classic Burgundian cuisine is the hallmark of the excellent restaurant. *Truite à la Crème* (trout in cream sauce), *Jambon Persillé* (ham in parsley aspic), *Coq au Vin*. Good value. Auxey-Duresses, 21190, Meursault, Côte d'Or. Tel: (80) 21.22.60. Meals 70–150F. Closed Monday night, Tuesday and 20 January–1 March.

The great white wine region starts with the small town of **Meursault** (1,733 inhabitants, 10Km south of Beaune on the D973 and D17E), dominated by the Gothic spire of its church. Meursault itself has no *grand cru* but is the best known of white Burgundies being recognised by connoisseurs, together with **Puligny** and **Chassagne-Montrachet**, as the 'best white wines in the world'.

Though dry, Meursault has a mellowness due to a high glycerine content, a nutty taste and full-blown aroma which make it a particularly distinctive and distinguished wine. Some reds are produced as well.

La Paulée de Meursault on the last (ie the Monday) of the *Trois Glorieuses*, after the Sunday auction at Beaune, is an important date, with a banquet to which each guest brings two bottles of his own wine, and a prize of 100 bottles of Meursault is given to the winner of a competition for the best literary work.

There is tasting at the **Château de Meursault** in the superb 14th century cellars. An exhibition of paintings on the theme of the vineyard and wine is also on show.

The **Ropiteau Frères**, growers and wine-merchants, offer wine-tasting in 17th century cellars, formerly owned by the Hospice of Beaune. (Open 9am–7pm, April–November, every day.)

The lyricism inspired by the wines of Burgundy is best illustrated by Alexandre Dumas who said that 'Montrachet should be drunk on one's knees with bare head'. The white wines of **Puligny-Montrachet** (528 inhabitants, 10Km south of Beaune on the N74) are drier and paler than Meursault, and have a slightly greenish tinge and a distinctive fruitiness which makes them perfect for drinking on their own.

The reds of **Chassagne-Montrachet** are full-bodied yet subtle.

The town of **Santenay** (1,008 inhabitants, 18Km from Beaune, on the N74 and D974), dominated by the spectacular belvedere of the **Montagne des**

Trois Croix, marks the end of the Côte d'Or. Santenay red wines, like those of Chassagne, are closer to those of the Côte de Nuits, being full-bodied with a distinct flavour.

The spring, the waters of which contain the highest lithium content of any in Europe, is renowned for relieving cases of gout and liver complaints. The small **Church of St Jean** is a mixture of styles, from the 13th century nave to the 15th century choir. The two wooden polychrome statues of St Martin and St Roch date from the 15th century.

Chagny (5,926 inhabitants, 16Km from Beaune on the N74 and N6) is a busy market town boasting a superb restaurant in an old Burgundian house converted into a very comfortable family-run hotel.

Hotels and Restaurants

Hôtel Lameloise A truly epicurean experience can be enjoyed within the walls of this 15th century house converted with great taste and attention to detail. Try the *Cassolette de Queues d'Ecrevisses* (fresh-water crayfish in their own juice), the *Salade de Cresson au Foie Gras Frais* (watercress salad with fresh foie gras) or the *Soufflé au Citron* (lemon soufflé). The wine list is a delight. 36 Place d'Armes, 71150, Chagny, Saône-et-Loire. Tel: (85) 87.08.85. 25 rooms, 140–280F. Meals 220–250F. Closed Wednesday, Thursday lunch-time and 27 April–13 May, and 29 November–17 December. Credit card: VISA.

Hôtel de la Poste Small hotel without restaurant. 17 Rue de la Poste, 71150, Chagny, Saône-et-Loire. Tel: (85) 87.08.27. 11 rooms, 130–160F. Closed 15 December–1 March, and Sunday out of season.

At **Chassey-le Camp** (6Km from Chagny by the D974 and D109; from Paris, Chalon-Nord exit, N6, 13Km; From Lyon, Chalon-Nord/Chagny exit, 13Km) is the **Auberge du Camp Romain**, a simple quiet modern hotel, with restaurant, and a wonderful view over a lovely valley. Chassey-le-Camp, 71150, Chagny, Saône-et-Loire. Tel: (85) 87.09.91. 11 rooms, 50–120F. Meals 50F. Closed Wednesday (October–March) and January.

From the same exit, 13Km to Mercurey (on the D978) and you can reach the **Hôtellerie du Val d'Or**. An excellent village inn with garden and rooms, offering traditional Burgundian food with great flair, and some *nouvelle cuisine* inspired dishes such as: *Emincés de Rognons de Veau aux Navets* (thin slices of calves' kidneys with turnips) or *Feuilleté de Légumes au Saumon Frais* (fresh salmon with young vegetables in flaky pastry). Good value. Grande Rue, Mercurey, 71640, Givry, Saône-et-Loire. Tel: (85) 47.13.70. 12 rooms, 80–170F. Meals 65–170F. Closed Sunday night (15 November–15 March), Monday, 1–15 September and school holidays at Christmas. Credit card: VISA.

BEAUNE
From Paris, Beaune/Chagny exit, 3Km
From Lyon, Beaune/Chagny exit, 3Km
Inhabitants: 19,972
Office de Tourisme: opposite the Hôtel-Dieu, *closed Christmas and New Year's Day*

Beaune, unlike Dijon, is a town at the very heart of the wine trade. It lives by and for wine, as the complex labyrinth of cellars under the town illustrates. Even the bastions of the old city ramparts have been taken over for wine storage.

The wines of **Beaune** have been renowned from the earliest times. It is only since the end of the 18th century that the full-bodied Nuits-St George became prized above the wines of Beaune, which drunk young have much subtlety and bouquet.

As well as being a city of wine, Beaune is a city of artistic treasures all linked, however, with the history of wine. This is admirably illustrated by the outstanding **Hôtel-Dieu**, with its world-famous auction in November of the Hospice wine, the proceeds of which go towards the running costs of the hospital. It has been called the greatest charity auction in the world. The **Hospices de Beaune** (comprising the **Hôtel-Dieu** and the **Hospice de la Charité**) own 53Ha of vineyards between **Aloxe-Corton** and **Meursault**. Since 1851 the wines of the *hospices* have been sold at a public auction held on the third Sunday in November. It is now an international event of great importance for the wine growers of Burgundy, as the prices fetched determine the general price each year. It is the main reason for the festivities known at the **Trois Glorieuses.** On Sunday (the second of the three days), the auction takes place in the market-hall, the day ending with a candlelit dinner inside one of the bastion cellars on the town-ramparts.

A Gallo-Roman city, Beaune was the main seat of the Dukes of Burgundy until the 14th century when they moved to Dijon. The fortifications date from that time. However, despite the fact that they moved their capital to Dijon, the Dukes still presided over the Appeal Courts and the *Grands Jours* (when the Dukes' council of barons, knights and lawyers sat as a high court) at Beaune itself. During these sessions the ducal court resided at the **Hôtel des Ducs**, rebuilt in the 15th century and now a **museum of wine.** Situated in the **Rue de l'Enfer**, near the Church of Notre Dame the *hôtel* is built in stone and wood used in the typically decorative Burgundian manner. The inner courtyard, with the low eaves of the high-pitched roof and the slender wooden beams of the open gallery, has the atmospheric quality of a stage set.

The **cuverie** displays a wine press and barrels, while the history of wine in Burgundy is outlined on the ground floor. Upstairs the headquarters of the Ambassade des Vins de France display two contemporary Aubusson tapestries from designs by Lurcat and Tourlière. (Guided tours at 9, 10 and 11am and 2, 3, 4 and 5pm. Closed 1 January, Christmas.)

The **Collegiate Church of Notre Dame**, off the Rue de la République, is one of the most striking examples of Burgundian Romanesque architecture, and shows the influence of Cluny. The most remarkable feature of the whole building is the transept tower topped by a bulbous tiled roof, with a lantern added in 1581 when it served as a watch tower. Inside notice the 16th century **Bouton Chapel** (first bay, south aisle) with a coffered ceiling, and the outstanding **Tournai tapestries** of the life of the Virgin, woven in wool and silk and commissioned in 1474 by Cardinal Jean Rolin.

From Notre Dame walk down the **Rue de la République** to the **Rue de l'Hôtel-Dieu** in which the famous **hôtel-Dieu** stands. Built between 1443 and 1451 by **Nicolas Rolin** as an act of piety to assure the salvation of his soul, the *Hôtel-Dieu* was designed as a refuge for the sick and impoverished of Beaune. Louis XI of France, in customary fine cynical form, remarked that 'It was only fitting that he who made so many destitute during his life should build them an almshouse before he died'. Be that as it may the *Hôtel-Dieu* is a marvellously well-preserved example of pure Flemish medieval architecture which has survived unaltered and untouched.

In true northern fashion the vast high-pitched slate roof, animated with dormers, weathercocks, pinnacles and a lead-fretted balustrade, is the main feature of the outer façade.

As you enter, notice on the oak door the magnificent **knocker** in the form of a lizard poised to catch a fly. Inside, the **cour d'honneur** is an extraordinary blaze of colour. The magnificence of the varnished tiles of the roof and the general conception of arcades, open galleries and crocketed gables make for a gay, glowingly rich ensemble 'more fitting for princely than poorly lodgings'.

The **well** in the centre of the courtyard adds the final touch to this elegant medieval scene.

The **Grande Salle des Pôvres (paupers' ward)** is a splendid sight inside with its impressive proportions (52m long) and the glowing many-coloured ceiling with beam-ends carved in the shape of sea-monsters. The twenty-eight four-poster beds face towards the altar of the chapel situated at the east end behind a screen, so that the patients could follow Mass. The beds were designed to hold two or four patients if necessary. Men and women were welcome in the paupers' ward until the young Louis XIV visited the hospital in 1658 and was so shocked that he ordered the women to be moved to another wing. The beds used to be covered with magnificent tapestries (now in the museum) on feast days. Notice near the entrance a Flemish Christ of Sorrows (14th century) carved from a single block of oak. The famous Roger Van der Weyden alterpiece (now in the museum) used to stand on the altar.

The **paupers' ward** was in use until 1948 when the main hospital was moved to modern premises just behind the *Hôtel-Dieu*, although the *Hôtel-Dieu* itself is still used as an old peoples' home, and the nuns in charge of it are under the same rule as their 15th century sisters. It is this historical continuity which makes Beaune hospice such a fascinating place to visit for the 20th century traveller.

A glimpse of the **kitchen** can be had on the way to the museum. It still caters for the 240 residents. Notice the small model of Maître Bertrand, who turns the spit, built in 1698 by a clockmaker of Beaune. In the **pharmacy** a collection of pewter and bronze vessels is displayed, together with some 18th century Nevers faience.

The most outstanding work in the hospice's **museum** is the famous Last Judgement **altarpiece** of **Rogier Van der Weyden**. Commissioned by Nicolas Rolin in 1443, it used to stand on the altar of the chapel of the *Grande Salle des Pôvres*. The impressive central panel of Christ at the Last Judgement, surrounded by saints and angels with the blessed on one side and the damned on the other, was seen only on Sundays and feast days. On the right wall the shutters of the altarpiece are displayed, to show the portrait of the donor, Nicolas Rolin, and his wife Guigone, with St Sebastian and St Anthony, patron Saints of the *Hôtel-Dieu*. The altarpiece is one of the masterpieces of International Gothic, and compares with the Van Eyck altarpiece of the Lamb at Ghent. The extreme naturalism of the treatment of details is striking, yet does not distract one's attention from the awesome grandeur of the whole. The overpowering presence of this piece makes all the other exhibits look pale. Yet it is worth looking at the tapestries of St Eligius and an original counterpane depicting St Anthony and the donor's monogram together with his wife's motto (*Seulle Etoile* – The only, or lonely, star) which appears all over the hospice. (Guided tour of the museum, 9–11.30am and 2–6pm, 1 April–December, otherwise 9–11am and 2–5pm, but until 6pm Sunday and holidays.)

A walk through the animated town reveals Beaune's lesser known treasures. From the *hôtel-Dieu* take the **Boulevard Bretonnière** and follow the ramparts to the **Bastion of St Martin** and the public garden in the **Place des Lions.** Nearby in the **Parc de la Bouzaise** a mini-zoo and childrens' games corner make it an interesting walk for the family.

Come back to the centre and the **Place Monge** with its 14th century **beffroi** and its statue by the sculptor Rude of Monge, the 18th century mathematician and physicist, who founded the École Polytechnique. Take the **Rue des Tonneliers** to have a look at the **Hôtel de la Rochepot**, a 16th century Italianate building with a lovely Gothic façade and two inner courtyards.

Follow the **Rue de Lorraine** and admire some 16th century houses at numbers 18–24.

The **Hôtel de Ville**, a 17th century former Ursuline convent, is off the Rue Lorraine and houses the **Musée des Beaux Arts**. Paintings and sculpture relating to local history are exhibited. (Open 9–12am and 2–5.30pm, Easter–November. Closed Tuesday, 1 May and 14 July.)

The **Church of St Nicolas**, on the N74 in the direction of Dijon, is reached from the Rue de Lorraine. The church was rebuilt in the thirteenth century, but the portal depicting the legend of St Nicolas saving the three maidens sold by their father is 12th century.

Hotels and Restaurants

Le Cep A luxury hotel in a beautiful 17th century house very comfortably converted with great taste and attention to detail. No restaurant but own cellar with wine tasting. 27 Rue Maufoux, 21200, Beaune, Côte d'Or. Tel: (80) 22.35.48. 21 rooms, 125–300F. Closed Thursday morning and 1 December–1 March. Credit cards: AE, EC.

La Poste A traditional luxury hotel with a classically gastronomic restaurant, and rooms with air-conditioning and soundproofing overlooking the ramparts on one side and the vineyards on the other. Specialities include: *Filet de Veau Sauce Légère au Citron* (veal fillet with light lemon sauce), *Sole à la Bourguignonne* (sole in wine sauce) and *Soupe de Moules au Safran* (mussel soup with saffron). 3 Rue Clémenceau, 21200, Beaune, Côte d'Or. Tel: (80) 22.08.11. 25 rooms, 235–665F. Meals 135–250F. Open all year. Credit cards: AE, DC, EC, VISA.

Central Comfortable centrally situated (therefore noisy!) hotel with an excellent restaurant serving traditional Burgundian cuisine: *Terrine de Carpe et d'Anguilles Marinées au Bourgogne* (carp and eel pâté marinated in Burgundy wine) and *Aiguillettes de Canard* (thin slices of duck). 2 Rue Victor Millot, 21200, Beaune, Côte d'Or. Tel: (80) 24.77.24. 22 rooms, 80–230F. Meals 72–160F. Closed 22 November–31 March. Credit card: VISA.

Rôtisserie de la Paix Excellent restaurant in an old converted barn on the outskirts of the town, offering traditional *haute cuisine* interpreted with individuality. Try the *Salade Tiède de Laperau* (hot rabbit salad) or the *Rognon de Veau au Basilic* (calf's kidneys with basil sauce) and the delicious sweets. 47 Faubourg Madeleine, 21200, Beaune, Côte d'Or. Tel: (80) 22.33.33. Meals 80–180F. Closed Sunday night, Monday, and February–beginning of March, and 1–15 August. Credit cards: AE, VISA.

At **Levernois** (5Km on the D970 and D111) is the **Hôtel Parc** (From Beaune/Chagny exit, D970, 2Km) A very quiet simple hotel in a converted farmhouse in the heart of the Burgundy countryside. No restaurant. Levernois, 21200, Beaune, Côte d'Or. Tel: (80) 22.22.51.

20 rooms, 74–115F. Closed 23 November–8 December and 1–15 March.

Garages
Citroën: 1 Route Pommard. Tel: (80) 22.28.14.
Fiat: 40 Faubourg Bretonnière. Tel: (80) 22.31.30.
Ford: 146 Route de Dijon. Tel: (80) 22.11.02.
Peugeot/Talbot: 135b Route de Dijon. Tel: (80) 22.27.00.
Renault: 78 Route de Pommard. Tel: (80) 22.25.48.

Festivals, Fairs and Sporting Events
November, third Sunday: second day of the **Trois Glorieuses, auction** of hospice wines in the covered market.

L'ARCHÉODROME
From Paris, Beaune–Tailly service area
From Lyon, Beaune–Merceuil service area

The Archéodrome 6Km south of Beaune on the *autoroute* the A6 is a fascinating example of a totally new concept in museums, particularly appreciated by children and well worth a visit, if only for curiosity's sake or to break the journey. It is situated directly by the side of the *autoroute*, with a hotel and a restaurant on the same service area.

The theme of this open-air museum is 'A Thousand Centuries of Human Life in Burgundy', prompted by the discovery of the fascinating tombstones at Nuits-St Georges, in the burial ground of the Bolards, and of a Gallo-Roman villa at Selongey. A great deal of serious scholarship has gone into this imaginative and evocative historical *tableau vivant*. Financed by the Paris–Rhin–Rhône Autoroute Company, this project has materialised in the shape of an exhibition hall built in the form of a walk-way, with photographs, reproductions of artefacts and models from prehistoric to Gallo-Roman Burgundy, around a patio with a reconstituted Gallic village. On a piece of land with no particular historical interest, a garden has been laid out with fields, trees, running water and seats, allowing the visitor to absorb the atmosphere of this illustrated journey back into history. The path takes the traveller past Stone Age huts, an ancient tomb in a tumulus, a reconstruction of the fortifications erected by Julius Caesar in front of **Alesia** (16Km north-east of Semur-en-Auxois), which brought about the defeat of the legendary Gallic chieftain Vercingétorix. The Gallo-Roman period is evoked with a small temple, a fanum (sanctuary), a necropolis with tombstones lining a Roman road and a Roman villa. (Open 10am–8pm, 1 May–30 September, otherwise 10am–6pm.)

TOURNUS

From Paris, Tournus exit, N6, 2Km
From Lyon, Tournus exit, N6, 2Km
Inhabitants 7,339
Office de Tourisme: Rue A. Thibaudet, 1 March–31 October

Tournus lies at the edge of the **Mâconnais** hilly region, on the right bank of the River Saône. It is a small intimate town where the warmth of the climate heralds the south. A pleasant place to have a leisurely meal or to spend a quiet night, Tournus marks the beginning of the **Mâconnais vineyard**, which stretches along the right bank of the river beyond Mâcon to **Romanèche-Thorins**, where it becomes the **Beaujolais** region. A Roman staging-post, Tournus was the scene in 200AD of the martyrdom of St Valerian. An abbey was built to house his relics, which in 875 were given by Charles the Bald to the monks of the Island of Noirmoutier, who were fleeing from the Norman raiders with the relics of St Philibert, their own saint. From then onwards the abbey became known as St Philibert's, but the yearly pilgrimage is in honour of both the saints whose relics are preserved there.

Coming from the N6 take the **Rue Albert Thibaudet**, passing through the **Porte des Champs**, the former gateway of the abbey precinct, of which only two towers remain. The **abbey** is one of the most beautiful monuments in Burgundy, part of the 'white mantle of churches' erected after the year 1000, although the two belfries date from the 12th century. The nave is preceded by a vast narthex (10th and 11th century), one of the few surviving examples of the early Romanesque style called 'Lombard', with pilasters and decorative blind arcades on the outside walls. The upper part of the narthex is a chapel dedicated to St Michael, in accordance with Carolingian tradition.

The nave is radiantly luminous in pale pink local stone with tall plain columns, built up of stone blocks, separating the central nave, with barrel vaulting, from the two side aisles, which have groin vaulting. The transept and the choir contrast with the rest of the building in the whiteness of their stonework and the sudden narrowing of proportions in order to accommodate the dimensions of the earlier crypt, which dates from the 10th century and is decorated with frescoes of the Virgin and Child and Christ in Majesty.

In the right hand aisle of the nave notice in the Chapel of Notre Dame la Brune the 12th century cedarwood Virgin and Child reliquary statue in the style of the Auvergne region.

Outside, on the right side of the church, a **cloister** (11th century) and the **chapter house** have been restored and are open to visitors. The **refectory**, a vaulted 12th century room with impressive dimensions, was used as a tennis court in the 17th century, hence the name *Le Ballon* still used to designate it.

Behind the Abbey of St Philibert, the **Musée Perrin-de-Puycousin** (or **Musée Bourguignon**) is housed in a 17th century building and displays wax figures in tableaux illustrating the people and life of Burgundy throughout the ages. (Guided tour 9–12am and 2–6pm, 1 April–31 October. Closed Tuesday.)

Tournus is the native town of the painter Greuze 1725–1805, and a small museum in the Rue du Collège is dedicated to his works and contains seven portraits, drawings and reproductions. To reach the **Musée Greuze** from St Philibert take the **Rue A. Bessard** and then the **Rue du Collège**. (Open 9–12am and 2–6pm, Palm Sunday–1 November. Closed Tuesday morning, Sunday and holidays and 1 May.)

The **Church of St Madeleine** overlooking the Quai de Verdun and the River Saône still has a 12th century Romanesque portal.

Hotels and Restaurants

Le Rampart A very comfortable modern hotel, on the N6, yet quiet, with an excellent restaurant offering specialities such as *Ris de Veau au Citron* (sweetbreads with lemon sauce) and *Grenouilles Sautées* (pan-fried frogs). 2–4 Avenue Gambetta, 71700, Tournus, Saône-et-Loire. Tel: (85) 51.10.56. 30 rooms, 120–250F. Meals 57–200F. Open all year. Credit cards: AE, DC, EC, VISA.

Greuze A quality restaurant in the classical tradition of the *grande cuisine* with delectable specialities such as *Quenelles de Brochet* (pike dumplings) and *Goujonnette de Sole au Citron Vert* (small pieces of fried sole with lime sauce). 4 Rue Albert Thibaudet, 71700, Tournus, Saône-et-Loire. Tel: (85) 51.13.52. Meals 140–250F. Closed Thursday, and 10–19 June and 16 November–5 December. Credit cards: AE, VISA.

Le Sauvage Excellent restaurant offering Burgundian specialities. Try the *Filet de Charolais Marchand de Vin* (fillet of Charolais beef with red wine and shallot sauce) or *Mousse de Brochet* (pike mousse). Place du Champ-de-Mars, 71700, Tournus, Saône-et-Loire. Tel: (85) 51.14.45. Meals 75–150F.

13Km from Tournus at Fleurville on the N6 is the **Château de Fleurville**. A very comfortable hotel in a 16th century château beautifully and tastefully converted, with an excellent restaurant offering unusual dishes such as *Quenelle au Fromage de Chèvre* (goat cheese dumpling) and *Turbotin à la Crème de Truffes* (turbot with truffle sauce). A lovely, peaceful place with its own garden – perfect for a quiet weekend. Fleurville, 71260, Lugny, Saône-et-Loire. Tel: (85) 33.12.17. 14 rooms, 170–190F. Meals 62–150F. Closed Monday and February. Credit cards: AE, DC, VISA.

Garages
Ford: 3 Avenue Gambetta. Tel: (85) 51.06.45.
Peugeot: 5 Avenue·du Général Leclerc. Tel: (85) 51.04.63.
Renault: 3 Route de Paris. Tel: (85) 51.07.05.

BRANCION
From Paris, Tournus exit, N6 and D14 from Tournus, 17Km
From Lyon, Tournus exit, N6 and D14 from Tournus, 17Km

Brancion is a very picturesque tiny medieval village perched at a height of 400m on a rocky promontory overlooking the pass linking Tournus to the **Grosne Valley.** It was the seat of a powerful barony in the Middle Ages.

Only the gatehouse remains of the town walls and the 10th century **château**, rebuilt by the Duke Philippe le Hardi in the 14th century, is now a ruin. But the narrow medieval streets invaded by grass and lined with old houses, the 15th century **covered market** and the small **Church of St Pierre** sitting proudly at the very end of the promontory all conjure up a more important and glorious past.

The remains of Josserand de Brancion, cousin of St Louis King of France and killed during the Seventh Crusade, are preserved in the church under a tombstone with his effigy. The 14th century frescoes decorating the walls were commissioned by Eudes the fourth Duke of Burgundy.

'Rural Burgundy is still largely Romanesque in its visual effect', said the archaeologist K.J. Conant. This continuity in tradition is very apparent despite subsequent alterations to original buildings, and when one looks down from the terrace of the château on the village and its church, the Valley of the Grosne, the hills of the **Charollais** and the **Morvan**, it is as if time has stood still. In fact the whole village seems to bask in a strange and pregnant silence. It is no surprise to hear that Celtic fires are still lit here on midsummer night. The site has the disquieting quality of an ancient place of worship.

Hotels and Restaurants
Montagne de Brancion A very quiet small family hotel in a secluded position in the wooded Mâconnais hills. No restaurant. Col de Brancion, 71700, Tournus, Saône-et-Loire. Tel: (85) 51.12.40. 20 rooms, 100–190F. Open all year.

Festivals, Fairs and Sporting Events
Sunday nearest 24 June: **midsummer Celtic bonfires.**

95

MÂCON
From Paris, Mâcon-Nord exit, N6, 8Km
From Lyon, Mâcon-Sud exit, N6, 6Km
Inhabitants: 39,587
Office de Tourisme: Avenue de Lattre-de-Tassigny, closed Sunday

Lying on the right bank of the River Saône, Mâcon, two hours away from Geneva and the Alps, four hours from the Mediterranean coast, is a turning point most travellers shoot past on their way south. However it will repay a more lingering visit.

The River Saône, 'so slow, one cannot tell which way it flows' according to Julius Caesar, expands into a natural lake, 5Km long and with an average width of 300m, at Mâcon. A marina has been built and provides a haven for those keen on water sports, such as rowing (Oxford and Cambridge regard with respect the black and gold local colours), sailing, water skiing, windsurfing, water jousting, water polo etc. Tennis, riding and golf complete this survey of an eminently sporty city.

The pleasures of the table are well catered for, with the delectable Mâconnais wines accompanying such delicacies as *Quenelles de Brochets* (pike dumplings), *Pochouse* (a fresh-water *Bouillabaisse* using pike, perch, tench, carp and eels with an onion and bacon sauce and, of course, white burgundy), *Poularde à la Crème* (grain-fattened chicken with a cream sauce) or *Friture de la Saône* (fried whitebait consisting mostly of baby roach). All this can be found in many establishments, both simple and expensive, in Mâcon itself and in the surrounding villages.

Mâcon, the Roman *Matisco*, was the seat of a powerful county in the Middle Ages. In the 6th century the Frankish King Childebert, on his way back from a victorious raid on Spain, presented to the town of Mâcon the relics of St Vincent which had been given to him in return for raising the siege of Saragossa. The saint's popularity in Burgundy dates from this time. He is the patron saint of vine growers and his feast day on 22 January is celebrated by the Confrérie des Chevaliers du Tastevin, with a procession in a different town or village every year.

Mâcon itself has suffered heavily from the iconoclastic fury of the Revolution and, later, thoughtless town development.

The old **Cathedral of St Vincent** was destroyed. Only the portal and the two west towers survive, on the Place de la Barre.

Nowadays, apart from a pleasant river-front with the 14th century **Pont St-Laurent**, Mâcon has little left of historical interest except the **Maison de Bois.** Situated at the corner of the Place aux Herbes, 22 **Rue Dombey**, reached from the **Quai Lamartine**, it is a Renaissance house decorated with slender columns and fine carvings of grotesque figures and fantastic animals. It is supposed to have been the headquarters of the Abbaye de Maugouvert (the Abbey of Misrule), a society devoted to the irresponsible pursuit of pleasure. At Mâcon it went beyond the rules of decency and was forbidden in 1625, with the threat of the death penalty for anyone who took the title of Abbot of Misrule.

The **Musée Municipal des Ursulines**, in the former 17th Century Ursuline convent, houses a collection of local prehistoric artefacts and ceramics as well as paintings of the French School from Le Brun and Greuze to Courbet, Monet, Picasso and Braque. (Open 10–12am and 2–6pm. Closed Tuesday, morning of Sunday and holidays, 1 January, 1 May, 14 July, 1 November and Christmas.)

The most famous son of Mâcon, the 19th century poet **Lamartine** has a **museum** dedicated to him at the **Hôtel Senecé, Rue Sigorgne** off the **Place aux Herbes**. Paintings, tapestries and furniture evoke the period, while documents relating to Lamartine's life and career as a politician and a poet are exhibited. (Open 2–5pm, 1 May–30 September.)

The **Maison de Lamartine**, 15 Rue Lamartine, was bought in 1804 by his father. Lamartine wrote his first poems there, and the *Méditations* which were the start of his literary career.

Hotels and Restaurants

Frantel Hôtel with **Le St Vincent Restaurant** A very comfortable hotel, with very quiet modern rooms looking on to the river, and a tennis court nearby. The restaurant serves local Bressane specialities and lighter *nouvelle cuisine* inspired dishes such as *Lapereau aux Raisins* (rabbit with grapes) or *Rognons de Veau à la Fleur de Tilleul* (calf's kidney with lime blossom). 26 Rue Pierre-de-Coubertin, 71000, Mâcon, Saône-et-Loire. Tel: (85) 38.28.06. 63 rooms, 219–316F. Meals 70–160F. Closed Saturday lunch-time. Credit cards: AE, DC, EC, VISA.

Bellevue Comfortable hotel with an excellent restaurant serving regional specialities with a personal touch. Try the *Volaille Pochée* (grain-fattened chicken poached in stock) or the *Pochouse d'Anguilles* (eel stew). 416–420 Quai Lamartine, 71000, Mâcon, Saône-et-Loire. Tel: (85) 38.05.07. 43 rooms, 120–350F. Meals 75–130F.

Auberge Bressane Bressane specialities are the hallmark of this very good restaurant. *Quenelles au Fromage de Chèvre* (goat cheese dumplings) and *Pâté d'Anguilles* (eel pâté) are part of the menu. Good value. 114 Rue du 28 Juin 1944, 71000, Mâcon, Saône-et-Loire. Tel: (85) 38.07.42. Meals 52–130F. Closed Tuesday, and 1–15 December. Credit cards: AE, DC, EC, VISA.

Au Rocher de Cancale An excellent fish restaurant serving seafood and specialities such as *Sardines Fraîches au Mâcon* (fresh sardines cooked in Mâcon wine). Very good value. 393 Quai Jean-Jaurès, 71000, Mâcon, Saône-et-Loire. Tel: (85) 38.07.50. Meals 40–110F. Closed Sunday night, Monday and 1–15 January.

Le Saint Laurent 300m on the other side of the river the Saint Laurent offers regional (and other) specialities such as *Brochet au Vin* (pike in wine sauce), *Mousse de Saumon à la Ciboulette* (salmon mousse with chives) and *Filet de Veau aux Chanterelles* (veal fillet with chanterelles). Very good value. 1 Quai Bouchacourt, 01620, Saint-Laurant-sur-Saône, Ain. Tel: (85) 38.32.03. Meals 40–140F. Closed Tuesday night, Wednesday and 15 November–15 December.

At **Vonnas** (19Km from Mâcon by the N79 and D80; from Paris, Mâcon-Sud exit, N79 and D80, 25Km; From Lyon, Belleville exit, D17 and D936, 26Km) is the **La Mère Blanc**, a luxurious hotel exquisitely furnished with antique furniture and beautifully appointed with balconies overlooking the river, nestling in the middle of a park with tennis court, heated swimming pool and a ravishing inner garden. An outstanding restaurant completes this taste of heaven. Gourmet dishes such as *Ecrevisses au Pouilly-Fuissé* (fresh-water crayfish in Pouilly-Fuissé stock), *Tartelettes d'Escargots* (snail tartlets), fresh goat cheeses and exquisite Petits Fours. A dream of a place. 01540, Vonnas, Ain. Tel: (74) 50.00.10. 25 rooms and suites, 185–1,100F. Meals 155–300F. Closed Wednesday, Thursday lunch-time and January. Credit cards: AE, DC, VISA.

At **Thoissey** (16Km from Mâcon, by the N79 and D933; from Paris, Mâcon-Sud exit, N6 and D7, 18Km; from Lyon, Belleville exit, D17 and D933, 12Km) is the **Hôtel du Chapon Fin.** A very comfortable hotel in a beautiful old house with a lovely garden. A very friendly welcome matches the smiling atmosphere and the delicious cuisine offering the best of Bressane tradition. Specialities include *Cassolette de Queues d'Ecrevisses* (fresh-water crayfish) and *Volaille à la Crème et aux Morilles* (grain-fattened chicken with cream and mushroom sauce). 01140, Thoissey, Ain. Tel: (74) 04.04.74. 25 rooms, 120–320F. Meals 110–180F. Credit card: VISA.

At **Montmerle-sur-Saône** (29Km from Mâcon by the N79 and D933; from Paris, Belleville exit, D17, 8Km; from Lyon, Belleville exit, D17, 8Km) is the **Castel de Valrose**, an excellent restaurant specialising in traditionally classical food such as *Mousse Chaude de Foies de Volailles* (hot chicken liver mousse) or *Sole à la Mousse de Homard* (sole with lobster mousse). With quiet rooms. 12 Boulevard de la République, Montmerle-sur-Saône, 01140, Thoissey, Ain. Tel: (74) 69.30.52. 5 rooms, 150F. Meals 95–200F. Closed Monday night, Tuesday and 2–15 January.

Garages

Austin/Morris/Triumph: 390 Rue Lacretelle. Tel: (85) 38.64.31.
BMW: 20 Rue Lacretelle. Tel (85) 38.46.05.
Citroën: 62 Rue de Lyon. Tel: (85) 38.01.74.

Peugeot/Talbot: Rue Bigonnet. Tel: (85) 39.16.66.
Renault: Carrefour Europe. Tel: (85) 38.25.50.

Festivals, Fairs and Sporting Events

May, second fortnight: **Foire Nationale des Vins de France** (national wine-tasting festival) (The **Maison Mâconnaise des Vins**, Avenue de Lattre-de-Tassigny, offers tasting of Mâconnais wines. **The Vignerons de St Vincent** are the local Bacchic association.)

LE MÂCONNAIS

The region stretching between **Tournus** and **Mâcon** on the right bank of the River Saône is one of the most attractive in France. Rising from the **Saône Valley** in gentle terraces the hills of the **Mâconnais** are on a human scale. Nature is gentle here, easily moulded to man's needs and aspirations, and has been softened and enriched by human ingenuity and industry.

The Mâconnais is a transition region between north and south with a milder climate than Northern Burgundy, reflected in the architecture. The flat roof with Roman round terracotta tiles replaces the pointed high-pitched slate or flat-tiled roofs of the north. Between the rich grazing land of the valleys and the wooded summits of the hills, the vineyards are stretched on the most exposed slopes, scattered in small patches wherever the soil and the morning sunlight allow them to flourish.

The first vineyards were planted by the monks of Cluny with **Chardonnay, Pinot** and **Gamay** grapes. The Mâconnais region merges into the **Beaujolais** south of Mâcon at **Romanèche-Thorins.** It includes the region of **Pouilly-Fuissé**, a great white wine produced by the *Chardonnay* grape. 'You do not sell a wine like that, you part with it', said a wine grower! The Pouilly-Fuissé is a wine of greenish golden tone, dry and strong, at first fruity then with a distinctive aroma as it matures. Other *crus* include **St Véran, Pouilly-Loche, Pouilly-Vinzelles** and **Mâcon Vire**, the favourite altar-wine of the saintly Curé d'Ars, who although he starved himself, insisted on the best for the service of God! Other white wines from *Chardonnay* grapes, light and fruity with a sweetish tang, are sold under the names of **white Burgundy, Mâcon Blanc** and **Mâcon Villages.** They are the perfect accompaniment to the dry goat cheese called **Chevrotons.** Until the 19th century red wines constituted the majority of the Mâcon production; now the Mâcon Rouge produced from *Gamay* grapes (**Gamay Noir à Jus Blanc**) represents only a third of the production and cannot really be compared with northern Beaujolais wines.

The development and promotion of the Mâcon region is due to a 17th century wine grower, Claude Brosse, born at Chasselas which produces a famous dessert grape. Built like a giant, Claude Brosse went up to Versailles in an ox-driven cart carrying two barrels of his best wines, in order to make them known at court. After a thirty-three day trip he attended High Mass at Versailles, where his gigantic size attracted the King's attention. Later, at an audience, he so impressed King Louis XIV that the monarch immediately tasted his wine and found it much better than the usual court wine from **Senlis** or **Beaugency.** Louis XIV bestowed his royal approval on Claude Brosse's wine, thereby assuring his fortune and the prosperity of the Mâconnais.

From Mâcon take the D54 and D172 to **Pouilly-Fuissé** (391 inhabitants, 8.5Km) a typical small village of prosperous wine growers. Taste the lovely, fragrant *grand cru* white wine and have a meal at a simple restaurant serving traditional French food prepared with love and care.

Carry on to **Chasselas**, a tiny village dominated by rocky formations, which produces a famous dessert grape the **Chasselas.** Keep on the D31 to reach **Solutré** (7.5Km), a small village of 374 inhabitants overshadowed by the dramatic shape of the **Rock of Solutré** rising from the vineyards like the gigantic prow of a half-sunk ship. It is a famous prehistoric spot which has given its name to a Stone Age, the Solutrean (15,000–12,000BC). In 1866, excavation at the foot of the rock revealed a charnel house containing the bones of about 100,000 animals which were hunted, killed and eaten here. The finds from the site are in the **municipal museum** at Mâcon, although a few objects are displayed in a small museum near the grocery at Solutré.

Hotels and Restaurants

Pouilly-Fuissé Enjoy here *Tête de Veau* (calf's head), *Grenouilles* (frogs) or *Andouillettes* (coarse sausage). Very good value. 71960, Pierreclos, Saône-et-Loire. Tel: (85) 35.60.68. Meals 40–70F. Closed 20–30 September, February, Tuesday night except in July and August, and Wednesday.

Le Relais de Solutré An excellent restaurant in a rustic inn with simple rooms, serving traditional French food such as *Grillades au Feu de Bois* (steaks grilled on a wood fire) and *Rognons de Veau Moutarde* (calf's kidneys in a mustard sauce). Good value. 71960, Pierreclos, Saône-et-Loire. Tel: (85) 37.82.67. 33 rooms, 130–150F. Meals 55–110F. Closed Monday and January.

The Mâconnais wine region is also the *Terre natale* (native land) of the poet **Lamartine**. From Solutré take the D54 to Davaye, then the D89 to reach the N79 and the **Château de Monceau**, one of the favourite houses of Lamartine now converted into an old people's home. He wrote his political *Histoire des Girondins* there in a summer house, in the middle of the vineyards called La Solitude. The *cour d'honneur*, chapel and terrace are open to visitors (9–12am and 2–6pm, June–September, closed Sunday).

From Monceau take the D45 to **Bussières** where the Abbé Dumont, friend of Lamartine, who portrayed him in *Jocelyn*, is buried in the village church. In *Jocelyn*, a love story, the nearby **Château de Pierreclos** (17th century) appears, as does Mademoiselle de Milly, the owner's daughter (as 'Laurence').

Carry on along the D45 to **Tramayes**, a picturesque road with a beautiful panoramic view over the Mâconnais hills and their arcadian landscape of woods, vineyards and fields, to reach **St Point** by the D22. St Point was Lamartine's favourite residence. Together with his English wife he redecorated it between 1833 and 1855 in the contemporary 'Troubadour' (Gothic) taste. Here he entertained the famous men of his time: Victor Hugo, Liszt, Lacordaire etc. His study has been preserved as it was in his lifetime and the private apartments can be visited. In the garden the stone bench where the poet used to meditate still stands under the same tree. Lamartine and his family are buried in the village church. The whole place is imbued with the elegiac tone of Lamartine's poetry and it is truly a moving pilgrimage to the very heart of a great man's inspiration. (Château open 9.30–11.30am and 2–5pm, closed Friday morning, and mornings of Sunday and holidays.)

A **reservoir** on the side of the D22 covers 15Ha and offers a variety of water sports including sailing, windsurfing etc.

Carry on from St Point to **Berzé-le-Châtel** where a medieval castle still dominates the hills around, which are covered with vineyards. It used to protect the access to Cluny abbey. (Open 10–12am and 2–6pm, Easter–1 November.)

From Berzé-le-Châtel take the N79 towards Mâcon and stop at **Berzé-la-Ville**, where the **Abbey of Cluny** owned a country house. St Hugh used to come here often to rest from his heavy duties. The **chapel** displays the only large-scale Romanesque paintings to survive from Cluny. On the oven-vault of the chancel there is an impressive Christ in Majesty over 4m high surrounded by apostles and attendants. He is seated on a cushion handing a scroll to St Peter. On the sides saints and martyrs venerated at Cluny are represented. These paintings, dating from the 12th century, show much affinity with the Byzantine mosaics of the Empress Theodora at Ravenna. (Open 9–12am and 2.30–6pm, Easter–1 November. Closed Sunday morning and Tuesday afternoon.)

From **Berzé-la-Ville** carry on to **Milly-Lamartine**. The squat plain villa where Lamartine spent a blissful childhood still stands behind its wrought-iron gate. After this pilgrimage in the atmospheric *Pays de Lamartine* (Lamartine country) go and spend a night amid the vineyards in a sleepy village where time has stood still. From the N79 take the D85 to **Igé**.

Hotels and Restaurants
Château d'Ige A very quiet luxurious hotel in a converted 13th century fortified château. A place to dream. With restaurant. Igé, 71960, Pierreclos, Saône-et-Loire. Tel: (85) 33.33.99. 6 rooms, 170–280F. 5 suites, 390F. Meals 80–120F. Closed 5 November–15 December, restaurant Thursday. Credit cards: AE, DC, VISA.

CLUNY
From Paris, Mâcon-Nord exit, go through Mâcon, then N79 and D980, 25Km
From Lyon, Mâcon-Sud exit, go through Mâcon, then N79 and D980, 25Km
Inhabitants: 4,680
Office de Tourisme: Rue Mercière, closed January

Cluny is indissolubly linked with the spiritual search of the Middle Ages and European history as a whole. The Cluniac order exercised a remarkable influence on the religious, political and artistic life of the West for over five centuries. It is a high point of Western civilisation not to be missed by the traveller. Excellent restaurants and comfortable hotels together with a camp site cater for the needs of modern visitors.

A visit to Cluny is truly a visit back through time as, until the Revolution, every century left its mark on the buildings. In 910 when St Berno and his monks founded the Abbey of William the Pious, Duke of Aquitaine, they were determined to reform the abuses which had beset the monasteries since Merovingian times. The practice of giving or selling abbacies to secular churchmen or laymen was circumvented by placing Cluny, like **Vézelay**, under direct obedience to the Holy See without feudal or episcopal ties. Pope Gregory VII expressed the special link which bound Cluny with Rome: 'Amongst all the monasteries founded beyond the Alps to the glory of Almighty God and to the blessed apostles Peter and Paul, there is one which is St Peter's own, and which is united with the Church of Rome by special right – Cluny. Dedicated since its foundation to the honour and defence of the Apostolic See, it has attained, under saintly abbots, by divine grace and mercy, such holiness that it surpasses all monasteries beyond the mountains in the service of God and in spiritual fervour. It has no peer, for there is not one Abbot of Cluny who has not been a saint.'

Under the guidance of saintly but worldly-wise abbots such as St Odo (917–942) the custom of plurality of abbaies was developed, with papal agreement. Abbots could gather under their rules other Benedictine houses, ensuring a uniformity of rule as well as strength and power against the assaults of rapacious neighbours, raiders and overlords. This policy established the tradition of a firmly regulated élite corps which could keep order in other religious houses. The Cluniac congregation soon became a power to be reckoned with. It was a strong asset in the establishment of a theocratic papacy, it promoted pilgrimages to **St James of Compostella** and helped to recover Moorish Spain. At Cluny popes resided, emperors and kings came for advice, and the abbots were entrusted with important and delicate diplomatic missions.

But **Cluny**, however involved in the temporal world, did not forget its spiritual mission, and Abbot St Odilo (994–1048) was a fervent promoter of the 'Truce of God', a peace movement, and the first to ask observance of All Souls' Day on the 2 November, as a feast in honour of all the faithful departed.

The main aim of every monastery was to create a replica of heaven on earth and it was to this end that the Middle Ages built their wondrous monuments to God's glory. Cluny had always been associated with artistic achievement. Romanesque religious fervour expressed itself in Gregorian chant and St Odo, a talented musician and choirmaster, had the wooden ceilings replaced by stone tunnel vaulting to achieve better acoustics. The second abbey, (**Cluny II**) built by St Mayeul in 955, was too small for the 200 resident monks and the assemblies of the chapters general. So the most important building contribution was made by St Hugh, who after a visit to Monte Cassino in 1083, resolved to make of Cluny a Gallic replica of Monte Cassino. When first built, **Cluny III** was the epitome of mature Romanesque, the largest and most beautiful church in Christendom, and it remained so until the building of **St Peter's in Rome.**

Cluny III heralded the principles of Gothic style with its impressive proportions, its soaring height and the deliberate attempt to bring about in the faithful a spiritual and emotional experience of heaven through the senses. 177m long (St Peter's is 186m), the church consisted of a narthex, two transepts, five bell towers and two towers, and could accommodate the entire 10,000 members of the order, standing. This truly magnificent building was senselessly and pitilessly destroyed by iconoclasts from Mâcon who used it as a quarry for building materials, from 1798 to 1823. Only the great south transept remains, supporting the handsome **Clocher de l'Eau Bénite (the Holy Water bell tower)**, together with a Flamboyant 15th century **chapel** with fifteen consoles carved in the shape of the Old Testament prophets projecting from the walls. The transept and chapel are reached along an airy 18th century cloister.

In the garden the 13th century abbey **granary** still stands. It consists of two rooms: the cellar, housing pieces of sculpture from the town and the abbey; and the upper room, with beautiful chestnut beams, exhibiting 10 capitals from the choir of the abbey, carved with allegorical motifs, and the altar in Pyrenean marble, all dating from 1095. The two models of Cluny were built from the plans of Professor K.J. Conant, the American archaeologist who did so much to bring Cluny back to life.

The monks of Cluny, wealthy and powerful, soon started to forget the true spiritual meaning of their life, and their abbey, from being the 'Light of the World', a centre where prayer, study and teaching were paramount, insensibly got caught in the trap of worldly magnificence. St Bernard vituperated against bishops 'who could not go four leagues from their houses without a retinue of sixty horses or more', and asked 'Does light only shine from a gold or silver candlestick?'

The former **abbatial palace** built in the 15th century, at the same time as the **Hôtel de Cluny**, the abbots' Parisian residence, dates from the time of the abbots' increasing love for luxury. This decadence carried on into the 16th century and the Wars of Religion brought further looting and destruction, which the Revolution completed. (Abbey open 9–11.30am and 2–6pm, 1 April–30 September. Otherwise 10–11am and 2–4pm. Closed Tuesday, 1 January, 1 May, 1 November, Christmas Day.)

From the abbey walk down the **Rue K.J. Conant** to the former abbatial palace, now the **Musée Ochier** housing architectural fragments from the abbey and objects which belonged to it, together with some 4,000 volumes coming from the abbey library and works by the 18th century artist Prud'hon, who was born at Cluny. (Open 9–12am and 2–6pm 1 July–15 September, and 10–12am and 2–4pm 1 November–15 March. Otherwise 9.30–12am and 2–5pm. Closed Tuesday and 20 December–15 January.)

The **Hôtel de Ville** just behind the Ochier museum is an Italianate house built at the end of the 15th century and beginning of the 16th by the Abbots Jacques and Geoffroy d'Amboise.

The **Tour des Fromages** in the Rue Mercière can be visited from the Office de Tourisme itself. From the top of the 120 steps there is a panoramic view over Cluny and its buildings. (Closed in January.)

The **Hara National** (stables) was built near the abbey precinct, of stones from the abbey itself. It houses about a hundred stallions which are sent to local stables during the period of March to July.

The **Church of Notre Dame** in the **Rue Mercière** stands in a small square with an 18th century fountain. It was built around 1100 and was enlarged in Gothic style at a later period.

The **Church of St Marcel** in the **Rue Prud'hon**, reached from the abbey by the **Rue Lamartine**, then the **Rue Filaterie**, turning right into the **Rue Prud'hon**, has a fine Romanesque bell tower with an elegant 15th century Gothic spire.

Hotels and Restaurants

Bourgogne Lamartine used to stay in this very comfortable hotel with some rooms overlooking the abbey, beautifully decorated, with an excellent restaurant offering traditional cuisine with a touch of originality: *Blanquette de Lotte aux Primeurs* (monkfish stew with young vegetables) or *Canard Escalope au Poivre Rose* (filleted duck with pink pepper). Place de l'Abbaye, 71250, Cluny, Saône-et-Loire. Tel: (85) 59.00.58. 18 rooms, 90–200F. Meals 80–180F. Closed Tuesday 15 November–1 February. Credit cards: AE, DC, VISA.

Moderne (1Km from Cluny by the D980) A lovely restaurant, with quiet rooms and a terrace overlooking the River Grosne, where one can eat such delectable dishes as *Escalope de Foie de Canard aux Noix* (duck livers with walnut) or the *Salade de Cresson aux Coquilles St Jacques* (watercress salad with scallops). Good value. Pont-de-l'Etang, 71250, Cluny, Saône-et-Loire. Tel: (85) 59.05.65. 15 rooms, 50–140F. Meals 50–130F. Closed Sunday night, Monday (15 September–15 June), February and 15–30 November.

Garages
Citroën: Tel: (85) 59.08.85.
Peugeot: Tel: (85) 59.09.72.
Renault: Tel: (85) 59.11.67.

Festivals, Fairs and Sporting Events
July, August, September: **exhibition of contemporary art**
August, Saturdays or Sundays: **concerts** and **recitals.**

Camping

LE BEAUJOLAIS
Mâcon-Sud exit

The Beaujolais Region takes its name from the town of **Beaujeu** whose nobles controlled the whole area. With its picturesque valleys and hills, the westerly slopes of which are covered with vineyards, the countryside has a rugged appearance which can be taken in in the wide view provided from the belvederes situated on many summits.

Wine has been produced here since Roman times. In the Middle Ages the city of **Lyon** consumed the region's entire production, hence the saying: 'Lyon is watered by three rivers, the Rhône, the Saône and the Beaujolais.' Today 90 million bottles of Beaujolais are produced every year, from the *Gamay* grape (*Gamay Noir à Jus Blanc*).

Beaujolais is a young red wine, tender and fruity, refreshing with a slightly sweet taste and better enjoyed if drunk chilled. Its particular qualities are due to the low content of tannin. In the region it is served on pots or *pichets* directly from the wood. It is a very easy wine to drink; indeed it is without the unpleasant after-effects of stronger wines. Specific aromas vary according to the composition of the soil. The **Côte de Beaujolais**, north of **Villefranche**, is the region of **Beaujolais-Village** and of the nine *grands crus:* **Moulin-à-Vent**, **Fleurie**, **Morgon**, **Chiroubles**, **Juliénas**, **Chénas**, **Côte-de-Brouilly**, **Brouilly** and **St Amour**. All are wines of real distinction. South of Villefranche is the region of **Beaujolais** and **Beaujolais Supérieur**.

Start from **Belleville** (Belleville exit, 1.5Km; 7,400 inhabitants; Office de Tourisme, 105b Rue de la République, closed morning, Saturday and Sunday). Belleville is the wine centre of the Beaujolais. A small town nestling in the middle of vineyards, its Romanesque **church** dates from the 12th century. It was formerly part of an Augustinian abbey built by the Seigneurs de Beaujeu. The impressive Romanesque portal gives access to a Gothic nave with carved column capitals depicting the cardinal sins. North of Belleville, 1.5Km by the N6 at **St Jean d'Ardières**, the **Maison du Beaujolais** offers wine tasting of the produce of eight co-operatives and an opportunity to try the entire range of *grands crus* together with their perfect accompaniment of local goat cheese and *charcuterie.*

Hotels and Restaurants

Le Beaujolais An excellent restaurant, with rooms, offering traditional regional specialities such as *Grenouilles Sautées Fines Herbes* (pan-fried frogs with chives) and *Coq au Vin*. 40 Rue du Maréchal Foch, 69220, Belleville-sur-Saône, Rhône. Tel: (74) 66.05.31. 10 rooms, 65–85F. Meals 60–150F. Closed Tuesday night, Wednesday and 15 November–15 December.

Garages
BMW/Datsun: N6, St Jean d'Ardières. Tel: (74) 66.39.69.
Citroën: N6, St Jean d'Ardières. Tel: (74) 66.42.40.
Peugeot: 171 Rue de la République. Tel: (74) 66.08.46.
Renault: 172 Rue de la République. Tel: (74) 66.17.15.

From Belleville take the D37 to **Cercié** and the D43 to the conspicuously isolated **Mont Brouilly** (6.5Km) with its **Chapel of Notre Dame du Raisin (Chapel of Our Lady of the Grape)** perched at 483m. Dating from 1857 it is the destination of a pilgrimage of wine-growers every year on 8 September. From the esplanade at the top, near the chapel, a panoramic view embraces the **hills of Beaujolais**, the **Saône Valley** and the **Dombes** region.

On the southern slopes of the **Mont Brouilly**, the **Côte de Brouilly** produces a fruity wine with a strong body and bouquet.

Go back to the D37 and drive down for 1Km on the other side of **Mont Brouilly** to **Quincié-en-Beaujolais**, by the D9 on the left, for a delicious meal.

Hotels and Restaurants

Auberge des Samsons On the D37 towards **Chaufailles**, this excellent inn in the heart of the **Beaujolais** region serves traditional specialities with a hint of *nouvelle cuisine*, meaning lighter, tastier dishes of subtle flavour such as: *Compote de Lapin à la Gelée de Sauternes et aux Oignons Confits* (rabbit in Sauternes aspic with pickled onions) and *Magret au Cassis et aux Nouilles Fraîches* (duck with blackcurrant and fresh pasta). Quincié-en-Beaujolais, 69430, Beaujeu, Rhône. Tel: (74) 04.32.09. Meals 72–150F. Closed Sunday night and Monday, and Christmas and January. Credit cards: AE, VISA.

From Cercié take the D68E and D9 to **Villié-Morgon** (11Km), passing the **Château de Corcelles**, a 15th century fortified castle built to protect the frontier between Burgundy and Beaujolais. A Renaissance gallery gives a light and gay appearance to the inner courtyard. The chapel has some very handsome Gothic wood panelling. The main wing houses a cellar for wine-tasting in the former guardroom, while the vat-house is one of the finest in the Beaujolais area. (Open 3–6pm 1 May–30 September. Closed Sunday and public holidays.)

From Villié-Morgon take the D68 to **Fleurie** (4.5Km, 1,416 inhabitants). The wine of Fleurie has a mellow colour, light and tender, and a distinctive feminine character: 'If Moulin-à-Vent is the King of Beaujolais, Fleurie is the Queen.'

Hotels and Restaurants

Auberge du Cep A quality restaurant in one of the best-known villages of the Beaujolais region with a great name serving delectable food on traditional lines but with a sense of innovation and a light tone. Sample the *Chanterelles Persillées* (chanterelles with parsley) or the *Escalope de Turbot aux Fèves Fraîches* (turbot fillet with fresh broad beans). Place de l'Eglise, 69820, Fleurie, Rhône. Tel: (74) 04.10.77. Meals 120–200F. Closed evenings (unless reserved), Sunday night and Monday and December.

Garages

Citroën: Tel: (74) 04.10.36.

From Fleurie follow the D32 to **Romanèche-Thorins** (7Km, 1,915 inhabitants). This small city has a stake together with **Chénas** in the famous *grand cru* of the **Moulin-à-Vent**.

The **Parc Zoologique René-Livet** (safari-park) gathers on 8Ha animals and birds from all over the world. It is an ideal excursion for families, with a miniature train, a picnic area with tables and a sports field. (Access via the Carrefour de la Maison Blanche on the N6. Take the D466E towards St Romain-des-Iles.) (Open 8am–8pm, 1 April–30 September. Otherwise 8.30–12am and 1.30–6pm.)

Hotels and Restaurants

Les Maritonnes (near the station) A very comfortable hotel with a garden with a fine restaurant offering specialities such as *Grenouilles Sautées Fines Herbes* (pan-fried frogs with chives) and *Fricassée de Volaille aux Morilles* (braised chicken with cream and mushroom sauce). 71570, Romanèche-Thorins, Saône-et-Loire. Tel: (85) 35.51.70. 20 rooms, 140–210F. Meals 100–210F. Closed 1 December–15 January, Sunday night and Monday out of season, Monday and Tuesday lunch-time in July, August and September.) Credit cards: AE, VISA.

From Romanèche-Thorins take the D266 to **Chénas** (6Km, 465 inhabitants.) Chénas shares with Romanèche-Thorins the production of the **Moulin-à-Vent** *grand crus*, the most distinguished Beaujolais of all. Manganese in the soil gives a robustness and body which makes Moulin-à-Vent a long-lived wine. The Chénas itself is much lighter. The windmill giving its name to the *grand cru* still stands by the side of the road to Chénas.

Hotels and Restaurants

Robin An attractive restaurant in a converted private house with a terrace and garden in the middle of the vineyards, serving excellent food in the traditional vein but with imagination. Try the *Emincé de Canard au Vieux Vinaigre* (thin slices of duck with a vinegar sauce) or *Charolais à la Bourguignonne* (Charolais steak with a red wine sauce). Aux Deschamps, Chénas, 69840, Juliénas, Rhône. Tel: (85) 36.72.67. Meals 90–180F. Closed Wednesday, February, evenings.

Follow the D266 to **Juliénas** (5Km, 649 inhabitants). One of the best-known Beaujolais names. Its strong, full-bodied wine can be tasted in the deconsecrated **church** decorated with Bacchic scenes.

Hotels and Restaurants

Hôtel des Vignes A very quiet simple family hotel in the middle of the Beaujolais vineyard. No restaurant. 69840, Juliénas, Rhône. Tel: (74) 08.43.70. 20 rooms, 115–160F.

ARS-SUR-FORMANS/VILLARS-LES-DOMBES
From Paris, Villefranche exit, D904, 4Km to Ars, then 19Km to Villars-les-Dombes
From Lyon, Villefranche exit, D904, 4Km to Ars, then 19Km to Villars-les-Dombes

Pay a visit to a pilgrimage centre before repairing to a good restaurant and enjoying a delicious meal in a garden after a walk in a bird sanctuary.

St Jean Baptiste Vianney was the parish priest of the small village of Ars-sur-Formans (518 inhabitants) in the Dombes from 1818 to his death in 1859. A strange, paradoxical man, torn by self-doubt and intolerance yet he had an extraordinary gift for individual conversion. He was so sought after at the height of his fame that he sometimes had to spend up to eighteen hours in the confessional. Unable to sleep and existing on a starvation diet he died as a saint at the service of his parish and parishioners. His body is kept in a reliquary inside the modern **basilica** built on to the simple village church which he had known, to accommodate the many pilgrims who come to pray to the saint who brought spiritual enlightenment in this isolated corner of the Dombes region. His heart is preserved in a special chapel, while the old **presbytery** nearby, where he lived, can be visited. The austere simplicity of the rooms evokes the character of the man in all his ascetic grandeur and strength. (Open 8–12am and 1.30–9pm, 1 April–30 September. Otherwise 9–12am and 1.30–6.30pm.) In 1929 he was named the patron saint of parish priests and every year an important pilgrimage is held on 4 August, the anniversary of his death.

Built on the right bank of the **River Chalaronne, Villars-les-Dombes** (1,859 inhabitants) is a small town with a Flamboyant Gothic church and two excellent restaurants well worth a stop on the way to the **Parc Ornithologique (bird sanctuary).** This latter covers 23Ha (10Ha are taken over by lakes for water fowls), and is a haven for 2,000 birds of 400 different species ranging from tropical birds in the *Maison des Oiseaux* (bird house) to peacocks, cranes, pelicans, flamingoes, ibises, ostriches etc. (Access by the N83, 1Km south of Villars.) (Open 8.30am–7pm, 1 April–31 October. Otherwise 8.30am–5.30pm.)

Hotels and Restaurants
La Table des Etangs In a small village 5Km north-east of Villars by the N83 and D70, a simple restaurant offers delicious food such as *Carpe en Salade à la Moutarde* (salad of carp with a mustard sauce) or *Grenouilles Sautées à la Persillade* (pan-fried frogs with a parsley sauce) on a terrace. Le Plantay, 01330, Villars-les-Dombes, Ain. Tel: (74) 98.15.31. Meals 60–180F. Closed Wednesday 15 September–30 June or Monday (1 July–14 September).

Auberge des Chasseurs At Bouligneux (4Km) north-west of Villars by the D2) this restaurant in its lovely garden is one of the best places in the Dombes area to taste the local specialities such as *Poulet de Bresse à la Crème de Morilles* (grain-fattened chicken with a mushroom and cream sauce) or *Col Vert aux Navets* (mallard with turnips) and some truly delectable sweets. A place to linger. Bouligneux, 01330, Villars-les-Dombes, Ain. Tel: (74) 98.10.02. Meals 80–170F. Closed Tuesday night, Wednesday, and 1–24 February and 20 August–1 September. Credit card: VISA.

TRÉVOUX
From Paris, Anse exit, D6, 6Km
From Lyon, Lyon–Rive Gauche exit, D433 and D933, 28Km
Inhabitants: 5,090

Trévoux is the capital of the former principality of the **Dombes**, founded in 1532 by François I after he had confiscated the lands of the Connétable de Bourbon who betrayed him. Nowadays Trévoux is a very quiet, pleasant provincial city with gardens and pretty houses cascading down to the right bank of the River Saône, in the centre of a region characterised by a multitude of lakes giving it a charm all its own. It is well worth visiting Trévoux on the way to **Mionnay** and the outstanding restaurant and hotel of **Alain Chapel**, one of the best chefs in France.

The creation of the **lakes** of the Dombes region goes back to the 14th century when the landlords realised how little attention they required in order to produce fresh-water fish (carp, tench, pike) and water fowl for their tables. Today the lakes are drained regularly every six or seven years and used as agricultural land for a year, so that the cereal production is important, as is cattle and horse breeding, all yielding a treasure trove of gastronomic delights.

Trévoux was the seat of an independent parliament until the mid-18th century. During the 17th and 18th centuries, Trévoux was one of the most important intellectual centres in France. Its printing press, founded in 1603, was very famous. It is here that in 1704 the Jesuits published the first edition of the *Dictionnaire de Trévoux* and fought for three years against Voltaire and the philosophers of the Encyclopedia.

The **Rue du Gouvernement**, overlooked by the **church**, was the scene of the writing and printing of the *Dictionnaire*. Numbers 3 and 9 in the **Grande Rue** were the Jesuits' **Maison des Pères**; the printing press was just opposite in the Rue du Gouvernement. Walking down the Rue du Gouvernement, admire the austere classical façades of several fine old houses whose back gardens look out from terraces over the River Saône.

At the end of the Rue du Gouvernement take the **Rue des Halles** and visit the **hospital** founded in 1686 by La Grande Mademoiselle, daughter of Gaston d'Orléans, brother of Louis XIII. the **pharmacy** displays an extensive collection of Nevers and Gien earthenware amid handsome wood panelling. (Open 9–11am and 3–6pm.)

Go up the **Rue de L'Herberie**, formerly part of the Jewish district, and turn right into the Grande Rue again the reach the **Montée de L'Orme** leading to the **château**, a medieval ruin with an octagonal tower commanding a splendid view over the Saône. Go down the **Montée des Tours** to the **Palais du Parlement**, built at the end of the 17th century. The **audience chamber** can be visited. It has a magnificent 17th century ceiling and paintings by Sevin.

From Trévoux take the D6 and D4 to **St-André-de-Corcy** (13Km) and the N83 to **Mionnay** (4Km from St-André-de-Corcy).

Hotels and Restaurants

Alain Chapel An outstanding restaurant where cuisine is raised to the level of great art. A meal enjoyed there is sure to leave unforgettable memories. Sample delights such as *Foie de Canard Chaud aux Navets Confits* (hot duck's livers with preserved turnips) or *Salade de Homard Tiède à la Moutarde* (hot lobster salad with mustard sauce) or *Gâteau de Foies Blonds* (mould of lightly cooked livers). A few rooms decorated with a discreet comfort and luxury to match the excellence of the restaurant look over a pretty garden. Mionnay, 01390, St-André-de-Corcy, Ain. Tel: (7) 891.82.02. 13 rooms, 300–400F. Meals 200–400F. Closed Monday, Tuesday lunch-time and January. Credit cards: AE, DC.

At **St Marcel** (3Km by N83) **Manoir des Dombes** A small quiet family hotel. Without restaurant. 01390, St-André-de-Corcy, Ain. Tel: (7) 881.13.37. 16 rooms, 120–250F. Closed January and Sunday out of season. Credit cards: AE, DC.

Garages

Renault: Trévoux. Tel: (74) 00.21.82.

COLLONGES-AU-MONT-D'OR
From Paris, Lyon exit, CD51 and D51, 25Km
From Lyon, D51, 9Km north

The restaurant of **Paul Bocuse** deserves a special entry of its own as a visit to it is a pilgrimage to the temple of modern French gastronomy. Not many French chefs are awarded the *Légion d'Honneur* and are as widely famous and celebrated as this marvellously creative man. So go and experience a legend, and taste the deliciously light yet exquisitely flavoured cuisine he offers. Examples from the menu are: *Mousse de Brochet au Coulis d'Ecrevisses* (pike mousse with a fresh-water crayfish sauce), *Saumon Cru à l'Aneth* (a sort of *Gravad Lax*, marinated raw fresh salmon with dill) and a delight of a raspberry *Soufflé*. This was voted by the specialists Gault and Millau 'Best Meal of the Year'. Try it! Pont de Collonges, 696660, Collonges-au-Mont-D'Or, Rhône. Tel: (7) 822.01.40. Meals 170–300F. Closed 5–26 August. Credit cards: AE, DC.

Autoroute du Soleil
Lyon–Salon de Provence (A7)

The **Rhône** is the vital artery of the region crossed by the A7 on its course to the Mediterranean coast. From **Lyon** to the sea the Rhône, the largest and most powerful of French rivers, flows majestically for 200Km among steep gorges, stark rocky promontories and soft fertile hills are covered with orchards and vineyards.

Twenty centuries of history look on this fast-flowing, busy waterway. Historic cities with Roman ruins, medieval castles and bridges stand side by side with the most advanced industrial and atomic developments. The **Compagnie Nationale du Rhône** is the overseer of the river traffic and its output of energy for electricity and the irrigation of the adjacent countryside.

The multiple activities of the Rhône Valley determine its landscape. From Lyon to **Vienne** large industrial complexes spread at the foot of green hills.

From Vienne to **Valence**, vineyards and orchards are to the fore, creating in the spring a glorious landscape of fragile pink and white blossoms, punctuated here and there by an old village.

Between **Tournon** and Valence, the **Corniche du Rhône**, a rocky crest running above the river, provides a staggering view all the way to the **Alps** and **Mont Blanc, Mont Ventoux** in **Provence** and, to the west, the hills of the **Vivarais.** Beyond **Montélimar** a starker landscape appears in which old fortressess alternate with 20th century developments such as the **Donzère-Mondragon** hydro-electric complex and the atomic centres of **Pierrelatte** and **Marcoule.**

At **Orange** the Rhône reaches the more smiling country of famous vineyards such as **Châteauneuf-du-Pape, Tavel** and **Beaumes-de-Venise.** It heralds a gentler way of life, together with a slowing down of the river which now stretches out to the Mediterranean with two arms, the **Petit** and the **Grand Rhône** (the small and large Rhône) in a delta laden with silt which becomes more and more saturated with salt as it nears the sea. It forms the vast natural reserve of the **Camargue**, a low marshy country of peculiar charm with its lagoons harbouring pink flamingoes, cranes etc, and the *Manades* (herds) of wild horses shimmering in the heat haze, like mirages, under the vast horizon.

Although prehistoric man has left many traces of his passage, the history of the valley is intimately linked with the history of Western civilisation. The Greeks who founded **Marseille** in 600BC used the Rhône to transport tin from Brittany. In Gallo-Roman times the Romans, who introduced the vineyards to the area, ferried wine on the river. The towns of Vienne and Lyon developed, and Lyon became the capital of the Gallic lands.

In the 5th century AD Vienne came to the fore when the *Burgondes* chose it as their capital. Abbeys, fortresses and cities were built during the Middle Ages. In 1419 the twice-yearly **Fair of Lyon**, decreed by the future Charles VII, made Lyon (one of the key places in the French kingdom because of its geographical position), one of the largest commercial centres of the medieval world. In 1450 Charles VII gave Lyon the monopoly of silk in France. From then on prosperity favoured Lyon and the Rhône Valley until the terrible massacres of the Wars of Religion. In this part of France, exposed very early in the 16th century to the Calvinistic creeds, the wars had a particularly savage and repressive effect. Religious fighting continued well into the 18th century with the resistance of the **Camisards** (from the word *Chemise*, shirt, as they were poor peasants), fervent Calvinists who carried on their struggle until the 1787 Edict of Tolerance decreed by Louis XVI. Protestantism, however, was not recognised officially until 1802 during the reign of Napoléon.

This part of France has nurtured many scientists and engineers, from **Montgolfier Brothers** in the 18th century (who made the first ascent in a balloon) to **Jacquard** who invented a silk-weaving mechanism bearing his name. **Ampère** the famous physicist and **Claude Bernard** the bio-chemist were both born in the region, while in Lyon the **Lumière Brothers** invented the first cinematograph, the ancestor of our movie camera.

GASTRONOMY

Abundance and variety are the characteristic features of the Rhône Valley, a place of transition between north and south. The meat from **Charollais**, the poultry from **Bresse**, game from the **Dombes** region, fish from local lakes and the Rhône, and fruit and vegetables from the valley, all unite to create a cuisine of hearty traditional values.

Specialities include: *Quenelles de Brochet* (pike dumplings), usually served with cheese and butter on top; *Poulet* or *Volaille de Bresse* (chicken with delicate white flesh, fed on corn and soaked in milk when killed, renowned throughout France). Bresse poultry can be cooked *Demi-Deuil* with thin slices of truffles inserted between skin and flesh in a *court-bouillon.*

Gras-Double is a form of tripe dish made from ox stomach cooked with onions. The *Saucisson de Lyon* (sausage) is renowned while the *Poulet à la Lyonnaise* (chicken) is cooked in a vinegar and onion sauce.

Sweets include the delicious *Beignets de Fleurs d'Acacia* (acacia blossom dipped in batter and deep-fried, eaten with sugar), while cheeses include: *Bleu de Bresse* (a mild soft blue cheese); *Mont d'Or* (with a savoury taste); and *Chevrotin de Mâcon* (a goat's cheese with a nutty taste, delicious with a glass of Beaujolais).

The **Côtes du Rhône** produce some magnificent red wines such as **Côte Rôtie** to the north, around Vienne, a fine heady wine with the fragrance of violets. Tain-l'Hermitage's *cru* **Hermitage** is a dark ruby coloured wine of great power and a raspberry flavour, while the celebrated **Châteauneuf-du-Pape** is a warm strong full-bodied wine which matures well, a lordly wine of great character. More ordinary reds include **Côtes du Ventoux, Côtes du Lubéron** and **Côtes du Vivarais.**

The famed **Tavel** rosé, tangy and orangy-pink in colour, is made from the *Grenache* grape. The **Lirac** is a second well-known rosé, fruity and fragrant. White wines include two famous rare *crus*, **Condrieu** and **Château-Grillet**, both produced from the *Viognier* grape. At **Dié**, southeast of Valence, the sparklingly fresh **Clairette de Dié Mousseux** is made from the *Clairette* grape (the *Brut* or very dry wine) or the *Muscat* grape (the *Demi-Sec*, or medium-dry wine). Near Châteauneuf-du-Pape the delectable **Muscat de Beaumes de Venise** is a golden and fragrant sweet wine of exquisite mellowness.

VIENNE
From Lyon, Condrieu/Ampuis exit, N7, 5Km
From Salon-de-Provence, Chanas/Annonay exit, N7, 26Km
Inhabitants: 28,753
Office de Tourisme: 3 Cours Brillier, closed Sunday out of season

Vienne is outstanding for its history, art and food. With a quiet hotel 9Km away, it is the perfect overnight stop before reaching Provence.

The *Vienne la Belle* (Vienne the beautiful) of Roman times and the *Vienne la Sainte* (Vienne the holy) of Christian times 'sits like an altar on the foot-hills of the noble Dauphiné region' wrote the poet Mistral. With its joint Roman and Christian past, the luminosity of its skies and the animated Saturday market, which takes over the centre of the town, Vienne already belongs to Provence.

Fifty years before Caesar's conquest of the Gauls, Vienne was already occupied by Roman legions. It soon became the capital of a vast province. In 200AD Christianity flourished and, after the collapse of the Roman Empire in 476, Vienne became the capital of the tribes of *Burgondes*. The Franks swept them away but each successive barbarian wave left its mark on Vienne itself. Under Carolingian rule in the 9th century the local archbishops became very powerful. Vienne was the seat of the 'primate of primates of Gaul'. Gui de Bourgogne, 1083–1119, the most famous, became Pope Calixte II. Several Councils of the Church were held in the city. However the French monarchs did not look kindly on this strong, independent church enclave in their kingdom, and from the 14th century onwards they fought to gain possession of the **Dauphiné** region, achieving their aim in the 17th century.

From the *autoroute* one arrives in the **Place du Jeu de Paume** with the 12th century **Church of St André le Bas** just off it with a **cloister** where the Festival of Sacred Music is held every summer.

Take the Rue des Clercs to the outstanding Roman **Temple of Augustus and Livia**, an elegant building of harmonious proportions dating from the early Roman occupation of the city. Take the Rue Joseph Brenier and the Rue Chantelouve for the **Roman portico**, the only vestige of a vast complex of Roman baths. Cross the **Archaeological Garden** and climb up to the **Mont Pipet**, the hill on which Vienne leans and which bears the **Roman theatre**. It is one of the largest of Roman Gaul and could accommodate 13,500 spectators. A temple used to stand above the tiers of seats. The view from the Mont Pipet, of Vienne and the Rhône Valley, is remarkable. (Open 9–12am and 2–6.30pm 1 April–15 October. Otherwise 10–12am and 2–4pm. Closed Tuesday 16 October–31 March, and 1 January, 1 May, 1 November, 11 November, Christmas Day.)

Go back to the lower part of the town, passing the **Musée des Beaux Arts et d'Archéologie** containing Gallo-Roman antiquities, notably a bronze statue of a dignitary from Vienne. (Opening times as for the Roman theatre.)

From the museum, go to the **Place de Miremont**, off which stands the **Cathedral of St Maurice**. Built between the 12th and the 13th centuries, it has Romanesque as well as Gothic features. The façade with three portals has some remarkable carvings depicting scenes from the Old and New Testaments. The interior, which has no transept, is very harmonious despite the fact that it was completed over four centuries. From the cathedral go down Rue Bosson to the **Church of St Pierre**, one of the oldest churches in France, dating from the 6th century with a beautiful three-tiered Romanesque tower. It now houses a **Lapidary museum** with a magnificent collection of Roman sculpture and mosaics. (Opening times as for the Roman theatre.)

The **Pyramid**, just off the N7 towards Valence, used to decorate the centre of the Roman theatre.

On the right bank of the Rhône, directly opposite Vienne, a Gallo-Roman city has been excavated at **St Romain-en-Gal**. (Open from 3.30pm, 1 March–15 November, Sunday and public holidays, and every day by appointment. Closed Tuesday.)

Hotels and Restaurants

La Pyramide A visit to the Pyramide, a shrine to good French food, is an experience not to be missed. Many great French chefs have been initiated at its altar: Chapel, Bocuse and the Troisgros brothers among others. The cuisine is in the grand gastronomic tradition, and includes *Terrine de Grives au Genièvre* (thrush pâté with juniper) and *Soufflé Glacé Grand Marnier* (cold Grand Marnier soufflé). 14 Boulevard Fernand Point, 38200, Vienne, Isère. Tel: (74) 53.01.96. Meals 220–300F. Closed Monday night, Tuesday and 1 November–15 December. Credit cards: AE, DC.

Le Bec Fin Just opposite the cathedral, with a comfortable dining-room, this restaurant serves regional specialities such as *Quenelles de Brochet* (pike dumplings) and *Tournedos aux Morilles* (tournedos with mushrooms). Good value. 7 Place St-Maurice, 38200, Vienne, Isère. Tel: (74) 85.76.72. Meals 46–120F. Closed 14–31 August, 22 January, 9 February, Sunday night and Monday. Credit Cards: AE, CB, EC, VISA.

At **Chonas l'Amballan** (9Km by the N7) is the **Domaine de Clairefontaine**. A very comfortable hotel and restaurant in a private house beautifully converted in its own park with tennis courts. Very peaceful and welcoming. Chonas-l'Amballan, 38121, Reventin-Vaugris, Isère. Tel: (74) 58.81.52. 17 rooms, 62–145F. Meals 45–130F. Closed Monday and 15 December–1 February. Credit Card: VISA.

Garages

BMW/Datsun: 57 Rue F. Bonnier. Tel: (74) 85.46.50.
Citroën: 163 Avenue du Général Leclerc. Tel: (74) 53.16.07.
Fiat/Lancia: 27 Quai Riondet. Tel: (74) 53.05.54.
Ford: 76 Avenue du Général Leclerc. Tel (74) 54.13.44.
Peugeot/Talbot: 140 Avenue du Général Leclerc. Tel: (74) 53.22.75.
Renault: 4 Cours Verdun. Tel: (74) 53.42.23.

Festivals, Fairs and Sporting Events

June, July, August: **Festival of Sacred Music** in the cathedral and the cloister of St André le Bas.

CONDRIEU
From Lyon, Condrieu/Ampuis exit, N86, 12Km

From Salon-de-Provence, Chanas/Annonay exit, D519 and N86, 20Km
Inhabitants: 3,190

Condrieu is a small market town lying at the foot of the hills producing the famous white wine, identified by the same name, from the rare *Viognier* grape. The small **Château-Grillet** vineyard of the same grape lies on the west bank of the river. The very small output of these wines can only be enjoyed on the spot – in the Vienne region and around Condrieu itself.

Condrieu is also the centre of the important trade of fruit and vegetables grown in the fertile Rhône valley.

The small port in the lower town is full of southern charm while from the D28, climbing up the hill, there is a vast panorama over the wide green river and its valley.

Hotels and Restaurants

Beau-Rivage A beautiful old house, covered in Virginia creeper and overlooking the Rhône, converted into a very comfortable hotel with a terrace on the river, a garden and rooms furnished with antiques, the Beau Rivage has an excellent restaurant offering such classics as *Pochouse du Rhône à l'Oseille* (fresh-water fish stew with sorrel) and *Matelote d'Anguilles* (eel stew in a red wine sauce). A wonderful place to relax. 2 Rue du Beau Rivage, 69420, Condrieu, Rhône. Tel: (74) 59.52.24. 24 rooms, 165–320F. Meals 130–230F. Closed 5 January–1 March. Credit cards: AE, DC, EC, VISA.

1Km across the bridge over the Rhône, at **Les Roches de Condrieu**, is the **Hôtel le Bellevue**. A comfortable hotel overlooking the Rhône on the other side of the river with a first-floor dining-room, with a panoramic view, where you can enjoy delicious food such as *Filet de Sandre au Vin Rouge* (fresh-water fish in a red wine sauce) and *Canard au Vinaigre et au Miel* (duck fillet in a honey and vinegar sauce). 1 Quai du Rhône, 38370, Les Roches de Condrieu, Isère. Tel: (74) 59.41.42. 20 rooms, 80–150F. Meals 70–170F. Closed Monday and 14–28 February and 4–14 August. Credit cards: AE, DC, VISA.

Garages
Citroën: Tel: (74) 59.53.24.

Festivals, Fairs and Sporting Events
March, last Sunday: **water regatta** on the Rhône (Lyon–Condrieu).
August, first Sunday: **water jousting** on the Rhône.

Camping

From the Tain-l'Hermitage/Tournon exit
Hotels and Restaurants

At **Mercurol** (4Km by the D532) is **L'Abricotine.** A very small modern family hotel among orchards, a white villa with a pretty garden. The restaurant serves dinners only. Very quiet and friendly. Route de Romans, Mercurol, 26600, Tain-l'Hermitage, Drôme. Tel: (75) 08.42.00. 9 rooms, 135–145F. Meals 37–40F. Closed 20 November–6 December.

From Tournon, opposite Tain-l'Hermitage, a small town at the centre of one of the most famous vineyards of the Côte du Rhône (**L'Hermitage**: the reds full-bodied with a delicate fragrance and a lovely ruby colour, and the whites golden dry wines), leave by the GR42 for St-Romain-de-Lerps. 15Km of a winding mountain road reveal wonderful sweeping vistas over thirteen different French departments, from the snowy peaks of the Alps to the summits of the Vercors. It is one of the most magnificent views over the Rhône Valley.

The small village of **St-Romain-de-Lerps** (from Lyon, Valence–Nord exit, N7, N533 and D287, 15Km; from Salon-de-Provence, Valence–Sud exit, N7, N533 and D287, 15Km) can be reached from Valence too.

Hotels and Restaurants

Château du Besset A wonderfully luxurious hotel in an old converted house with a heated swimming pool, stables and tennis courts and beautiful antique furniture. A wonder of style, taste and elegance, with a restaurant to match. Try the *Terrine de Homard aux Truffes* (lobster pâté with truffles) or the *Mousseline de Rouget au Basilic* (red mullet mousse with basil). St-Romain-de-Lerps, 07130, St Péray, Ardèche. Tel: (75) 44.41.63. 10 rooms, 800–1,300F. Meals 230–300F. Closed January–May and 10 October–31 December. Credit cards: AE, DC, VISA.

At **St Peray** itself is the **Hôtel Les Bains**. A very quiet family hotel in a large garden with an excellent restaurant proposing traditional food at very good prices. 14 Avenue du 11 Novembre, 07130, St Péray, Ardèche. Tel: (75) 60.30.13. 35 rooms 60–145F. Meals 40–80F. Closed during school holidays and Christmas. Credit cards: AE, DC, EC, VISA.

From St Peray visit the romantic ruins of the **Château de Crussol**, taking the road passing the **Château de Beauregard.** A car park enables the visitor to leave his car and walk up the path to the 200m high rocky promontory dominating the valley. On top the only remaining part of the 12th century fortress of the ambitious and powerful **Crussol** family is a **watch tower** from which the view over the sweeping landscape is well worth the climb.

VALENCE
From Lyon, Valence–Nord exit, N7, 4Km
From Salon-de-Provence, Valence–Sud/Grenoble exit, N7, 4Km
Inhabitants: 70,307
Office de Tourisme: Place du Général Leclerc

Valence, built on terraces overlooking the river, is a key communications centre for the Rhône Valley. Very comfortable hotels and excellent restaurants make it a pleasant stopping place.

Valence was an important medieval market town with a renowned university founded by Louis XI at which the famous writer **Rabelais** was a student. The Wars of Religion saw terrible massacres led by the legendary bloodthirsty **Baron des Adrets** 'a wild beast'. Napoleon was an officer cadet at the Military Academy of Valence in 1785.

Arriving from the N7 drive to the vast terrace of the **Champ de Mars** overlooking the Rhône and commanding a magnificent view of the eyrie of **Crussol** with its striking white rock and picturesque ruins. The old town lies on the right. Walk to the **Apollinaire Cathedral**, a large Romanesque building partly rebuilt in the 17th century as it was badly damaged during the Wars of Religion. The **museum** nearby in the former **bishop's palace** houses a large collection of drawings by the 18th century painter Hubert Robert, together with a collection of gems and stones, furniture, and paintings dating from the 16th to the 19th century. (Open 9–11.45am and 2–5.45pm. Closed public holidays.)

On the other side of the cathedral the **Pendentif** is a small 16th century classically inspired building designed as a mausoleum for the Mistral family.

Behind the cathedral, at number 57 in the Grand Rue, the **Maison des Têtes** displays a wealth of remarkable Renaissance carvings.

Hotels and Restaurants
Hôtel Pic A magnificent restaurant in elegant surroundings with a few, very comfortable, rooms overlooking a pretty garden. The food is exquisite. Sample the *Truffes aux Navets* (truffles with parsnips) and the excellent Condrieu wines. 285 Avenue Victor Hugo, 26000, Valence, Drôme. Tel: (75) 44.15.32. 5 rooms, 170–200F. Meals 160–300F. Closed Sunday night, and 4–28 August, and school holidays in February and Wednesday. Credit cards: AE, DC.

Hôtel Europe Small comfortable family hotel nicely furnished with sound-proofing. No restaurant. 15 Avenue Félix Faure, 26000, Valence, Drôme. Tel: (75) 43.02.16. 26 rooms, 60–160F. Credit card: VISA.

Chaumont A very good restaurant, with rooms, offering traditional food on a nice terrace. Very good value. 79 Avenue Sadi-Carnot, 26000,

Valence, Drôme. Tel: (75) 43.10.12. 11 rooms, 41–71F. Meals 28–110F. Closed Saturday and December.

At **Pont-de-l'Isère** (9Km north by the N7) is the **Chabran**. A quality restaurant in a lovely garden with some very comfortable modern rooms beautifully appointed. The food is delicious. Try the *Sole aux Artichauts* (sole with artichokes) or the *Chevreau Rôti à l'Ail* (roast kid with garlic). 47th Parallèle N7, 26600, Tain-l'Hermitage, Drôme. Tel: (75) 58.60.09. 12 rooms, 110–200F. Meals 100–300F. Closed Sunday night and Monday. Credit card: VISA.

Garages
BMW: N7, south exit. Tel: (75) 44.20.97.
Citroën: 126 Route de Beauvallon. Tel: (75) 44.31.24.
Ford: 287 Avenue de Romans. Tel: (75) 42.54.44.
Peugeot/Talbot: 125 Avenue Félix Faure. Tel: (75) 44.11.66.
Renault: 105 Avenue Sadi-Carnot. Tel: (75) 43.93.23.

Festivals, Fairs and Sporting Events
July: **summer festival** in the old town with chamber music concerts.

From the Loriol/Privas/Crest exit
Hotels and Restaurants
At **Baix** (7Km by the N104 and N86) is **La Cardinale**. Old manor house luxuriously converted into a paradise hotel with 7 rooms in the main house and 10 at the *Résidence*, 3Km away in a beautiful garden by the river. The cuisine matches the idyllic décor. Try the *Blancs de Volaille Truffés* (chicken breasts with truffles) or *Mousse de Rouget au Beurre d'Ecrevisses* (red mullet mousse with fresh-water crayfish butter). Baix, 07210, Chomérac, Ardèche. Tel: (75) 62.85.88. 17 rooms, 330–500F. Meals 135–200F. Closed Thursday and 2 January–15 February. Credit cards: AE, DC, VISA.

At **Mirmande** (10Km by the N7, or 5Km from the Montélimar–Nord exit is **La Capitelle**. A lovely place to spend a night, in a pretty village, this beautiful medieval house offers quiet comfortable rooms overlooking the Rhône Valley. The restaurant only serves dinners. Mirmande, 26370, Loriol, Drôme. Tel: (75) 61.02.72. 15 rooms, 90–210F. Meals 55F. Closed Tuesday night and November–10 March.

MONTÉLIMAR
From Lyon, Montélimar-Nord exit, N7, 13Km
From Salon-de-Provence, Montélimar-Sud exit, N7, 10Km
Inhabitants: 29,149

Office de Tourisme: Allée Champ de Mars, closed Sunday

Once on the main road to the south (the N7), since the advent of the *autoroute*, Montélimar has become a quiet city, sprawled on the left bank of the **Rambion River**, with some luxurious hotels and restaurants.

Montélimar owes its name to the medieval *Mont Adhemar* fortress built by the local noble family. The old **château** to the east of the town, off the Rue St-Martin, stands on a hill overlooking the river and still has a 12th century keep surrounded by 15th century ramparts.

Montélimar's speciality is the famous **nougat**, made with honey and almonds.

Hotels and Restaurants

Relais de l'Empereur Luxury hotel in which Napoléon once slept; his room can be visited and is furnished in the style of the period, as are most of the other rooms. An excellent restaurant offers classical cuisine such as *Salade Caroline* with *Foie Gras* and *quail's eggs* and delicious sweets. 1 Place Max-Dormoy, 26200, Montélimar, Drôme. Tel: (75) 01.29.00. 40 rooms, 95–350F. Meals 135–300F. Closed 11 November–20 December. Credit cards: AE, DC, EC.

At **L'Homme-d'Armes** (4Km north by the N7) is **La Bastide.** A delicious restaurant in a beautiful 15th century house overlooking the Rhône and offering excellent cuisine such as *Magret de Canard à l'Aigre-Doux* (fillet of duck in sweet-and-sour sauce) and *Gigot au Foie Gras* (leg of lamb with foie gras). L'Homme-d'Armes, 26200, Montélimar, Drôme. Meals 95–200F. Closed Wednesday and February. Credit cards: AE, DC.

At **Montboucher-sur-Jabron** (5Km east by the D169) is **Le Castel.** A very quiet small hotel in a 13th century converted house with gardens and swimming pool and a marvellous view over the Rhône Valley. The restaurant serves regional specialities. Montboucher-sur-Jabron, 26740, Montélimar, Drôme. Tel: (75) 46.08.16. 10 rooms, 220–350F. Meals 105–150F. Closed 5 January–5 February, and Sunday night and Monday lunch-time. Credit card: DC.

At **Le Poët Laval** (20Km east by the D540, 545 inhabitants). This small village on top of a rocky hill retains many medieval houses and the ruins of a stronghold once belonging to the Knights of Malta. The old **temple**, in the village, houses a **library** and the **Musée du Protestantisme en Dauphiné (Museum of Protestantism in the Dauphiné Region).**

Les Hospitaliers A medieval house in this outstanding village converted into a very comfortable hotel with a swimming pool and delicious gourmet cuisine: *Lotte aux Agrumes* (monkfish with orange and grapefruit sauce) with delectable Côtes du Rhône wines. Au Vieux Village, Le Poët Laval, 26160, La Bégude-de-Mazenc, Drôme. 20 rooms, 110–280F. Meals 100–200F. Closed 15 November–1 March. Credit cards: AE, DC.

Garages
BMW: 44 Avenue J. Jaurès. Tel: (75) 51.83.65.
Citroën: 9 Avenue J. Jaurès. Tel: (75) 01.20.55.
Ford: Route Châteauneuf. Tel: (75) 01.39.16.
Opel: Avenue du Teil. Tel: (75) 01.08.07.
Renault: Route Valence. Tel: (75) 01.77.00.
Talbot: Route Marseille. Tel: (75) 01.33.44.

From the Bollène exit
ST-RESTITUT
From Lyon, Bollène exit, D160, 10Km
From Salon-de-Provence, Bollène/Pierrelatte exit, D160, 10Km
Inhabitants: 453

This picturesque old village has an interesting Provençal Romanesque **church** with classically inspired details particularly on the porch. An intriguing **funerary tower** adjacent to the west wall is supposed to have been built over the tomb of St Restitut.

Hotels and Restaurants
The **Auberge des Quatre Saisons** is a very comfortable hotel beautifully decorated and furnished with antique furniture, with a restaurant to match the warmth of the welcome. Try the *Daube Provençale* (beef stew with garlic, olives and vegetables) and the delicious sweets. Place de l'Eglise, St-Restitut 26130, St-Paul-Troix-Châteaux, Drôme. Tel: (75) 04.71.88. 12 rooms, 105–245F. Meals 40–130F. Closed 15 January–1 February and 15 November–1 December. Credit card: AE.

SOLÉRIEUX
From Lyon, Bollène exit, D160, 18Km
From Salon-de-Provence, Bollène/Pierrelatte exit, D160, 18Km

Hotels and Restaurants
Ferme St-Michel A tiny hotel, very peaceful and comfortable, with a swimming pool in the garden. With restaurant. Good value. Route de la Baume, Solérieux, 26130, St-Paul-Trois-Châteaux, Drôme. Tel: (75) 98.10.66. 10 rooms, 130–175F. Meals 45–90F. Closed Sunday night and Monday.

ROCHEGUDE
From Lyon, Bollène exit, D994 and D8, 10Km
From Salon-de-Provence, Bollène/Pierrelatte exit, D994 and D8, 10Km

Hotels and Restaurants
Château de Rochegude A château, standing in a large park with gardens, tennis courts and swimming pool, beautifully converted into an elegant and comfortable hotel. Marvellous outlook. With restaurant. 26130, Rochegude, Vaucluse. Tel: (75) 04.81.88. 25 rooms 180–660F. Meals 130–170F. Closed 5 October–late April.

ORANGE
From Lyon, Orange/Carpentras exit, 2Km
From Salon-de-Provence, Orange exit, 2Km
Inhabitants: 26,468
Office de Tourisme: Avenue Charles de Gaulle, closed Sunday out of season

Orange is a small town, quietly dozing in the sun at the foot of an isolated hill in the Rhône Valley, with two outstanding Roman monuments. A quiet hotel and excellent restaurant make it a pleasant halt.

Once a Celtic market town, **Orange** became a great Roman city of 80,000 people with all the trappings of grandeur: a theatre, an amphitheatre, a gymnasium, a triumphal arch, baths and temples. Of these only the **triumphal arch**, commemorating the victory of Caesar over Pompey in 49AD, (just off the N7 as one arrives from Lyon) remains, together with the **classical theatre.** The latter, built on the green slopes of the hill of St Eutrope, is still an impressive sight. Its vast proportions and excellent state of preservation create a powerful atmosphere. It is used as the centre of a festival every summer. Built in 120AD its front was described by Louis XIV as 'the finest wall in the Kingdom of France'. A colossal **statue of Augustus** stands in a central niche and gives a final touch of imperial grandeur to the whole. Behind the stage the excavations of a former temple and gymnasium, part of a large capitol, can be visited. (Open 8am–6pm Easter–30 September. Otherwise 9–12am and 2–5pm.)

Follow the Montée des Princes d'Orange-Nassau to reach the top of the **Colline St-Eutrope**, once the site of the fortified castle of the **Orange-Nassau** family and destroyed by order of Louis XIV. The Orange-Nassau family originated in the small 13th century principality of which **Orange** was the capital. Heirs to the German Duchy of Nassau, they extended their territory to the Netherlands. In 1689 **William Prince of Orange and Nassau** was asked to rule over England with his wife Mary. The ruling house of the Netherlands comes from a separate branch of the family.

In the old part of the town the **cathedral** is built in Provençal Romanesque style.

Hotels and Restaurants

Arène A peaceful small family hotel. No restaurant. Place Langes, 84100, Orange, Vaucluse. Tel: (90) 34.10.95. 30 rooms, 120–180F. Closed November. Credit cards: DC, EC, VISA.

La Pigraillet Lovely restaurant overlooking the town and the theatre, serving delicious food. With a garden and a swimming pool. Try the *Maquereaux Marinés* (marinated mackerel) and the delectable sweets. Colline St-Eutrope, 84100, Orange, Vaucluse. Tel: (90) 34.44.25. Meals 80–105F. Closed Monday and November–March. Credit cards: AE, DC.

Garages

Citroën: Route d'Avignon. Tel: (90) 51.65.00.
Fiat: 28 Avenue Arc de Triomphe. Tel: (90) 34.69.04.
Ford: 78 Avenue Maréchal Foch. Tel: (90) 34.24.35.
Peugeot: Avenue Maréchal Foch. Tel: (90) 34.24.11.
Renault: N7. Tel: (90) 34.02.68.
Talbot: Route de Lyon. Tel: (90) 34.04.16.

Festivals, Fairs and Sporting Events

July and early August: **Festival** in the classical theatre featuring opera, drama, ballet, concerts.

CHÂTEAUNEUF-DU-PAPE
From Lyon, Orange exit, D976 and D17, 15Km
From Salon-de-Provence, Orange exit, D976 and D17, 15Km
Inhabitants: 2,113
Office de Tourisme: Place Portail, closed Sunday and Monday morning

At the centre of the celebrated vineyards producing the famous **Côte du Rhône** wine (a strong, warm, full-bodied red), Châteauneuf-du-Pape is a small town dominated by the impressive ruins of the 14th century **castle** built by the Avignon popes and commanding a magnificent view over the Rhône Valley.

Hotels and Restaurants

Hostellerie des Fines Roches (3Km on the D17) A gourmet restaurant with rooms and a wonderful view over the vineyards, offering delicious cuisine. Sample the *Truffe en Chausson* (truffle vol-au-vent) and the mouth-watering sweets. 84230, Châteauneuf-du-Pape, Vaucluse. Tel: (90) 39.70.23. 7 rooms 180–350F. Meals 140F. Closed Sunday night, Monday and January.

La Mule du Pape Excellent restaurant serving delicious Provençale food such as *Pâté de Rouget au Pastis* (red mullet pâté with Pastis). Place de la

Fontaine, 84230, Châteauneuf-du-Pape, Vaucluse. Tel: (90) 39.73.30.
Meals 60–160F. Closed Monday night, Tuesday. Credit Card: VISA

VILLENEUVE-LÈS-AVIGNON
From Lyon, Avignon-Nord exit, N107, 13Km
From Salon-de-Provence, Avignon-Sud exit, N7, 16Km
Inhabitants: 10,234
*Office de Tourisme: 1 Place Ch. David, closed Monday; and Tour Philippe
le Bel, closed Tuesday*

Villeneuve-lès-Avignon is a small town directly facing the large fortified
city of Avignon. Its very comfortable hotels and excellent restaurants
make Villeneuve a very welcome halt.

As the Rhône was the frontier of the Kingdom of France in the 13th
century the Tour de Philippe le Bel was built in order to protect the end of
the **St Bénezet Bridge**, the Avignon bridge made famous by the song.

On the arrival of the popes in Avignon, Villeneuve became a city of
cardinals and enjoyed great prosperity. Palaces, churches and monasteries were built and trade boomed, until the Revolution reduced it all to
ashes and decay. The main monument now is the ruined **Chartreuse du
Val de Bénédiction**, a monastery founded in 1356 by Pope Innocent VI.
His tomb is in the **church.** The **cloister** still survives together with the
papal chapel and some 14th century frescoes.

Go by the Chemin des Chartreux to the **Fort St André.** Built by the
French kings in the 14th century, it used to encompass the monastery and
a village of St André. The fortified gateway is still standing, and the 12th
century **chapel** has simple Romanesque lines.

Go down the Montée du Fort St André to the Rue de la République to
reach the 14th century **collegiate church** housing two remarkable **statues
of the Virgin and Child**: a 14th century polychrome ivory masterpiece and
a 13th Century marble double-faced statue illustrating joy and grief.
(Open daily expect Sunday mornings and Tuesdays. Ring the bell for
admission, at the south end of the choir.)

The **municipal museum** (Rue de l'Hospice) is housed in the 17th
century former hospital and exhibits a famous 15th century painting of
the Coronation of the Virgin by the Avignon artist Enguerrand
Charouton, and other paintings and furniture. (Open 10–12.30am and
3–7.30pm 1 April–30 September. Otherwise 10–12am and 2–5pm.
Closed Tuesday and February.)

Time permitting the traveller should cross over to **Avignon** itself to visit
the impressive 14th century fortified **Popes' Palace** and the **Museum of
Medieval Art** in the **Archbishop's Palace** where there is a remarkable
collection of medieval painting and sculpture.

Hotels and Restaurants

La Prieuré A luxury hotel in a 13th century priory with some rooms in the medieval buildings and some modern ones around a large swimming pool in a green setting. The cuisine is on a par with the surroundings. *Tournedos aux Morilles* (tournedos with mushrooms) and *Lotte* (monkfish) are served in the superb dining-rooms or on the terrace. 7 Place du Chapitre, 30400, Villeneuve-lès-Avignon, Gard. Tel: (90) 25.18.20. 29 rooms, 300–600F. Meals 250F. Closed 2 November–3 March. Credit cards: DC, EC, VISA.

Les Cèdres A family hotel in a converted private house with a park and a swimming pool. Cosy and comfortable. No restaurant. 39 Avenue Pasteur, 30400, Villeneuve-lès-Avignon, Gard. Tel: (90) 25.43.92. 23 rooms, 65–170F. Credit card: VISA.

La Magnaneraie Excellent restaurant serving very good traditional food. Try the *Saumon Frais à l'Echalotte* (fresh salmon with shallot sauce). 37 Rue Camp de Bataille, 30400, Villeneuve-lès-Avignon, Gard. Tel: (90) 25.11.11. Meals 90–180F. Closed February. Credit cards: DC, EC, VISA.

At **L'Isle sur la Sorgue** (from Lyon, Avignon-Nord exit, D942 and N100, 24Km; from Salon-de-Provence, Nîmes/Cavaillon exit, D938, 16Km) is the **Hostellerie la Grangette.** A small family hotel in the middle of the Provençal countryside, with a swimming pool in a lovely garden. With restaurant. L'Isle sur la Sorgue, 84740, Velleron, Vaucluse. Tel: (90) 20.00.77. 17 rooms, 150–200F. Meals 100–150F.

At **Noves** (from Lyon, Avignon-Sud exit, D28, 2Km; from Salon-de-Provence, Avignon-Sud exit, D28, 2Km) is the **Auberge de Noves.** A luxury hotel in a beautiful converted old Provençal house, very peaceful and comfortable with a beautiful view over the countryside, a swimming pool, a tennis court in the large park and gourmet food to match. Try the *Moules à la Menthe* (mussels with mint sauce) and the *Grâtin de Fraise* (a delicious strawberry sweet). 13550, Noves, Bouches-du-Rhône. Tel: (90) 94.19.21. 22 rooms, 260–600F. Meals 140–300F. Closed Wednesday lunch-time (15 October–1 July) and 1 January–15 February. Credit card: VISA.

Garages (in Avignon)

Austin/Morris/Rover: 4 Boulevard Limbert. Tel: (90) 86.39.58.
BMW: Avenue de Marseille. Tel: (90) 88.54.84.
Citroën: Route de Marseille, N7. Tel: (90) 87.05.45.
Fiat: Boulevard St-Roch. Tel: (90) 82.44.15.
Ford: N7. Tel: (90) 82.16.76.
Opel: Avenue de Marseille. Tel: (90) 88.50.47.
Peugeot/Talbot: Rue Reine Jeanne. Tel: (90) 82.15.51.
Renault: Route de Marseille. Tel: (90) 87.08.51.

Festivals, Fairs and Sporting Events
April: **St Mark's day carnival** through the streets of the town.

GORDES
From Lyon, Cavaillon exit, N100 and D15, 17Km
From Salon-de-Provence, Nîmes/Cavaillon exit, D2 and D15, 17Km
Inhabitants: 1,574
Office de Tourisme: Place du Château, 15 June–15 September

Gordes is a small picturesque village clinging to a rocky hill, with a very comfortable hotel, making it a marvellous place to stay and from which to explore the Provençal countryside around.

Arriving from the D15 the view over the village is remarkable. The 16th century **château**, built on the site of a medieval fortress, has a stern machicolated façade to the north and a more smiling appearance to the south. Inside notice the Renaissance chimney on the first floor.

The château houses the **Vasarely Museum**, containing the work of this modern abstract painter and sculptor. (Open 10–12am and 2–6pm.)

Along the D15 from Cavaillon take the road leading to the **Village des Bories**, which has some fascinating ancient drystone crofts with pointed roofs, creasing a landscape of timeless, eerie primitiveness.

Visit **Sénanque Abbey**, by the D15 towards Cavaillon then the D177. A very well-preserved Cistercian abbey, Sénanque is now the venue for concerts of Gregorian chant and medieval music from 15 July to 15 August, as well as being an exhibition centre and the home of the Commission of Saharan Studies. (Open 9–12am and 2–7pm.)

Hotels and Restaurants
La Mayanelle Small comfortable hotel with magnificent view over the countryside. Excellent food served in a medieval décor. Try the *Canard aux Olives* (duck with olives). 84220, Gordes, Vaucluse. Tel: (90) 72.00.28. 10 rooms, 120–180F. Meals 120–150F Closed Tuesday and 2 January–1 March. Credit cards: AE, DC, EC, VISA.

Les Bories A delicious gourmet restaurant, in the depths of the marvellous Lubéron countryside, serving delectable dishes such as *Rouget au Basilic* (red mullet with basil) or *Gigot de Cabri Rôti* (roasted leg of kid). Route de Sénanque, 84220, Gordes, Vaucluse. Tel: (90) 72.00.51. 2 rooms, 180–200F. Meals 140–210F. Closed Wednesday and 30 November–1 January. Lunch only.

At **Pont-Royal** (from Lyon, Senas exit, 9Km; from Salon-de-Provence, Senas exit, 9Km) is the **Moulin de Vernègues**. A very comfortable hotel in an old royal shooting lodge in a large park beautifully adapted with swimming pool and tennis courts. With restaurant. Pont-Royal, 13370,

Mallemort-en-Provence, Bouches-du-Rhône. Tel: (90) 59.12.00. 37 rooms, 210–450F. Meals 110–190F. Open all year. Credit cards: AE, DC.

ST-RÉMY-DE-PROVENCE
From Lyon, Cavaillon exit, N99, 17Km
From Salon-de-Provence, Cavaillon exit, N99, 17Km
Inhabitants: 7,970
Office de Tourisme: Place J. Jaurès, closed Sunday and public holidays except morning during the season

St-Rémy is a sleepy small Provençal town with some outstanding Roman remains. Very comfortable hotels and excellent restaurants make it a most pleasant halt at the very heart of Provence.

Lying at the centre of the fertile alluvial plain of the Rhône delta, St-Rémy is an important market centre for flowers and vegetable seeds. The town is clustered around the Place Favier. The 19th century **church** retains a 13th century bell tower. Two museums stand close together at one corner of the *Place*. One of these is the **Musée du Folklore Provençal des Alpilles** (museum of Provençal folklore). A large 16th century house built around an inner courtyard exhibits a collection of local art, including the famous **santons** (Provençal Christmas cribs) and Provençal costumes, together with mementoes of two famous men related to the town, one the late 19th century poet **Mistral**, bard of Provence, and the other the famous 16th century sage **Nostradamus**, who was born at St-Rémy. (Open every day except Tuesday from 1 June–30 September. Otherwise Saturday and Sunday.)

The other museum is the **Musée Archéologique** (archeological museum), in the 16th century **Hôtel de Sade.** The museum displays the finds excavated at Glanum, including two marble busts of Octavia and Julia. (Opening times as for the folklore museum.)

Leave St-Rémy by the Avenue Pasteur, heading south. To the left a small cluster of monastic buildings, the **Priory of St Paul de Mausole** has a 12th century Romanesque church and cloister. **Van Gogh** spent some time here between 1889 and 1890, painting his marvellous Provençal landscapes alternatively lyrically happy or tormented and gnarled like an olive tree.

Further on (1Km), on the right lies the **Plateau des Antiques**, where two of the most handsome Roman buildings on French soil recall the glorious past of the rich city of **Glanum.** A sacred spring on this plateau overlooking the Durance Valley and the Mont Ventoux was the focus of a Gallic settlement in 600BC. Forty years later it developed into a Greek style city with a vast complex of forum, temples, baths, houses etc.

The Germanic invasions devastated the site, which was rebuilt after

Caesar's victory at Marseille in 49BC and destroyed again by barbarians in 3AD except for the **mausoleum** and **triumphal arch**, known as the *Antiques*. The mausoleum, dating from the early 1st century AD, is a memorial to the grandsons of the Emperor Augustus who died in their youth. It is a small three-storey monument with a square base decorated with bas-relief carvings of fighting warriors, surmounted by a four-sided arcade with a columnar rotunda and a conical roof above. The triumphal arch is earlier than the mausoleum. Little remains of its former grandeur, but the elegant proportions and the high quality of the carving point to the strong Greek influence which was prevalent at Glanum. The excavations of the site have revealed intriguing levels of superimposed buildings from the earliest times to the Roman period.

The **sacred spring** still flows in a basin of Greek ashlar masonry. The remains of several Gallic and Roman temples stand nearby. Vestiges of a forum, fortifications, baths and houses can be seen all over the site. (Open 9–12am and 2–6pm 1 March–30 September. Otherwise 10–12am and 2–5pm. Closed Tuesday, 1 October–28 February, 1 January, 25 December.)

Hotels and Restaurants

Hôtel des Alpilles A luxury hotel off the D31 in a lovely 19th century château where Lamartine and Chateaubriand stayed. Beautifully converted and furnished with antiques, it stands in a large park with a swimming pool and a barbecue by the pool. No restaurant. 13210, St-Rémy-de-Provence, Bouches-du-Rhône. Tel: (90) 92.03.33. 17 rooms, 300–400F. Closed 1 January–1 April. Credit cards: AE, DC, VISA.

Château de Roussan A beautiful 18th century house built on the site of Nostradamus's house by his descendants, in a lovely poetic garden with fountains and pools, converted into a private hotel. A place in which to retreat from the turmoil of the outside world in its comfortable old walls. No restaurant. Route de Tarascon, 13210, St-Rémy-de-Provence, Bouches-du-Rhône. Tel: (90) 92.11.63. 19 rooms, 100—230F. Closed 20 October–20 March. Credit card: AE.

Auberge du Mas de Nierne A friendly Provençal inn serving sunny Mediterranean specialities: *Aubergines Provençales* (aubergines with tomatoes, onions, herbs and garlic) and *Daubes* (beef stew with tomatoes, onions etc). Route d'Orgon, 13210, St-Rémy-de-Provence, Bouches-du-Rhône. Tel: (90) 92.00.88. Meals 100F.

Villa Glanum Just by the *Antiques* site, a small hotel with a pretty terrace, offering traditional Provençal food. 46 Avenue Van Gogh, 13210, St-Rémy-de-Provence, Bouches-du-Rhône. Tel: (90) 92.03.59. 8 rooms, 78–120F. Meals 60–120F. Closed 1 December–10 January and Monday. Credit card: AE.

Garages
Citroën: 22 Boulevard Mirabeau. Tel: (90) 92.09.34.
Ford: Tel: (90) 92.01.24.
Peugeot: 29 Avenue Fauconnet. Tel: (90) 92.10.21.
Renault: Route de Tarascon. Tel: (90) 92.00.35.

Camping

LES BAUX-DE-PROVENCE
From Orange, Cavaillon exit, N99 and D5, 23Km
From Salon-de-Provence, Nîmes/Cavaillon exit, N99 and D5, 23Km
Inhabitants: 367
Office de Tourisme: Hôtel de Manville, 1 April–30 October, closed Tuesday

Les Baux is an old medieval and Renaissance village standing in a most spectacular and atmospheric landscape. It is a very intriguing place to visit, and hotels with gourmet food and ranging from the simply comfortable to the luxurious make it a marvellous overnight stop.

Rising from the sheer side of a promontory forming part of the **Alpilles** range, in a white rocky landscape of lunar desolation called the **Val d'Enfer** (hell valley), les Baux has a magical impact on the visitor.

Les Baux was the medieval stronghold of proud warlords who controlled over eighty towns and villages. From the 11th to the 14th century it was a thriving city of 6,000 souls and the centre of a famous Court of Love.

The lords of les Baux allied themselves to the noblest families: one member became Prince of Orange; another married the Countess of Provence. Decline started at the end of the 14th century, and in 1426 the independent state became part of Provence and then of France. In the 17th century Louis XIII had the fortress destroyed as it had by then become a Protestant stronghold.

The village can only be reached on foot. Arriving from the D27, park at the entrance. Two villages coexist: the lower one, still lived in with houses, shops, restaurants etc; and the upper one, the ruined fortress or *Ville Morte* (dead city).

Go through the **Porte des Mages** and follow the steep, cobbled main street, noticing as you go along the **Hôtel de Manville**, now the hôtel de ville and **Musée d'Art Modern** (museum of modern art) with Renaissance decorative details on its façade. (Open 9.30–12am and 2–6.30pm 15 March–31 October.)

The **Hôtel des Porcelets** nearby is the **Musée Archéologique** (museum of archaeology) and displays finds from the old fortress excavations going back to Roman times. (Opening times as for museum of modern art.)

The **Church of St Vincent**, a Romanesque building standing on the minute Place St-Vincent, is the scene of the famous nativity play enacted every Christmas by the local shepherds (*Fête du Pastrage*).

The **White Penitents' Chapel** at the end of the cliff has been decorated by the Provençal painter Yves Brayer. Higher still the **Lapidary museum** is in the Hôtel de la Tour du Brau in the *Ville Morte*.

The ruins of the fortress include a colossal 13th century **keep** commanding a vast panorama over the Rhône delta and the Camargue. The ravishing small Renaissance building known as the **Pavillon de la Reine Jeanne** and praised by the Provençal poet Mistral stands apart from the village. (Access from the Porte Eyguières and down the path.)

Hotels and Restaurants

L'Oustau de Boumanière A luxury hotel in an old Provençal house standing at the foot of the village in a wonderful position, with swimming pool, tennis and riding. The food is of the same highest quality: *Agneau à la Crème d'Estragon* (lamb with tarragon mousse) and *Pigeon Farçi au Foie Gras* (pigeon stuffed with foie gras). Au Val d'Enfer, Les Baux de Provence, 13520, Maussane-les-Alpilles, Bouches-du-Rhône. Tel: (90) 97.33.07. 26 rooms, 475–660F. Meals 180–245F. Closed Tuesday, Wednesday and 15 January–1 March. Credit cards: AE, EC, VISA.

La Cabro d'Or Very comfortable hotel in a large garden with swimming pool, tennis and riding, and an excellent restaurant offering delicious dishes such as *Ragoût de Volaille aux Courgettes et Tomates* (chicken stew with courgettes and tomatoes). Au Val d'Enfer, Les Baux de Provence, 13520, Maussane-les-Alpilles, Bouches-du-Rhône. Tel: (90) 97.33.21. 19 rooms, 250–390F. Meals 120–250F. Closed Sunday night and Monday (October–April) and 15 November–20 December. Credit cards: AE, DC, VISA.

Bautezar A charming small hotel in the village itself and overlooking the Val d'Enfer. Rue Frédéric Mistral, Les Baux de Provence, 13520, Maussane-les-Alpilles, Bouches-du-Rhône. Tel: (90) 97.32.09. 10 rooms. With restaurant ½ pension 145–210F. Closed Wednesday, 5 January–10 February.

La Benvengudo Nestling in an isolated site on the D78F, this lovely and very comfortable hotel is beautifully furnished and offers excellent Provençal cuisine: *Mousse de Loup au Fruit de Mer* (sea bass mousse with seafood). Les Baux de Provence, 13520, Maussane-les-Alpilles, Bouches-du-Rhône. Tel: (90) 97.32.50. 18 rooms, 150–220F. Meals 80–120F. Closed November and January, and Sunday.

Festivals, Fairs and Sporting Events

June, last Sunday: **Folklore Festival of St Jean**
15 July–15 August: **Festival of Les Baux** (ballet, concerts etc)

July–September: **painting exhibitions**
24 December: **midnight Mass** with the **nativity play** and the **shepherds' festival**.

SALON-DE-PROVENCE
From Orange, Salon-de-Provence exit, 4Km
From Nice, Salon/Arles exit, 4Km
Inhabitants: 35,587
Office de Tourisme: 56 Cours Gimon, closed Sunday except morning in season

Salon is a busy market town in the midst of olive tree orchards. Some excellent hotels and restaurants make it a very pleasant halt.

Salon's main claim to fame lies in the extraordinary 16th century visionary **Michel Nostradamus.** Trained as a doctor, he travelled widely in France and Italy. Having found a cure against the plague he refused to disclose his secret to his colleagues and was struck off the doctors' register. He then retired, took up astrology and wrote the astonishing prophecies called the *Centuries* which have intrigued and frightened the world ever since. Catherine de Medici befriended him and he became personal physician to Charles IX.

The other famous son of Salon is the 16th century civil engineer **de Craponne**, who cut the canal bearing his name which irrigates the Crau Plain.

Arriving from the A7 from Cavaillon, the **Church of St Laurent** stands on the left. It is a magnificent example of Provençal Gothic from the 14th century. Notice in the fourth chapel on the left a 14th century alabaster Virgin and the **Tomb of Nostradamus.** (He died at Salon in 1566.)

The centre of the town revolves around the Place Croustillat, a picturesque, animated square with a 17th century **belfry** and a lovely 18th century **fountain.** Go to the left to the **hôtel de ville**, a 17th century building standing at the edge of the old town. The **Church of St Michel** dates from the 12th century and has a beautiful tympanum.

The old **Emperi Castle** dominates the town. A medieval castle, it was remodelled in the 17th century and was the residence of the archbishops of Arles, lords of Salon. It now houses the **Musée National d'Art et d'Histoire Militaire (national museum of military art and history)**, a survey of the history of the French Army from Louis XIV to 1918. (Open 10–12am and 2.30–6.30pm. Closed Tuesday, 1st January, Christmas Day.)

The **house of Nostradamus** is now a **museum.** It stands in the Rue Nostradamus, off the Place Croustillat.

Hotels and Restaurants

Abbaye de Sainte Croix A beautifully converted 12th century abbey, now a very luxurious hotel in a marvellous position, with a swimming pool in the garden. A fine restaurant offers Provençal cuisine with inventiveness: *Poissons Crus aux Herbes* (marinated raw fish with herbs) and *Escargots à l'Aneth* (snails with dill). Route du Val de Cuech, 13300, Salon-de-Provence, Bouches-du-Rhône. Tel: (90) 56.24.55. 22 rooms, 340–650F. Meals 100–200F. Closed Monday and 1 December–15 January. Credit cards: AE, DC, VISA.

Francis Robin Excellent restaurant serving traditional *haute cuisine: Civet de Homard* (lobster stew) and *Anguillettes de Canard aux Mangues* (thin slices of duck with mangoes). 1 Boulevard G. Clemenceau, 13300, Salon-de-Provence, Bouches-du-Rhône. Tel: (90) 56.06.53. Meals 98–180F. Closed Sunday night, Monday and February. Credit cards: AE, DC, EC.

Garages

Citroën: 306 Avenue Michelet. Tel: (90) 53.29.64.
Ford: 302 Boulevard du Maréchal Foch. Tel: (90) 56.21.19.
Peugeot: 83 Boulevard de la République. Tel: (90) 56.23.71.
Renault: 245 Allée Craponne. Tel: (90) 53.32.02.

Festivals, Fairs and Sporting Events

July: Celebration of the **anniversary of Nostradamus's death** (2 July 1566)
July: **Nuits de l'Emperi** (festival at the Château d'Emperi – plays and concerts).

La Provençale
Salon de Provence–Menton (A8)

The A8 from **Salon-de-Provence** to **Menton** starts at the heart of **Basse Provence** to reach the **Côte d'Azur** (or **Riviera**) through **Haute Provence**, the evocative region of light, warmth and vibrant colours that begins at **Orange.**

Following the **Rhône** on its way to the Mediterranean, Basse Provence is a fertile area of orchards and vineyards nurtured by the rich silt of the river. Its geographical features and wine areas are dealt with in the section on the **Vallée du Rhône.** In contrast to the low alluvial plain around the **Camargue, Haute Provence** is a country of rocky limestone crests and mountains heralded by **Mont Ventoux**, the highest Provençal peak culminating at 1,909m east of Orange, the **Lubéron** range south of **Gordes** and the **Alpilles** between **Avignon** and **Arles**, all running west–east. **Mont Ste-Victoire**, to the east of **Aix-en-Provence**, follows this pattern too. It is not, as its name suggests, a single peak but a white calcareous rocky ridge of angular formation dominating the whole plain. The **Ste Baume** *massif*, south of **St-Maximin**, is covered on its northern side by a thick forest, sacred to the Celts, of more northerly tree species such as the beech.

The **Maures** and **Esterel** ranges, along the coast, are covered with a thick blanket of pine, chestnut and cork trees (cork manufacturing is the major local industry), and the **Maquis**, a scrubland of lemon and orange trees together with aromatic plants: thyme and lavender, broom and heather. The higher country behind **Cannes** and **Nice** consists of rocky plateaux in which rivers have carved picturesque gorges such as the **Gorges du Loup**.

Between the mountains, where the cultivated areas are restricted to small terraces, fertile valleys produce the major Provençal products: wheat, wine and olives, while the coast itself has been taken over by tourism and the ensuing development of the large metropolis of **Cannes**, **Nice** and **Monte-Carlo** into centres of social and wordly delights.

Deep picturesque bays called **Calanques** are cut into the calcareous coast from **Marseille** to **Toulon**, the most famous being around **Cassis**. The **Maures** coast between **Hyères** and **St-Raphaël**, the southern edge of the mountain range, curves into gulfs at **St-Tropez** or at the old port of **Fréjus.**

The red porphyry **Esterel** forms an abrupt and chaotic, but picturesque, sight over the sparklingly blue sea. Small bays alternate with deep *Calanques.* From Cannes to Nice, sandy beaches line the coast, the only rocky promontory being the **Cap d'Antibes**, but there is an abrupt change to rocks on the Riviera from Nice to **Menton**, with the southern edge of the **Alpes Maritimes** plunging into the sea, creating a varied landscape of rocks and terraces cut through by a triple-level road: the **Corniche**, which gives access to luxurious villas standing in cascading gardens.

The coast is well protected and offers a warm climate even during the winter months, while the upper country can be bitterly cold and serves as a refuge in the summer from the scorching heat of the lower lands. The **Mistral**, a strong, northerly, cold, dry wind blows over the whole country during the winter and is funnelled through the Rhône Valley all the way to **Valence.** The **Sirocco** is a dry, burning, south wind bringing sandy dust from **North Africa**, drying up rivers and provoking violent storms with resulting flooding from mountain torrents.

The former Roman **Provincia**, Provence is the oldest civilised part of France. In 600BC the Greeks founded **Marseille**, bringing with them the basis of the present economy: the olive tree, the fig tree, the walnut and cherry trees, the exploitation of vineyards and the use of coins, replacing barter.

Nice, Antibes and the main ports became commercial centres, and remained so until the Celtic invasions in 400BC. The Roman conquest brought a new wave of prosperity. **Fréjus** was founded by Julius Caesar in 49BC, and during the first three centuries of our era Aix, Arles, Nîmes, Nice and Antibes were developed. The **Aurelian Way**, one of the most important traffic arteries of the Roman Empire, linked **Rome** to Arles via Nice, Antibes, Fréjus and Aix. Every *Mille* (1,478m) a high milestone indicated the distance on this cobbled road 2.5m wide. One of these stones is still standing at St-Raphaël. Staging-posts along the way welcomed riders and horses and offered rest and food. The N7 follows the ancient route of the Aurelian Way.

The dual Greco-Roman influence moulded the features which have remained most characteristic of the area to this day. Remnants or the whole of important monuments – amphitheatres, temples, baths, triumphal arches etc – are dotted around Provence. The **Provençal Romanesque** Christian architecture which flourished in the 12th century relied heavily on Roman prototypes in its structural forms and decorative motifs.

Christianity, which reached Provence in the 5th century, had a profound influence on the country's traditions, many of which have survived intact to this day. The Barbaric invasions marked a dark age. Provence became an independent kingdom in the Carolingian era, only to be devastated again by the Saracen raiders who terrorised the country for a century.

The Middle Ages saw renewed prosperity, with towns developing and becoming independent under the rule of the **Comtes de Provence**, of the **Anjou** family, who made Aix-en-Provence the centre of their court. The most famous is **René d'Anjou** in the 15th century, 'le Bon Roi René' (good King René).

Provence became part of France at the end of the 15th century, although recurring individual revolts went on for many centuries. Nice belonged to the **Duke of Savoie**, later passing to the rule of the **King of Sardignia** and finally being attached to France in 1860 by way of a referendum.

A land of legends and traditions from Greek to Christian times, Provence's folklore is best illustrated by the festivities surrounding **Christmas.** Since the 16th century **cribs** had been a popular way of expressing religious piety. In the 18th century, during the Revolution when churches were closed to worship, a maker of church statues called **Jean-Louis Lagnel** started making small, brightly painted clay figures which people could have at home. They were called *Santouns* ('small saints') in the Provençal. These **Santons** (as they are now called) soon included local figures as well as the Holy Family – the shepherd, the fisherman, the midwife, the blind man, the mayor etc. But the most representative among these of the true, delightful Provençal spirit is the **Ravi**, a naive poet, heir of the medieval troubadors, who – with arms thrown open – seems to keep exclaiming, 'It is all so beautiful, so very beautiful' in front of the miracle of Christmas. These scenes are now enacted every Christmas as a form of **nativity play**, just as **mystery plays** used to be in the Middle Ages. At Les Baux angels and pipe players accompany the local shepherds, who bring to the altar a small cart drawn by a ram carrying a new-born lamb as the symbol of the infant Jesus.

Provence in the 20th century is the land of **festivals**. Some 200 are held every year all over the country bringing together all aspects of artistic endeavour: painting, music, ballet, opera etc. Aix-en-Provence was a pioneer in the field, but Avignon, Orange, Nîmes, Carcassonne and Arles have followed suit.

Artistic creativity is intimately linked with Provence. Modern painters particularly have been attracted to the vibrant quality of Mediterranean light, which brings every detail into sharp focus, giving outlines of sculptural quality. Furthermore artists have fed on the country's immutable past and the continuity which gives a sense of timelessness to everyday life. Van Gogh, Cézanne, Matisse and Picasso are among the most famous and the greatest who favoured Provence as an abode.

Van Gogh, living at **St-Rémy**, expressed very well the dual quality of the country through his own schizophrenic temperament. His lyrical depictions of fragile almond blossom in the spring are so representative, in their ethereal dewy transience, of the quality of tenderness and delicacy which is part of Provence, while his black tormented cypresses, raising their tortured shapes to the burning sky, reflect the starker, darker side of the country, the implacable fight between nature and man under a scorching sun.

Cézanne, who lived all his life, and died, at **Aix**, probed into the timeless quality of Provence and tried to reach its very essence by using the colour so exalted by the Provençal light; colour to create light, shade, reflection, forms and the surrounding atmosphere, as in the Mont Ste-Victoire series of paintings.

Matisse represents the primeval, unadulterated *joie de vivre* of Provence. He spent most of his last thirty years at **Nice**, creating in his own words 'An art of balance, devoid of troubling and depressing matter'. His gloriously sensual, hedonistic celebration of life is the ultimate expression of the 'nearly religious' feeling he had for life itself, a very Mediterranean concept harking back to classical times.

This classical past, ever present in Provençal life, customs and buildings, has been strongly felt and powerfully expressed by Picasso, more than any other modern painter. Of Mediterranean origins, he spent much of his life in Provence, living and dying at **Mougins.** Part of his work represents the vital link between 20th century art and the Greco-Roman past which forms the very basis of our society.

GASTRONOMY

The cuisine of Provence is more Mediterranean than French. Aromatic herbs such as thyme, rosemary, fennel, basil and oregano, the olive and its rich oil, the abundant tomato and pungent garlic all combine to create a sunny *cuisine* which exploits to the full the succulent young vegetables and the fruit, the fresh products from the sea and the lambs raised in the upper lands.

Specialities include fish dishes, like *Aigo Saou* a fish soup served with *Rouille*, a delicious strong orange-coloured mayonnaise with saffron, garlic and pepper or *Aïoli*, a garlic and olive oil mayonnaise. Another is *Bouillabaisse*, the classical speciality of the coast. Of lengthy preparation it requires many sorts of fish including *Rascasse* (Scorpion-fish) and is eaten with the *Bouillon* (stock) separately from the fish, together with *Rouille* or *Aïoli. Bourride* is a creamy fish soup containing crayfish. *Soupe au Pistou* is a vegetable soup with basil and Parmesan cheese, bound together with olive oil and garlic. *Ratatouille* is a vegetable stew of courgettes, aubergines, tomatoes, garlic, onions etc in olive oil. *Pissaladière* is a Provençal pizza with onions, anchovies and olives. *Pieds et Paquets* consist of sheep's trotters with small parcels of mutton tripe cooked in white wine. *Brandade de Morue* is a thick mousse of salted cod with cream, olive oil and garlic.

Cheeses include *Banon*, a goat cheese wrapped in chestnut leaves or coated in peppercorns (au poivre). *Poivre d'Ane* is flavoured with rosemary or savory.

Sweets are plentiful and include all the delicious glacé fruit as well as many almond-based small cakes like the *Calissons* of Aix (small lozenge-shaped marzipan cakes).

Wines from the Provence area are fresh and fragrant and most often white, such as **Cassis** or **Rosé Côtes de Provence**, dry and drunk cool. Some reds are produced, such as **Bellet**, from above Nice, delicate and fragrant, with a fruity flavour, while the white of the same name is comparable to Chablis. **Bandol** is the best red of the Côtes de Provence and matures well being a full bodied, dark ruby red strong wine.

La Palette, opposite the Mont Ste-Victoire, produces strong full-bodied reds like a **St Emilion** and dry whites which mature as well as the reds.

BEAURECUEIL
From Salon-de-Provence, Aix-Est exit, N7 and D58, 10Km
From Nice, Le Canet exit, N7 and D58, 8Km
Inhabitants: 459

In the marvellous Provençal countryside, dominated by the **Mont Ste Victoire**, beloved 'motif' of **Cézanne**, a tiny village offers the welcome of a comfortable hotel and a gourmet restaurant.

Time permitting, stroll in the Old Town of **Aix**, admiring its handsome houses, and visit the **Musée Granet** in the former **Priory of the Knights of Malta**, near the **Church of Jean de Malte**, with its outstanding collections of Old Master paintings together with a room dedicated to Cézanne who spent much of his life painting Mont Ste-Victoire, the rocky promontory of powerful presence looming over the countryside for miles.

Cézanne's studio can be visited, in **Avenue Paul Cézanne.**

Hotels and Restaurants
Le Logis du Maistre A quiet comfortable modern hotel, with swimming pool, offering traditional Provençal food: *Caneton aux Olives* (duck with olives). Beaurecueil, 13100, Aix-en-Provence, Bouches-du-Rhône. Tel: (42) 28.90.09. Meals 90–100F. 8 rooms, 220–250F. Closed Tuesday January–Easter.

Relais Ste-Victoire A gourmet restaurant in a marvellous site offering inventive cuisine such as *Filet de Lotte à la Crème de Poivrons* (monkfish fillet with red pepper mousse). Beaurecueil, 13100, Aix-en-Provence, Bouches-du-Rhône. Tel: (42) 28.94.98 and 28.91.34. Meals 85–200F. Closed Sunday night, Monday and 15 January–15 February. Credit card: EC.

CASSIS
Off the A52 (the Gardanne–Toulon autoroute) La Bédoule exit, D1, 51Km
Inhabitants: 5,831
Office de Tourisme: Place Baragnon, close Tuesday out of season

Cassis is a small Provençal fishing port of great charm and a resort with three beaches on the rocky coast. Very comfortable hotels and excellent restaurants make it a lovely place in which to stay.

Cassis is reached by the D1, which runs through the vineyards producing the Cassis wines. These are a delicately fragrant red and a fine dry white particularly enjoyable with seafood and fish, especially the urchins for which Cassis is famous. The port nestles in the hollow of a bay surrounded by picturesque rocky cliffs covered with woods to the east and surmounted by the romantic ruins of a medieval castle. The site of Cassis has been an inspiration to many artists from the poet **Mistral** to the modern school of painters, the **Fauves**, which included **Matisse, Derain, Vlaminck** and **Dufy.**

The exploration of the **Calanques**, the gorges deeply carved in the soft limestone of the coast, makes a fascinating excursion. The red-brown rocks against the deep blue sky and sea create a vibrantly beautiful sight of typical Mediterranean charm. Boat trips to the Calanques are organised from the port (Quai St-Pierre).

Hotels and Restaurants
Les Jardins du Campanile Very comfortable hotel in the midst of bougainvilleas, lemon and orange trees with swimming pool. No restaurant. Route de Marseille, Rue Auguste Favier, 13260, Cassis, Bouches-du-Rhône. Tel: (42) 01.84.85. 30 rooms, 220–290F. Closed 10 October–1 April. Credit cards: AE, DC.
Les Roches Blanches Comfortable hotel in a Provençal house with a magnificent view over the port and the sea, sitting on a rocky promontory in a garden. With restaurant. Route des Calanques, 13260, Cassis, Bouches-du-Rhône. Tel: (42) 01.09.30. 34 rooms, 100–300F. Meals 60F. Closed November–March. Credit card: DC.
La Presqu'île A beautiful Provençal house with a terrace is the setting for a high-quality restaurant serving delicious food such as *Rouget en Papillote Verte* (red mullet in a spinach leaf) and *Poissons Crus Marinés* (raw fish in olive oil and herbs). Quartier du Port Miou, 13260, Cassis, Bouches-du-Rhône. Tel (42) 01.03.77. Meals 140–240F. Closed Sunday night and Monday. Credit cards: AE, DC.
Le Flibustier An elegant restaurant serving excellent classic *haute cuisine* such as *Daurade à l'Oseille* (sea bream with sorrel). Cap Naio, 13260, Cassis, Bouches-du-Rhône. Tel: (42) 01.02.73. Meals 75–180F. Closed Thursday and March. Credit cards: AE, DC.

Festivals, Fairs and Sporting Events
Several times a year: **water jousting** in the port.
29 June: celebration of the **feast day of St Peter**, patron saint of fishermen.

ST-MAXIMIN-LA-STE BAUME
From Salon-de-Provence, St-Maximin exit, N560, 2Km
From Nice, Marseille/St-Maximin exit, N560, 2Km
Inhabitants: 4,578

St-Maximin lies at the bottom of a dried up lake between the River Arc and the River Argens. It is the focus of one of the many Provençal legends about the lives of saints. A very comfortable hotel 12Km away makes it a pleasant halt.

St-Maximin was a small Gallo-Roman village which became famous in the 13th century through the discovery of the **tombs of St Maximin and St Mary Magdalen.** According to legend, Mary Magdalen, the repented sinner forgiven by Christ, lived with the Virgin for thirteen years after Jesus's death. Then, with her brother Lazarus, her sister Martha and other holy people incuding St Maximin, they were put, by the Jews, aboard a boat without sails or oars and abandoned to the tide. After a perilous journey they finally landed at the spot on the **Camargue** coast known since as **Stes-Maries-de-la-Mer**. It is a place of pilgrimage for gypsies, from all over the world, who come to venerate St Sarah, the black servant who came with Mary Magdalen and Martha.

The legend tells how Mary Magdalen started to preach the Gospel with St Maximin (who became the first Bishop of Aix), then decided to become a hermit in order to expiate her sins and retired in a cave, which can be visited, in the Ste-Baume mountain. She spent thirty-three years there in prayer and contemplation. Nearing death she went down to the plain again, to receive Communion from St Maximin. The place where this took place, at the entrance to St-Maximin, is marked by a small monument called the **Petit Pilon**. St Maximin buried her in the village itself.

During the Saracen raids, the relics of St Mary Magdalen were hidden away. In 1279 Charles d'Anjou, Comte de Provence, rediscovered them and built a Dominican **convent** and **basilica.** During the Revolution the Dominicans were sent away but the basilica was saved from destruction through the intervention of Lucien Bonaparte (brother of Napoléon), who used it as a food store.

The convent is now a cultural centre, the **Collège d'Echanges Contemporains**, where conferences, concerts and other events take place. The basilica is the most important Gothic building in Provence. It was started in 1295 and finished in 1532, yet the whole is very harmonious. The choir is a rich 17th century decorative ensemble of stalls, marble panelling and main altar, contrasting with the simplicity of the nave. Notice the **altarpiece of the Passion of Christ** by the 16th century Venetian painter of Flemish origin, **François Ronzen.** It depicts the oldest known view of the popes' palace at Avignon. The **crypt** holds a tomb dating from the 5th century and contains four fine Gallo-Roman sarcophagi and the relic of the skull of St Mary Magdalen.

Hotels and Restaurants
At **Nans-les-Pins** (12Km by the N560 and D80) is the **Domaine de Châteauneuf.** A beautiful 18th century house converted into a very comfortable hotel with a swimming pool in a park and two tennis courts. With restaurant offering traditional food. 83860, Nans-les-Pins, Var. Tel: (94) 78.90.06. 20 rooms, 185–500F. Meals 105–200F. Closed 1 December–1 April. Credit cards: AE, DC, EC, VISA.

Garages
Ford: Tel: (94) 78.00.89.
Peugeot: Tel: (94) 78.00.45.
Renault: Tel: (94) 78.01.04.

BRIGNOLES
From Salon-de-Provence, Brignoles exit, 2Km
From Nice, Brignoles exit, 2Km
Inhabitants: 10,482
Office de Tourisme: Place St-Louis, closed Saturday afternoon and Sunday

An important market town, Brignoles was known in the Middle Ages for its prunes, but in the 16th century the fruit trees were destroyed in the Wars of Religion. 'Brignoles' **prunes** now come from **Digne** and the main products of the 20th century Brignoles are bauxite, marble and **wine**. Brignoles is the wine capital of Provence and an exhibition and fair is held there every year in the first fortnight of April.

The Old Town, with its narrow cobbled streets, tumbles down a small hill topped by the former **Palace of the Comtes de Provence.** It is now the **Musée du Pays Brignolais** and has on display the oldest Gallo-Roman Christian work of art, the **Sarcophagus of the Gayole** (300AD), remarkable for the beauty of its carving, and some mementoes of St Louis d'Anjou. (Open 9–12am and 2.30–6pm. Closed Monday and Tuesday and October.)

The **Church of St Sauveur** has a fine Romanesque portal. Notice nearby a handsome 13th century house.

Hotels and Restaurants
At **La Celle** (2Km by the D554) is the **Hostellerie de l'Abbaye de la Celle.** Built on the site of a 12th century Benedictine abbey, with the church (notice a 9th century Christ inside) and the chapter house still standing,

this very comfortable hotel, in a 17th century house furnished with antique Provençal furniture, has a large garden with swimming pool and a lovely terrace where one can eat in the open air. With restaurant. 83170, La Celle par Brignoles, Var. Tel: (94) 69.08.44. 30 rooms, 90–280F. Meals 80–150F. Closed 15 September–15 May.

At **Flassans-sur-Issole** (from Salon-de-Provence, Brignoles exit, N7, 17Km; from Nice, Le Luc/Toulon exit, N7, 12Km) is **La Grillade au Feu de Bois.** A comfortable hotel in an attractive Provençal house on top of a hill overlooking vineyards with a park and swimming pool. A restaurant serves grills and Provençal specialities. Flassans-sur-Issole, 83340, Le Luc, Var. Tel: (94) 69.71.20. 7 rooms, 170–250F. Meals 90–120F. Open all year. Credit cards: AE, DC, VISA.

Garages
Citroën: Route de Nice. Tel: (94) 69.01.83.
Peugeot/Talbot: Route d'Aix, N7. Tel: (94) 69.21.23.
Renault: Zone Industrielle. Tel: (94) 69.23.28.

Festivals, Fairs and Sporting Events
April, first fortnight: **exhibition and fair of the wines of Provence**

LE THORONET
From Salon-de-Provence, Le Luc exit, D17, 12Km
From Nice, Le Luc/Toulon exit, D17, 12Km

Hidden in woody hills on the banks of a stream, the Cistercian **Abbey of Le Thoronet** dates from the 12th century. The **church**, of Provençal Romanesque style, has no central doorway; the monks entered by the side entrance leading from the cloister. The interior has the austere majesty of the Cistercian style, devoid of decorative detail. The **Cloister** of trapezoidal shape shows the same sobriety of line. The **chapter house** dates from the early Gothic period and displays the only carvings in the whole abbey on the capitals of its two columns. Above the chapter house is the **monks' dormitory**, which can be visited. (Open 10–12am and 2–6pm 1 June–30 September. Closed Tuesday.)

Hotels and Restaurants
Relais de l'Abbaye (3Km north-west of aux Bruns by D84 to Carcès). In the beautiful landscape of a peaceful valley surrounded by vineyards and forests this quiet Provençal inn will serve you delicious regional food. With comfortable peaceful rooms. Le Thoronet, 83340, Le Luc, Var. Tel: (94) 73.87.59. 5 rooms, 80–150F. Meals 85–130F. Closed Monday night and Tuesday.

FRÉJUS

From Salon-de-Provence, Puget-sur-Argens/Fréjus/St-Raphaël exit, N7, 5Km
From Nice, Puget-sur-Argens exit, N7, 5Km
Inhabitants: 30,801
Office de Tourisme: Place Calvini, closed Saturday afternoon out of season; also at Fréjus-Plage, Boulevard de la Libération, June–September

Fréjus is an attractive Provençal city with some outstanding monuments and a sandy beach 1.5Km away. Comfortable hotels and excellent restaurants make it a pleasant overnight stop.

Built on a rocky plateau overlooking the sea, Fréjus is an ancient city founded by Caesar in 49BC. Pompey made it an important port and Augustus developed it as a Roman colony. At its height it numbered 25,000 inhabitants. The military port declined in the first century AD as the Roman Empire basked in peace. In the 10th century the Saracens destroyed the city which Bishop Riculphe brought back to life. The seat of an admiralty during the Rennaissance, Fréjus was sold during the Revolution and the port filled in.

Extensive archaeological remains give an idea of the grandeur of Roman Fréjus. On the road to **Cannes** (the N7), arches and pillars from the **aqueduct** still stand, as do vestiges of the **ramparts** and the ruined **theatre** (in a street lined with the foundations of Roman houses).

The **amphitheatre**, the oldest in Gaul, lies off the Rue H. Vadon (reached via the Avenue de Verdun). Greatly damaged, it was designed for a public consisting mostly of soldiers from the legion colony and therefore lacks the elegance and style of the amphitheatres of Nîmes and Arles. It is still used for bull-fights in the summer.

The centre of Fréjus revolves around the Place de la Liberté. Take the Rue Sièyes to reach the important fortified **bishop's city.**

Entering the **cathedral** one passes some magnificent Renaissance carved doors depicting scenes from the life of Christ and the Virgin. The **baptistry** is on the right. The oldest in France, it dates from the 5th century. Inside are some Roman marble columns. The cathedral belongs to the beginning of Provençal Gothic and was built on the site of a Roman temple to Jupiter and a 10th century fortified church. Of simple lines it displays some noteworthy 15th century choir stalls. From the narthex a staircase leads up to an exquisite small **cloister** dating from the late 12th century. Two storeys high, it now has only one gallery, the ceiling of which is decorated with fascinating 14th century paintings. Upstairs, the **archaeological museum** has a collection of Roman antiquities from the excavations of Fréjus, including mosaic and jewellery, sculptures etc. (Open 9–12am and 2–6pm 1 April–30 September; 9.30–12am and 2–4.30pm 1 October–31 March. Closed Tuesday and 1 May.)

Hotels and Restaurants

Les Résidences du Colombier (3Km by the D4) A hotel/club with Provençal bungalows in a park enclosing a swimming pool, tennis courts etc. With restaurants. 5Km from the beach. Route de Bagnols, 83600, Fréjus, Var. Tel: (94) 51. 45.92. 60 rooms, 225–360F. Meals 100F. Closed 4 October–3 April. Credit cards: DC, EC, VISA.

Auberge du Vieux Four A welcoming inn in the centre of Fréjus offering delicious traditional food including fish specialities. With comfortable rooms upstairs. 57 Rue de Grisolle, 83600, Fréjus, Var. Tel: (94) 51.56.38. 8 rooms 120–150F. Meals 110–165F. Closed Sunday, Monday night, and 20 September–20 October and school holidays in February. Credit cards: DC, VISA.

Garages

Citroën: 151 Avenue de Verdun. Tel: (94) 51.52.65.
Fiat: 1264 Avenue de Lattre de Tassigny. Tel: (94) 51.30.74.
Ford: 449 Boulevard de la Mer. Tel: (94) 51.38.39.
Peugeot: 1370 Avenue de Lattre de Tassigny. Tel: (94) 51.33.00.
Renault: N7. Tel: (94) 51.40.61.
Talbot: Boulevard de la Libération. Tel: (94) 51.23.19.

Festivals, Fairs and Sporting Events

July–August: **Bullfighting** in the ancient amphitheatre.

From the Les Adrets exit

Hotels and Restaurants

At **Callian** (10Km by the D37) on the banks of the **Lac de St Cassien**, formed by a dam on the **River Biançon**, is the **Auberge du Puits Jaubert**. An excellent restaurant, with rooms, in an old Provençal house, near the Lac of St Cassien, offering delicious inventive *cuisine*, such as *Soupe Froide de Queues d'Ecrevisses* (cold fresh-water crayfish soup) and *Langoustines à la Mousse de Cresson* (Dublin Bay prawns with watercress purée). Route du Lac de Fondurane, Callian, 83440, Fayence, Var. Tel: (94) 76.44.48. 8 rooms, 86–100F. Meals 65–150F. Closed Tuesday and January.

At **Fayence** (17Km by the D37 and D19; 2,146 inhabitants), a typically Provençal village named after Faenza in Italy because of its earthenware production, is **France**, an excellent traditional restaurant offering *Poulet Sauté aux Pignons* (sautéed chicken with pine kernels) and delicious sweets and ices. Very good value. 1 Rue du Château, 83440, Fayence, Var. Tel: (94) 76.00.14. Meals 40–100F. Closed Wednesday night, Thursday and 15 May–15 June and 15 December–15 January.

Moulin de la Camandoule 3Km south-west of Fayence by the D19, an old olive mill has been converted into a very comfortable hotel with a swimming pool in a large park. A restaurant offers excellent traditional food: *Filet de Boeuf aux Morilles* (beef fillet with Morilles mushrooms). Chemin Notre Dame des Cyprès, 83440, Fayence, Var. Tel: (94) 76.00.84. 11 rooms, 100–240F. Meals 95–160F. Closed Tuesday except July and August, and 1 October to first week before Easter. Credit card: VISA.

MIRAMAR
From Salon-de-Provence, Mandelieu/La Napoule exit, N98, 10Km
From Nice, Cannes/Mandelieu/La Napoule exit, N98, 10Km

Hotels and Restaurants
Saint Christophe A luxury hotel overlooking the sea in a spectacular setting with lifts down to the private beach; a private marina offers snorkelling, waterskiing and surfing. Restaurant with a panoramic view. Red Roc Beach, Miramar, 06590, Théoule-sur-Mer, Alpes-Maritimes. Tel: (93) 75.41.36. 40 rooms, 285–575F. Meals 120F. Closed October–May.

Père Pascal An excellent restaurant serving delicious fish specialities. Good value. 16, Avenue du Troyes Miramar, 06590, Théoule-sur-Mer, Alpes-Maritimes. Tel: (93) 90.30.11. Meals 55–150F. ßlosed Thursday, and November and December. Credit cards: AE, VISA.

MOUGINS
From Salon-de-Provence, Cannes/Grasse exit, N285, 0.5Km
From Nice, Cannes/Grasse exit, N285, 0.5Km
Inhabitants: 8,492

Hotels and Restaurants
Mougins, on top of a hill overlooking Cannes, has to be a halt on the **Riviera.** It counts several fine restaurants, among them **Roger Vergé's** famous **Moulin.**

Moulin de Mougins A very famous restaurant offering truly matchless cuisine in lovely surroundings, with a few luxurious rooms if one wants to stay and be thoroughly self-indulgent and hedonistic. Make a special event of a meal there and sample the *Turbot à la Crème de Safran* (turbot with saffron sauce) or the *Terrine de Rascasse* (scorpion-fish pâté). Quartier Notre Dame de Vie, 424 Chemin du Moulin, 06250, Mougins, Alpes-Maritimes. Tel: (93) 75.78.24. 5 rooms, 300–550F. Meals 270–400F. Closed Monday and 20 October–20 December. Credit cards: AE, DC, VISA.

Relais de Mougins Exellent restaurant with lovely décor, serving classical *haute cuisine* such as *Foie Gras* and *Pigeonneau à l'Ail* (pigeon with garlic). Place de la Mairie, 06250, Mougins, Alpes-Maritimes. Tel: (93) 90.03.47. Meals 175–300F. Closed lunch-time except Sunday in August; also closed Sunday night, Monday and 1 November–22 December. Credit card: VISA.

Hôtel de France A lovely Provençal restaurant with a terrace and rooms, offering delicious regional food such as *Canette à la Tomate et Olives Vertes* (duckling with tomatoes and green olives) and *Soupe de Moules au Curry* (curried mussel soup). Place du Commandant Lamy, 06250, Mougins, Alpes-Maritimes. Tel: (93) 90.00.01. 6 rooms, 130–150F. Meals 105–160F. Closed February, March, Sunday night and Monday out of season: Credit card: VISA.

St PAUL-DE-VENCE
From Salon-de-Provence, Cagnes-sur-Mer exit, D2, 10Km
From Nice, Cagnes-sur-Mer exit, D2, 10Km
Inhabitants: 1,974
Office de Tourisme: Maison Tour, Rue Grande, closed November and Tuesday

St Paul-de-Vence is an old fortified village well worth a visit despite its enormous tourist influx. The old town retains its 16th century ramparts and the view over the valley to the sea is breathtaking. A wide range of hotels and restaurants make of St Paul a marvellous place to stay.

Walk up the Grand Rue to the **church**, a Romanesque building restored in the 17th century. Notice the paintings inside and ask to see the **treasury**, which consists of gold and silver religious objects. In the chapel of the baptismal font notice an alabaster Virgin from the 15th century.

Walk round the **ramparts** built by François I and admire the wide view over the mountains and hills of the upper country.

From St Paul go on to visit the **Fondation Maeght** north-west of the village. Standing on a hill in the midst of pine trees, with a view of the valley all the way to the sea, this **museum** is dedicated to modern art. Sculptures stand in the gardens and terraces, reflected in the pools while fountains play. It is a lovely place to spend the afternoon, visiting the well laid out gallery with choice pictures by **Kandinsky**, **Miró**, **Chagall**, **Matisse** etc, and strolling on the terraces and in the gardens where the abstract shapes of the sculptures take on an elemental quality and blend so well with the Provençal landscape beyond. Children love it. They clamber on to the pieces of sculptures experiencing the *joie de vivre* that a Miró or **Calder** wanted to express through their works.

A very pleasant cool and shady cafeteria serves drinks and snacks. Do not miss the **chapel**, where there is a poignant 12th century Crucifix.

(Open 10–12am and 3–7pm 1 May–30 September, 10–12.30am and 2.30–6pm 1 October–30 April.)

Hotels and Restaurants

Mas d'Artigny A very luxurious hotel in a large park with apartments giving on to a private patio, garden and individual swimming pool. The restaurant offers food to match the high standard of accommodation, from traditional *haute cuisine* to regional dishes. Chemin de Salettes, 06570, Saint Paul-de-Vence. Alpes-Maritimes. Tel: (93) 32.84.54. 81 rooms and apartments, 220–1,060F. Meals 140–250F.

La Colombe d'Or A beautifully decorated Provençal house converted into a luxury hotel in Old St Paul, with a swimming pool in the garden. With restaurant. 1 Place du Général de Gaulle, 06570, St Paul-de-Vence, Alpes-Maritimes. Tel: (93) 32.80.02. 24 rooms, 400–560F. Meals 150F. Closed 5 November–18 December. Credit cards: AE, DC.

Le Hameau (On the D7) A comfortable hotel with a cosy atmosphere, in a lovely garden overlooking the sea. No restaurant. 528 Route de la Colle, 06570, Saint Paul-de-Vence, Alpes-Maritimes. Tel: (93) 32.80.24. 14 rooms, 130–270F.

Morateur An excellent restaurant in old St Paul offering traditional Provençal *cuisine*. 98 Rue Grande, 06570, St Paul-de-Vence, Alpes-Maritimes. Tel: (94) 32.81.91. Meals 60–150F. Closed Sunday night and Monday and first Monday in November to 18 December.

VENCE

From Salon-de-Provence, Cagnes-sur-Mer exit, D36, 15Km
From Nice, Cagnes-sur-Mer exit, D36, 15Km
Inhabitants: 12,796
Office de Tourisme: Place Grand Jardin, closed Sunday except morning in season

Vence is a lovely old town built on a rocky promontory between two gorges. Excellent hotels and restaurants make it a pleasant overnight stop 10Km from the sea.

Vence was an important Roman city and became the seat of a bishopric in the Middle Ages. It has retained from this past vestiges of its ramparts and a 15th century square tower, near the **Porte du Peyra**, dating from the same period. The **Place du Peyra** is a picturesque sight with its fountain in the centre of the small cobbled square.

The **cathedral** is Romanesque and has been much altered. Inside notice the 15th century stalls in the upper gallery and their fascinating misericords. From the Old Town go up the Avenue des Poilus, passing the Chapelle des Pénitents, and on to the Avenue Matisse (the N210), to visit the **Chapelle du Rosaire**, designed and decorated by **Henri Matisse** for a Dominican convent. It is a small white-washed place in which the stained-glass windows create an endlessly moving pattern of light and colour, such as Matisse would have enjoyed. The very simplicity of the interior and its graphically silhouetted motifs invite one to silence, contemplation and prayer. (Open 10–11.30am and 2.30–5.30pm Tuesday and Thursday. Otherwise by appointment only. Tel: (94) 58.03.26.)

Hotels and Restaurants
Château du Domaine St Martin A very luxurious hotel in a beautiful setting, with a swimming pool and a spectacular view over the hills. A restaurant offers gourmet cuisine such as *Pâtes Fraîches aux Truffes* (fresh pasta with truffles) and *Charlotte au Chocolat Amer* (bitter-chocolate sweet). Route de Coursegoules, 06140, Vence, Alpes-Maritimes. Tel: (94) 58.02.02. 27 rooms, 450–850F. Meals 195–300F. Closed Wednesday, December–March. Credit cards: AE, DC, EC, VISA.
Miramar Comfortable hotel with a lovely view and cosy rooms. No restaurant. Plateau St Michel, 06140, Vence, Alpes-Maritimes. Tel: (94) 58.01.32. 17 rooms, 180–240F. Closed November. Credit card: AE.
Les Portiques Excellent restaurant in the old part of Vence offering delicious food such as *Lotte au Safran* (monkfish with saffron) and *Tarte Soufflée au Citron Vert* (lime soufflé flan). 6 Rue St Véran, 06140, Vence, Alpes-Maritimes. Tel: (94) 58.36.31. Meals 120–150F. Closed Sunday, Monday and 1–20 January.

Garages
Mercedes/Talbot: 39 Avenue Foch. Tel: (94) 58.01.21.

Festivals, Fairs and Sporting Events
Easter Sunday and Monday: **Solemn Mass** and **Provençal folk dancing**

BEAULIEU-SUR-MER
From Salon-de-Provence, Nice Promenade des Anglais exit, 6Km
From Menton, Nice Centre exit, 6Km
Inhabitants: 4,273
Office de Tourisme: Place de la Gare, closed Saturday afternoon except during season and Sunday

One of the oldest and most famous resorts on the Riviera, Beaulieu-sur-Mer enjoys a particularly pleasant climate.

Hotels and Restaurants
La Réserve A very luxurious hotel with gardens and a swimming pool by

the sea and a restaurant offering delicious food: *Brouillade de Fruit de Mer au Basilic* (seafood in olive oil and basil) and exquisite sweets. 5 Boulevard du Général Leclerc, 06310, Beaulieu-sur-Mer, Alpes-Maritimes. Tel: (93) 01.00.01. 50 rooms, 250–870F. Meals 165–300F. Closed 1 December–10 January.

La Résidence Modern family hotel with terraces and a garden. No restaurant. 9bis Avenue Albert I, 06310, Beaulieu-sur-Mer, Alpes-Maritimes. Tel: (93) 01.06.02. 21 rooms, 210–390F. Closed 1 November–20 December. Credit card: AE.

La Pignatelle An excellent restaurant serving delicious Provençal food: *Lasagne au Four* and *Tripes Niçoises* (tripe with tomatoes, onions, garlic etc). Good value. 10 Rue Quincenet, 06310, Beaulieu-sur-Mer, Alpes-Maritimes. Tel: (93) 01.03.37. Meals 38–100F. Closed Wednesday.

VILLEFRANCHE-SUR-MER

From Salon-de-Provence, Nice Promenade des Anglais exit, 6Km
From Menton, Nice Centre exit, 6Km
Inhabitants: 6,863
Office de Tourisme: Square F. Binon, closed Monday out of season and Sunday

Villefranche is a small bustling fishing port built on woody slopes in the curve of a most beautiful bay between **Cap Ferrat** and **Mont Boron.** Villefranche owes its name to the Comte de Provence, Charles II of Anjou, who founded it in the 14th century and gave it trade franchises. It has retained a lovely 17th century atmosphere with its narrow cobbled streets tumbling down to the port, and the 16th century **Fortress** dominating the whole colourful scene.

In the port the **Church of St Michel** dates from the 17th century, as does the tiny **Fishermen's Chapel of St Pierre**, which was decorated by **Jean Cocteau** with graphic frescoes, of great sobriety and power, on themes from the Gospels. (Open 9–12am and 3–7pm 15 June–15 September. Otherwise 9–12am and 2–5pm.)

Hotels and Restaurants

Hôtel Welcome and **Restaurant le St Pierre** A very comfortable hotel in which Jean Cocteau stayed when painting the Chapel of St Pierre, with a very good restaurant serving traditional food such as *Sole Soufflée à l'Estragon* (sole soufflé with tarragon). 1 Quai Courbet, 06230, Villefranche-sur-Mer, Alpes-Maritimes. Tel: (93) 55.27.27. 35 rooms, 150–335F. Meals 88–200F. Closed 1 November–20 December. Credit cards: AE, DC, EC.

La Campanette Very friendly restaurant serving delicious Provençal food such as *Gâteau d'Oignons Doux* (onion flan with tomato sauce). 2 Rue Baron de Bres, 06230, Villefranche-sur-Mer, Alpes-Maritimes. Tel: (93) 80.79.98. Meals 75–150F. Closed Sunday and 15 January–15 February. Credit cards: AE, VISA.

Vauban A comfortable restaurant with pretty 18th century décor and a garden. No restaurant. 11 Avenue du Général de Gaulle, 06230, Villefranche-sur-Mer, Alpes-Maritimes. Tel: (93) 80.71.20. 12 rooms, 180–240F. Closed 15 November–15 February.

Fetivals, Fairs and Sporting Events

Shrove Tuesday: **nautical festival and carnival** in the marina of La Darse

ÈZE

From Salon-de-Provence, La Turbie/Monaco exit, D2564, 4Km
From Menton, Monaco/Roquebrune exit, D2564, 10Km
Inhabitants: 1,860
Office de Tourisme: Mairie (town hall), closed Saturday afternoon and Sunday

Eze is a strange village perched on a rocky promontory overlooking the sea and commanding a magnificent view of Cap Ferrat. **George Sand** and **Nietzsche** are among the celebrities who have enjoyed the charm of the village, steeped in the Middle Ages, and the natural beauty of its situation.

Explore the narrow cobbled streets, noticing the **Chapelle des Pénitents Blancs** dating from 1306, and climb up the hill to the **Jardin Exotique**, a tropical garden laid out around the ruins of a 14th century **castle** destroyed in the 17th century. From the top the view over the coast and glittering sea is breathtaking. (Open 8am–8pm 1 July–15 September; 9–12am and 2–5pm 16 September–30 June.)

Spend a night in one of the hotels in the Old Town and wander down to the **Parfumerie Fragonard** to visit the factory where pure flower essence is distilled in order to make scents, soaps, cosmetics etc. (Open every day.)

Hotels and Restaurants

Château de la Chèvre d'Or A medieval mansion converted into a luxury hotel with the most amazing view over the coast and Cap Ferrat. A restaurant offers gourmet food to match the situation and décor. Try *Pigeonneau aux Gousses d'Ail* (pigeon with garlic) and *Huîtres Chaudes au Champagne* (oysters in a champagne sauce). Moyenne Corniche, Rue Barri, 06360, Eze Village, Alpes-Maritimes. Tel: (93) 41.12.12. 9 rooms and apartments 280–750F. Meals 175–250F. Closed Wednesday

(October–Easter) and 15 November–15 February. Credit cards: AE, DC, VISA.

La Couletta An excellent restaurant serving specialities such as *Ecrevisses à la Purée de Poivrons Rouges* (fresh-water crayfish with red peppers) and *Pigeon au Pistou* (pigeon with a basil sauce). Place Charles de Gaulle, 06360, Èze Village, Alpes-Maritimes. Tel: (93) 41.05.23. Meals 150F. Closed Sunday night, Monday, December and January. Credit cards: AE, DC.

Le Nid d'Aigle Above the old village an excellent restaurant serving delicious Provençal specialities such as *Bourride* (fish soup with aioli) and *Lapin aux Herbes* (rabbit with herbs). Very good value. Rue du Château, 06360, Èze Village, Alpes-Maritimes. Tel: (93) 41.19.08. Meals 32–120F. Closed Thursday and 15 November–20 December.

PEILLON
From Salon-de-Provence, Nice-Est exit, D21, 10Km
From Menton, Nice-Centre exit, D21, 10Km
Inhabitants: 898

Peillon is a very picturesque village perched on the top of a rocky promontory.

Hotels and Restaurants
Auberge de la Madone A lovely Provençal house with a terraced garden; an excellent restaurant serving deliciously light Provençal dishes, which can be enjoyed in the garden. Try the *Pintadeau au Marc de Muscat et Fruits Frais* (guinea fowl with fresh fruit and brandy) or the *Tourton des Pénitents* (savoury cake with chives, almonds and pine kernels). Peillon, 06440, L'Escarène, Alpes-Maritimes. Tel: (93) 91.91.17. 19 rooms, 120–220F Meals 60–150F. Closed Wednesday and 15 October–15 December.

SAINTE AGNÈS
From Salon-de-Provence, Menton–Sospel exit, D22, 13Km
From Menton, Menton–Sospel exit, D22, 13Km

Hotels and Restaurants
Le Saint Yves A small comfortable hotel overlooking Menton and the coast. With restaurant. Ste Agnès, 06500, Menton, Alpes-Maritimes. Tel: (93) 35.91.45. 7 rooms, 115F (full-board only). Closed Friday and 15 November–15 December.

La Languedocienne
Orange–Collioure (A9)

The A9 runs through **Lower Provence**, on the western side of the Rhône delta, and the marshy **Camargue** to the **Languedoc plain**, bordered to the north by the **Cévennes** and **Causses** mountains, and on to **Roussillon**, a valley following the curve of the Mediterranean coast at the foot of the Pyrenees. Lower Provence, between **Orange** and **Nîmes**, is a country of rich orchards nurtured by the fertile silt of the Rhône delta. Luscious white peaches and golden sun-ripened apricots are a particular delight. Uzès is the centre of a truffle market from November to March.

Lower Languedoc is composed of three distinct landscapes. The **Garrigues** are sun-drenched limestone hills of a stark and forbidding appearance, with only a few clusters of stunted oak trees and aromatic shrubs to relieve their bareness. They form the southern outer edge of the Causses, Cevennes and **Minervois** mountains, and include the **Corbières** range. Between the Garrigues and the coast, vineyards take over the plain around **Lunel** and **Frontignan**, producing the **Muscat** wine.

The coast consists mostly of vast sandy beaches with large lagoons created by the sand and gravel brought down by the Rhône. On these sandy soils vineyards have taken over from olive trees and the cultivation of cereals. Around the **Grau du Roil, Chasselas** grapes are grown for the table.

The Roussillon plain is a luminous Mediterranean region covered with tropical vegetation: oleanders and orange trees grow wild. The local nectarines, peaches, cherries and apricots are the first to reach the markets all over France, thanks to the warm climate and the sheltered geographical position. The vineyards produce the naturally sweet Muscat wine.

Fishing is an important part of the economy of the Languedoc-Roussillon coast. **Tunny** is fished from March to December and **sardines** from February to October. **Anchovy** is caught from small fishing boats, particularly around Collioure, and tinned in various factories. Apart from the deep-sea fishing, the **lagoons** provide **eels, grey mullet, sea bass, sea bream** etc. Seafood is particularly rich with the development of **Ostreiculture** and **Mytiliculture** (oyster and mussel breeding) around the bay of **Thau** near the port of **Sète** in the Languedoc and the **Etangs de Leucate** in the Roussillon.

Throughout history the Languedoc-Roussillon region has been devastated by successive invasions from the **Celts** to the **Huns, Visigoths** and **Arabs**, and torn apart by religious strife. The most famous and tragic campaign was the 13th century savage persecution of the **Cathar heretics**, the **Albigensian Crusade.** The whole country still seems moulded by the appalling suffering and ravages undergone at that time. Sad reminders of bloody fights, the picturesque ruins of once-proud fortresses stand desolate and forlorn on their eyries. The names of **Béziers, Carcassonne** and **Montségur** conjure up the atrocities of this ruthless extermination.

The word *Cathar* comes from the Greek and means 'pure'. The Catharist doctrine, which can be traced to the 3rd century Persian **Manichean** sect, spread through the Middle East and the Balkans to southern Europe. The basic creed rested on the dual principle of Good and Evil as two separate entities represented by two different gods – one of goodness and all things spiritual, the other of evil, embodied in wordly and physical matter – and on the belief of the reincarnation of the soul.

The Cathars advocated celibacy and suicide, both negating the physical side of human nature, in order to consecrate their lives to attaining a high level of spirituality and becoming *pur* or *parfait* (perfect) through the rigorous observance of chastity, poverty, fasting etc after partaking of their only sacrament, the *Consolatum*, in order to avoid reincarnation. They would then retire from the world, living in communities and going around the country preaching their precepts. The ordinary follower could carry on his life as usual and receive the *Consolatum* on his deathbed to free his soul from the reincarnation cycle.

The appeal of this simple and austere doctrine was irresistible in the Middle Ages, when some of the notables of the church were living in great luxury and corruption. Both aristrocrats and peasants embraced it wholeheartedly. The church, feeling threatened and considering it a dangerous heresy, set out to eradicate it.

At first persuasion was used: **St Dominic** became an ascetic and went out preaching austerity and discipline like the *Parfaits*. But when the papal legate, **Pierre de Castelnau,** was murdered at St Gilles in 1208 the Pope excommunicated the **Comte de Toulouse,** who was accused of complicity, and gathered an army of crusaders from all over Europe to fight the heretics.

Béziers was rased to the ground and its entire population massacred. Carcassonne fell and atrocious persecutions and killings went on, encouraged by the **Inquisition** who kept the fires of the *auto-da-fé* burning.

It was not until 1229 that some sort of peace settled over the country with the **Treaty of Meaux** (or Paris), placing the Languedoc under French rule. The Wars of Religion were particularly ferocious in this part of France, converted early on to Protestantism. They lasted on and off for over two centuries, ending with the **Camisards' Revolt** in the early 18th century and the subsequent 1787 **Edict of Tolérance** ending the persecutions.

GASTRONOMY

The food and drink of the Languedoc-Roussillon is varied and copious, drawing inspiration from ancient Roman and Arab dishes. The famous *Cassoulet* of Castelnaudary, Toulouse and Carcassonne had an ancestor in Gallo-Roman mutton stew with white beans.

The ingredients available in this region are varied, abundant and of unmatchable freshness. Sheep graze on the Causses hills, while the forest yields game of all sorts and the 'buried empress', the **truffle.** Geese and ducks are fattened to perfection. **Fish** is plentiful both from the Mediterranean (red mullet, anchovies, sardines, and tunny, together with **seafood** – mussels and oysters) and the mountain rivers (trout, pike, tench etc). The orchards are annually the earliest in France to produce succulent fruit.

The specialities of the region include: *Aigo Bouillido* (a soup made of garlic, herbs, eggs and *croûtons*); *Boles de Picoulat* (meat balls with tomatoes); and *Cargolade* (a Catalan dish of snails from the vineyards).

Goose and duck provide the various *Foie Gras, Confits* (cooked and preserved in their own fat) and *Salmis* (also from pigeon, an ancient dish of complex execution involving stripping the flesh off the bone of the roasted bird to make a thick sauce with the left-overs, which is then poured over the pieces).

The coast offers many fish dishes: *Bourride* (fish stew with herbs); *Bouillabaisse* (see under Provence, here called *Boullinade*); and *Langouste au Banyuls* (crayfish with Banyuls wine sauce).

Sweets are plentiful: *Alléluias* from Castelnaudary; *Amellonades* (*brioche* with sweet almonds); *Fouace* (*brioche* with angelica); *Galichous* (marzipan with pistachio nuts); *Nemes* (aniseed cake); *Oreillettes* (deep-fried batter cakes flavoured with orange water); *Soleil* (almond cakes with orange water); and *Touron* (almond cake with pistachio nuts, hazel-nuts and preserved fruit).

The Côtes du Languedoc and Roussillon produce half of France's good *Vin Ordinaire* and *Vin du Pays*, mostly strong full-bodied reds from the Aude, Gard and Hérault areas. Names include **Côtes du Roussillon, Minervois, Corbières, Fîtou,** and **Côteaux du Languedoc,** all made from the **Carignan** grape. White wines include the **Blanquette de Limoux,** a naturally sparkling wine, light and fresh, known since the 16th century and made from the **Clairette** and **Mauzac** grapes. Its name comes from the white fluff under the leaves of the *Mauzac* grape. **Limoux Nature** is a white still wine, and **Vin Vert** is a green wine from the Roussillon, light and refreshing.

The most characteristic wines of the area are the various still sweet wines made from the *Muscat* grape, introduced to the area by the Greeks. The gravelly soils around **Lunel** and **Frontignan** in Languedoc yield this deliciously mellow and musky wine, praised by the poet **Paul Geraldy:**

Nowadays some stern Gentlemen,
Sit, grumbling, sipping dry wines,
It is a taste which comes from England . . .
For the wine favoured by Voltaire
Was the Muscat of Frontignan.

In the Roussillon, apart from the *Muscat*, the **Grenache, Macabeo** and **Malvoisie** grape produce natural sweet wines, warm and scented, perfect for drinking as an aperitive, simply chilled. These wines include **Banyuls, Maury, Muscat de Rivesaltes** and **Rivesaltes.**

PONT-DU-GARD
From Orange, Remoulins exit, N100, 4Km
From Perpignan, Remoulins/Avignon/Marseille exit, N100, 4Km

For the harmony of its three-tiered arcaded structure, the daring audacity of its span, the sheer beauty of its golden stones against the luminous blue sky in the wild Garrigue country of the torrential **River Gard**, the aqueduct known as Pont-du-Gard has been looked upon as one of the world's wonders ever since it was built.

In 18BC it was built on Agrippa's order to provide pure fresh water for the town of Nîmes, from a source near Uzès. It was in use until the 9th century when it became choked up with lime deposits. Having fallen into disrepair it was restored by Napoléon III in the 19th century.

It is possible to walk either on the first level, along the watercourse, (or if you do not suffer from vertigo!) along the stone roof which offers magnificent views over the Garrigue.

Hotels and Restaurants
Hôtel le Vieux Moulin (by the D981, on the left bank). A very comfortable hotel in a converted old mill on the River Gard just opposite the famous Pont. A garden stretches to the river and you can dine outside, with the magnificent view, enjoying typical Provençal cooking. 30210, Pont-du-Gard par Remoulins, Gard. Tel: (66) 37.14.35. 17 rooms 105–260F. Meals 80–145F. Closed Tuesday, and 1 November–5 February.

At **Castillon-du-Gard** (4Km by the D228) is **Le Vieux Castillon.** A luxury hotel in a beautiful old village with a lovely garden and a swimming pool. With restaurant. Castillon-du-gard, 30210, Remoulins, Gard. Tel: (66) 37.00.77. 21 rooms 250–450F. Meals 115–150F. Closed January–March. Credit card: VISA.

UZÈS

From Orange, Remoulins exit, N100, D19 and D981, 19Km
From Perpignan, Remoulins/Avignon exit, N100, D19 and D981, 19Km
Inhabitants: 7,387
Office de Tourisme: Hôtel de Ville, closed Saturday and Sunday out of season

Uzès is a fascinating medieval market town beautifully restored and overlooking the Garrigue. A very comfortable hotel makes it a perfect overnight stop.

The seat of a diocese from the 5th century to the Révolution, Uzès is a city of towers. Five dominate the pink-tiled sloping roofs of the old houses. The **Tour des Evêques** (bishops' tower), now the **clock tower**, the Bermonde, and the Vicomte in the ducal palace, and the Fenestrelle on the cathedral, all date from the 12th century and symbolise the power of their respective owners – king, bishop or Comte.

Arriving from the D981 walk to the Place du Marché and the **ducal palace**, a rectangular building dominated by its square tower, the **Bermonde.** The courtyard, with its lovely small garden, contains yet another tower, the **Tour Vicomte.** The Renaissance façade dates from the 16th century and was built by the royal architect Philibert, who built the **Tuileries Palace** in Paris. Classical influence is tempered by the French love for decorative details and an innate sense of harmonious proportions.

Inside the apartments display fine period furniture and mementoes relating to the Uzès family. (Ducal palace open 9.30–12am and 2.30–5pm. Closed Wednesday and Saturday in winter.)

The neighbouring **Hôtel de Ville** has an 18th century courtyard. Go from there to the Place de l'Evêché where the 17th century former **bishop's palace** is now a library and a small museum. Opposite, the **Hôtel de Castille** boasts a grand entrance with columns similar to those of the **Château de Castille** passed on the D981 and belonging to the same family.

The 17th century **Cathedral of St Théodorit** has a 19th century west front and contains a fine 17th century organ and two paintings by Simon de Chalons worth noting: an Ascension of Christ and a Resurrection of Lazarus. The adjacent 12th century **Tour Fenestrelle** is unique in France because of its tiered circular shape. It belonged to a Romanesque church destroyed during the Wars of Religion.

Linger in the **Promenade J. Racine** to enjoy the view over the Alzon ravine and the surrounding Garrigue, a limestone crest at the foot of the Massif Central, fragrant with wild plants and flowers such as lavender, thyme and rosemary.

Nearby the 17th century **Jean Racine Pavilion** is the house where the writer stayed for a year before his Parisian fame. Carry on into Le

Portalet to the **Musée di Rodo**, a railway and vintage-car museum. (Open 10–12am; also 3–7pm Palm Sunday–1 November; otherwise Sunday and public holidays 2–7pm, Closed Tuesday.)

Take the Boulevard Victor Hugo to the **Church of St Etienne**, an harmonious 18th century church, and reach the **Place de la République**, also called the **Place aux Herbes** from the time when it was a medieval 'herb' market. It has been beautifully restored and has great character and atmosphere with its golden stone houses above the arcaded ground-floor gallery running all round the square and sheltering shops and cafés. Every Saturday it is the scene of a lively market where truffles are sold from November to March.

Hotels and Restaurants

Hôtel d'Entraigues A comfortable hotel in a 17th century converted house just a few minutes away from the Fenestrelle Tower. With restaurant. Place de l'Evêché, 8 Rue de la Calade, 30700, Uzès, Gard. Tel: (66) 22.14.48. 20 rooms, 145–190F. Meals 80F. Credit cards: DC, EC, VISA.

Château d'Arpaillargues, Hôtel d'Agoult 4Km from Uzès by the D982, the owner of the Hôtel d'Entraigues, Mr Savry, manages this beautiful 18th century mansion furnished with antiques and exquisitely decorated, with a restaurant offering food to match the romantic surroundings (Liszt's mistress Marie d'Agoult used to live here.) Try the *Terrine de Lapereau Mariné au Céleri et aux Noix* (pâté of marinated rabbit with celery and walnuts) or *Lotte à l'Estragon* (monkfish with tarragon). A lovely park with a swimming pool completes this idyllic place. 30700, Uzès, Gard. Tel: (66) 22.14.48. 28 rooms, 240–380F. Meals 110–180F. Closed 15 October–15 March. Credit cards: DC, EC, VISA.

Garages

Citroën: Champ de Mars. Tel: (66) 22.22.64.
Peugeot: Avenue de la Gare. Tel: (66) 22.59.01.
Renault: Route d'Alès. Tel: (66) 22.60.99.

NÎMES
From Orange, Nîmes–Est exit, N86, 4Km
From Perpignan, Nîmes–Ouest/Garons/Marseille exit, 4Km
Inhabitants: 133,942
Office de Tourisme: 6 Rue Auguste

Nîmes is a city outstanding in the beauty of its Roman monuments and of its 18th century gardens, laid out around the famous **Nemausus spring**, which gave its name to the town. Very comfortable hotels and excellent restaurants make a stay in Nîmes most pleasant.

Nîmes, founded by Augustus, was one of the jewels of the Roman Empire. The collapse of the latter, and the subsequent barbaric invasions by Germanic tribes, brought ruin to the once flourishing city. During the Rennaissance François I was a benefactor, but the Wars of Religion once again ravaged the town which only came back to prosperity in the 18th century.

Arriving by the N86 aim for the Esplanade Charles de Gaulle. The **Arènes (amphitheatre)** lies nearby, off the Boulevard de la Libération. The oval structure is well preserved with its two-tiered, round-arched arcades, and used to accommodate 21,000 spectators. After many vicissitudes it is now used again, in the summer, for Provençal and Spanish bullfights. (The Provençal version does not include the *Mise à Mort* – the killing of the bull).

From the amphitheatre walk to the **Maison Carrée.** Inspired by Greek temples and built in the 1st century BC, it is the best preserved Roman temple in existence, being externally complete. The delicately carved Corinthian columns create a rhythmical harmony of great elegance. In the **Cella** (inner sanctum), reached through the **Portico**, a **Musée des Antiques** exhibits sculpture and artefacts, notably a colossal marble statue of Apollo, a white marble head of Venus (the 'Vénus de Nîmes') and a bronze head of a god.

Turn into the Quai de la Fontaine to reach the gardens, laid out around Roman remains including the **Temple de Diane** dating from the 2nd century AD. The name is misleading – the 'temple' was in fact a grand staircase hall preceding the establishment of the baths. The **Jardin de la Fontaine** takes its name from the ancient fountain still flowing in the Roman architectural structure and incorporated in the overall 18th century design. With mirror-like pools, promenades lined with balustrades and tall pines and cedars standing out against a setting of lawns and flowers, the Jardin de la Fontaine is a romantic place, where flood-lit recitals and concerts are given on summer evenings.

The squat octagonal **Tour Magne** overlooks the garden and was part of the Roman ramparts. From the top of its 140 steps, the view over the Alpilles and the Garrigue is magnificent.

The **Musée des Beaux Arts**, in the Rue Cité-Foulc reached from the Place des Arènes, houses an extensive collection of Old Masters (Brueghel and Bassano among others), sculpture and Venetian glass. (Open 9–12am and 2–5pm. Closed Tuesday.)

The **Cathedral of St Castor** was rebuilt in the 19th century, but the tower dates from the 11th to the 15th century.

The culinary speciality of Nîmes is *Caladons*, a delicious almond cake.

Hotels and Restaurants

Imperator A lovely old house with an inner garden, beautifully converted into a luxury hotel in the heart of the old Nîmes. An excellent restaurant serves traditional classic cuisine such as *Brandade Niçoise* (cod mousse with cream, olive oil and garlic). Quai de la Fontaine, 30000, Nîmes, Gard. Tel: (66) 21.90.30. 60 rooms, 240–395F. Meals 100–200F. Closed 15 December–1 March. Credit cards: AE, DC, EC, VISA.

Le Louvre A comfortable hotel overlooking a quiet square with a very good restaurant serving traditional food such as *Magret de Canard aux Morilles* (duck fillet with Morilles mushrooms). Good value. 2 Square de la Couronne, 30000, Nîmes, Gard. Tel: (66) 27.22.75. 35 rooms, 110–300F. Meals 45–140F. Credit cards: AE, DC, EC, VISA.

La Farigoule Gourmet food in lovely restaurant. Try the *Pigeon Rôti à l'Ail* (roast pigeon with garlic) and the *Ris de Veau Braisé aux Truffes* (sweetbreads with truffles). 15 Rue Pierre Semard, 30000, Nîmes, Gard. Tel: (66) 67.83.29. Meals 100F-150F. Dinner only. Closed Sunday and public holidays, August.

Garages

Austin/Morris/Rover/Triumph: Boulevard Périphérique. Tel: (66) 84.07.98.
BMW: 2532 Route de Montpellier. Tel: (66) 84.78.11.
Citroën: 2290 Route de Montpellier. Tel: (66) 84.04.40.
Ford: 655 Avenue du Maréchal Juin. Tel: (66) 84.08.01.
Peugeot: 1667 Avenue du Gard. Tel: (66) 84.60.08.
Renault: 1412 Avenue du Maréchal Juin. Tel: (66) 84.60.00.

Festivals, Fairs and Sporting Events

June–September: **bullfighting** in the old amphitheatre

AIGUES-MORTES

From Orange, Gallargues exit, N313 and D979, 18Km
From Perpignan, Gallargues exit, N313 and D979, 18Km
Inhabitants: 4,536
Office de Tourisme: Place St-Louis, 1 April–30 September, closed Monday; and at the Mairie *(town hall) 15 November–31 March, closed Saturday and Sunday*

Aigues-Mortes is an amazing medieval fortified city which has come down to the 20th century in its original state. A very comfortable hotel and a very good restaurant make it an unusual place in which to stay.

Aigues-Mortes sits in the middle of the **Camargue** lagoons and dry marshes, transformed into vineyards in the 19th century and producing the **Listel** wine or **Rosé des Sables**, a light, subtle rosé wine. The town was once a thriving port. It was created in the 13th century by Louis IX (St Louis) when planning the 7th Crusade to Egypt. Although King of France, he did not own a port on the Mediterranean shores. A local monastery gave him the small fishing village at the end of a marshy tongue of land, known as *Aigues-Mortes* (dead waters) because of its desolate position.

Aigues-Mortes became a privileged town under St Louis and his son Philippe le Hardi. Some 15,000 souls lived within its ramparts. Decline came with the gradual silting up of the port and now Aigues-Mortes is surrounded by marshes, saltflats producing sea salt, and lagoons where wildlife flourishes.

The **ramparts**, with their golden stone and medieval outline on the intensely blue sky, are a magnificent and evocative sight. Forming a rectangle they are punctuated at regular intervals by twenty watch towers marking the corners, sides and gateways of the city. At the north-west corner, the **Tour de Constance** was built in the 13th century over an earlier one built by the Comte de Toulouse, married to Constance de France (hence the name). Inside, a tiny chapel, Louis IX's **oratory**, and the **Knights' Hall** still survive. Protestant prisoners were held here in the 18th century.

The simple **Church of Notre Dame des Sablons** dates from the 13th century. There is a sweeping view of the Camargue from the top of the tower. (Open 9–12am and 2–6.30pm.)

Continue on the D979, which follows the ancient causeway which used to link Aigues-Mortes to its port. **Le Grau-du-Roi** (4,082 inhabitants) is the old port of Aigues-Mortes, once a fishing village but now a summer resort with a **camp site**. 3Km south the modern resort of **Port Camargue** has been developed and offers beach and water sport amenities and a **camp site.**

Hotels and Restaurants

Les Ramparts A very comfortable hotel in an old house furnished with antiques, with a restaurant offering delicious Provençal food. Try the *Agneau au Pistou* (lamb with basil) or the *Soupe de Moules au Thym* (mussel soup with thyme). 6 Place Anatole France, 30220, Aigues-Mortes, Gard. Tel: (66) 51.82.77. 19 rooms, 190–310F. Meals 69–160F. Closed November–February. Credit cards: DC, EC, VISA.

La Camargue A marvellous restaurant with great atmosphere in a 16th century house and delicious Provençal food at very good prices. 19 Rue de la République, 30220, Aigues-Mortes, Gard. Tel: (66) 51.86.88. Meals 45–120F. Closed November, and Tuesday except in July and August. Credit Card: DC.

Le Spinaker Modern hotel with bungalows around a swimming pool and a gourmet restaurant offering delectable dishes. Sample the *Crevettes aux Petits Légumes* (prawns with tender vegetables) or the *Turbot aux Tagliatelles* (turbot with fresh pasta) in the marvellous dining-room overlooking the port. Pointe du Môle, Port Camargue, 30240, Le Grau-du-Roi, Gard. Tel: (66) 51.54.93. 20 rooms, 190–210F. Meals 110–150F. Closed Sunday night and Monday, and January and February. Credit card: VISA.

Garages
Citroën: Tel: (66) 51.04.52.
Peugeot: Tel: (66) 51.96.55.
Renault: Tel: (66) 51.81.10.

Festivals, Fairs and Sporting Events
August, 1–20: **Festival of Aigues-Mortes** – theatre, concerts etc.
October, second week: **Abrivado** – traditional festivity involving the letting loose of bulls in the streets

Camping

PÉZENAS
From Orange, Agde/Pézenas exit, D13, 12Km
From Perpignan, Agde/Pézenas exit, D13, 12Km
Inhabitants: 8,058
Office de Tourisme: Boutique du Barbier Gély, closed Sunday except July and August

Pézenas is a fascinating small 17th century city whose past still lives in its beautifully preserved buildings. With its hotels and restaurants in period houses it is a most attractive and atmospheric place to spend a night.

Built on a small hill in the centre of a rich plain covered with vineyards, Pézenas was a fortified city in Roman times famed for its cloth market. Its trade activity increased in the Middle Ages and in 1456 the **General Assembly of Languedoc** was held here. The importance of the town grew even further when it was decreed the seat of the Languedoc government. Pézenas became the Versailles of the region when Armand de Bourbon, Prince de Conti, fostered a lavish way of life in this estate of the **Grange des Près**, famous for the grandeur and beauty of its formal gardens. The small court soon acquired great lustre and sumptuous festivities attracted noblemen, artists and writers. **Molière**, lured by the glittering assembly, performed at Pézenas with his **Illustre Théâtre** and earned applause and fame, not only at the Conti Court but also in the public market place, where he performed his own plays as well as the Italian *Commedia dell' Arte* from 1650 to 1656, when he settled in Paris.

The death of the Prince of Conti marked the decline of the town. In order to resurrect this glorious past, the visitor must walk along the picturesque old streets where small shops, as much as grand houses, dating from the 15th to the 17th century, provide a powerful evocation of another age.

The Syndicat d'Initiative at the *Office de Tourisme* in the **Maison du Barbier Gély**, off Place Gambetta, has mapped out an itinerary with arrows and numbers and an explanatory leaflet. (The house of Barbier Gély was the house where Molière spent his years at Pézenas.)

The **Maison Consulaire**, a 16th and 17th century house where the General Assemblies of Languedoc were held, stands on the Place Gambetta.

The **Musée Vulliod-St Germain** is just off on the right in the Rue Paul Alliés. Mementoes from Molière's stay, furniture and Aubusson tapestries are displayed. (Open 10–12am and 2–7pm. Closed Monday except July and August; also closed Tuesday in December.)

On the left of the Maison Consulaire, in the Rue Albert Sabatier, the **Hôtel de Flottes-de-Sébasan** has an 18th century façade and some Rennaissance decorative features.

Go down the Rue de la Foire, admiring the various shops and façades, to the **Church of St Jean**, dating from the mid 18th century, with beautiful period furniture. Continue down the Rue Conti to the **Hôtel d'Alfonce**, the best preserved 17th century house in Pézenas. It was used by Molière as a theatre. The entrance has a lovely galleried terrace, while the inner courtyard contains a two-storeyed loggia.

The culinary speciality of Pézenas is *Petit Pâté* (minced lamb with caramel, in pastry.)

Hotels and Restaurants

Genieys A small hotel with a garden and an excellent restaurant serving delicious dishes such as *Salade de Foie Gras Truffé* (salade of *foie gras* with truffles). Good value. 9 Avenue A. Briand, 34120, Pézenas, Hérault. Tel: (67) 98.82.03. 20 rooms, 60–125F. Meals 45–150F. Closed Sunday night December–Whitsun, and Monday September–end June; also 1–9 March and 7–30 November. Credit card: EC.

Le Beffroi Simple traditional cooking in a beautiful old house. Grills and *Daurade à l'Aioli* (sea bream with garlic mayonnaise). Very good value. 16 Rue de la Triperie-Vieille, 34120 Pézenas, Aude. Tel: (67) 98.82.03. Meals 40–100F. Closed Sunday, and January and February.

Garages

Citroën: Route d'Agde. Tel: (67) 98.11.27.
Peugeot: Route de Béziers. Tel: (67) 98.14.94.
Renault: Place Poncet. Tel: (67) 98.14.22.

Festivals, Fairs and Sporting Events
July–August: Pézenas festival – **Mirondela del Arts** – with arts and crafts exhibitions in the old shops and studios, theatre, concerts, folk dancing etc.

From the Narbonne–Sud Exit
ORNAISONS
From Orange, Narbonne–Sud exit, D113 and D24, 15Km
From Perpignan, Narbonne–Sud exit, D113 and D24, 15Km

Hotels and Restaurants
Relais du Val d'Orbieu An old mill sited in the middle of the Corbières vineyards and converted into a very comfortable hotel with a swimming pool and a patio on which one can eat out of doors delicious food such as *Foie Gras à la Purée d'Oignons* (foie gras with onion mousse). Ornaisons, 11200, Lézignan-Corbières, Aude. Tel: (68) 27.10.27. 18 rooms, 190–290F. Meals 100–180F. Closed 1 November–20 March. Credit cards: AE, DC, EC.

PORT-LA-NOUVELLE
From Orange, Sigean exit, D9B, 10Km
From Perpignan, Sigean exit, D9B, 10Km
Inhabitants: 4,036

Spend the night in a simple but comfortable hotel near the wild lagoons of **Sigean** and visit the safari park, the Réserve Africaine de Sigean, set in a fascinating landscape of bare white hills of the Garrigue and the blue lagoons between golden sands.

The Réserve Africaine de Sigean (access indicated from the N9) is a strikingly beautiful place with African wild animals – zebras, lions, leopards etc – and birds – pink flamingoes, cranes, pelicans etc – in freedom in what looks remarkably like their natural habitat. Picnic areas, cafeterias and a restaurant with a panoramic view make it a perfect family excursion. (Open 9am–6pm in summer, 10am–4.30pm in winter.)

Port-la-Nouvelle itself is a small town with a busy port and a vast sandy beach.

Hotels and Restaurants
La Rascasse A simple, friendly, welcoming hotel with a restaurant serving excellent fish specialities. Avenue de la Mer, 11210, Port-la-Nouvelle. Aude. Tel (68) 48.02.89. 45 rooms, 60–80F. Meals 35–150F. Closed 2 January–2 February. Credit cards: AE, VISA.

At **Sigean**, off the N9 on the way to Narbonne, is the **Château de Villefalse**. A private house converted into a comfortable hotel with a garden and swimming pool, and a restaurant offering regional specialities. 11130, Sigean, Aude. Tel: (68) 48.21.53. Rooms 105–230F. Closed December–March.

From the Perpignan–Nord Exit
ST LAURENT-DE-LA-SALANQUE
From Orange, Perpignan–Nord exit, D83 and D11, 10Km
From Perpignan, Perpignan–Nord exit, D83 and D11, 10Km

Hotels and Restaurants
Auberge du Pin A simple country hotel with a friendly atmosphere and nice regional food. *Terrine de Rougets* (red mullet pâté) and *Salade d'Ecrevisses* (fresh-water crayfish salad). 15 Avenue du Maréchal Joffre, 66250, St Laurent-de-la-Salanque, Pyrénées-Orientales. Tel: (68) 28.01.62. 20 rooms, 88–180F. Meals 45–130F. Closed Monday, and 2 January–28 February and 15–30 September.

Garages
Citroën: Tel: (68) 28.01.08.
Renault: Tel: (68) 37.01.07.

CÉRET
From Orange, Le Boulou/Perthus exit, D115, 8Km
From the frontier, Le Boulou exit, D115, 8Km
Inhabitants: 6,189
Office de Tourisme: Avenue Georges Clémenceau, closed morning out of season, Saturday, Sunday and public holidays

Céret is a small Catalan town nestling in the middle of orchards; its cherries are renowned. The Old Town is surrounded by pleasant promenades or **Cours** lined with plane trees, where some fragments of the ramparts still survive: a gateway and three towers. A monument to **Picasso**, who made Céret the 'Mecca of Cubism' stands in an arcade. The **monument aux morts (war memorial)** in the Place de la Liberté is by Maillol.

The Vieux Pont, called the **Pont du Diable**, dates from the 14th century. It daringly spans the River Tech with one single arch of 45m. In Boulevard Maréchal Joffre the 13th century **Church** stands on one side. On the other the **Musée d'Art Moderne** displays an outstanding collection of modern painting gathered by the painter **Pierre Brune.** Picasso, Braque and Juan

Gris came to work in Céret before World War I, at the time they were experimenting with Cubism. Their works are exhibited together with works by Matisse, Chagall, Dufy etc. (Open 10–12am and 3–7pm 1 June–30 September. Otherwise 10–12am and 2–4pm. Closed November.)

Hotels and Restaurants

La Terrasse au Soleil Very comfortable quiet hotel in a lovely house with a garden and swimming pool. Delicious food with a hint of *nouvelle cuisine*, such as *Canard aux Pêches* (duck with peaches). Route de Fontfrède, 66400, Céret, Pyrénées-Orientales. Tel: (68) 87.01.94. 12 rooms, 200–250F. Meals 75–150F. Closed December–March, Monday and Tuesday.

La Châtaigneraie A comfortable hotel in a secluded villa with magnificent views and a swimming pool in the garden. With restaurant. Route de Fontfrède, 66400, Céret, Pyrénées-Orientales. Tel: (68) 87.03.19. 8 rooms, 150–240F. Meals 90F. Closed 16 October–31 March.

Pyrénées Quiet simple hotel with a garden. Restaurant for guests only. 7 Rue de la République, 66400, Céret, Pyrénées-Orientales. Tel: (68) 87.11.02. 22 rooms, 75–145F. Meals 70F. Closed 1 November–1 January.

Garages

Citroën: 8 Place du Pont. Tel: (68) 87.00.75.

Festivals, Fairs and Sporting Events

August, third Sunday: **Festival of the Sardane** (the very ancient and popular Catalan dance).

COLLIOURE

From Orange, Le Boulou/Le Perthus exit, D618 and N114, 28Km
From the frontier, Le Boulou/Le Perthus exit, D618 and N114, 28Km
Inhabitants: 2,839
Office de Tourisme: Avenue C. Pelletan, closed morning out of season except Monday

Collioure is a very attractive small fishing port lying in a bay at the bottom of a rocky cliff. This picturesque site was a favourite holiday place of the Fauve painters Matisse, Dérain and Dufy, who painted it in brilliant hues. It is a very pleasant place to spend the night and loiter in the old port.

An old medieval fortified town as well as a port, Collioure's most characteristic view is that of the old town between its church and the ruins of the 12th century **castle.** It is an essentially French Mediterranean sight with its two small ports on either side and the colourful small fishing boats with nets drying in the bright sunshine.

The **church** was rebuilt in the 17th century. Its **tower** used to be a **lighthouse.** Inside the nine altarpieces dating from the beginning of the 18th century are noteworthy.

Hotels and Restaurants

La Frégate A very comfortable hotel with a fine restaurant offering delectable regional specialities, particularly fish and seafood such as *Loup de Mer au Coulis de Tomates* (sea bass with fresh tomato sauce) and anchovies fished at Collioure. 24 Quai de l'Amirauté, 65190, Collioure, Pyrénées-Orientales. Tel (68) 82.06.05. 22 rooms, 150–250F. Meals 80–200F. Closed December and January.

Les Caranques Very peaceful small hotel on the sea looking over the port of Collioure, with bathing available from the rocks. Restaurant on a terrace only for guests (half-board). Route de Port-Vendres, 65190, Collioure, Pyrénées-Orientales. Tel: (68) 82.06.68. 16 rooms, 75–175F. Closed 10 October–1 April.

Casa Pairal A beautifully decorated hotel, very peaceful with a swimming pool in a garden. No restaurant. 66190, Collioure, Pyrénées-Orientales. Tel: (68) 82.05.81. 24 rooms, 150–220F. Closed 5 November–1 April.

La Bodega An excellent restaurant serving delicious regional dishes such as *Rougets aux Tomates et Citrons* (red mullet with a tomato and lemon sauce) and *Clafoutis* (fruit flan usually with cherries). 6 Rue de la République, 66190, Collioure, Pyrénées-Orientales. Tel: (68) 82.05.60. Meals 60–180F. Closed Monday night, Tuesday (15 September–30 June) and 12 November–25 December. Credit cards: AE, DC, VISA.

Garages

Renault: Tel: (68) 82.08.34.

Festivals, Fairs and Sporting Events

Good Friday: **Procession of the Brotherhood of Penitents**

L'Aquitaine
Paris–Bordeaux (A10)

The A10 runs across the **Ile de France** and the region of the **Hurepoix** where historic places like **Dourdan** evoke a past, very often bloody, of wars and conquests. Woods on the hills, meadows and market gardens in the valleys create a varied landscape.

The northern part of the **Orléanais**, called the **Beauce**, is reached next, a vast plateau of uniform flatness constituting one of the main granaries of France with its extensive crops of wheat, sugar beet and fodder produce spreading under an immense horizon. Few trees and rivers break the monotony of this 'deep swell and ocean of wheat fields' as the Orléans poet Charles Péguy so aptly described it.

Etampes is the only tourist spot in this vast agricultural expanse. The southern part of the Orléanais belongs to the **Loire Valley** (the **Val de Loire**), which the A10 follows from **Orléans** to **Tours**, crossing the **Touraine** before branching off south to the **Poitou**, the **Aunis** and **Saintonge** and finally the **Bordelais** region.

The **Loire Valley** is the most privileged place on earth. The gentleness of the climate, the geographical position midway across France, the sheer abundance of nature have made it the Garden of France in the real as much as in the metaphorical sense. Everything is on a human scale and the hand of man has moulded, fashioned and embellished even further a landscape of soft feminine curves, limpid waters, blossoming gardens and mellowing vineyards and orchards, while the deep ancestral forests retain a wealth of wildlife to complete this overflowing cornucopia.

Douceur de vivre (gentle living) is truly alive in this country of natural beauty, prosperity and refined civilisation. 'Do not ask me why I love the Touraine', said Balzac, a native of Tours, 'I love it as an artist loves Art.' This lyrical line evokes the charm of this opulent region where the Loire sensuously flows blue between golden sandbanks, having dug its bed deep into the soft white *tuffeau* (chalk) of the valley. Here, as at **Vouvray**, grottoes house both wine – in deep cellars – and people – in their *troglodytique* houses (houses in the rocks).

Until the mid 19th century the Loire was a highway celebrated by poets and writers, including Charles d'Orléans, La Fontaine, Madame de Sévigné, Balzac and Victor Hugo. Freight and travellers, with coaches on rafts, used to be ferried on sailing boats until the invention of the steam boats in 1832. However the birth of the railway proved fatal to the river traffic, and in 1862 the last boat company ceased trading. Now only a few stone quays recall those adventurous days, while the Loire, capricious and treacherous, lies sleepily, coiled like a mermaid amid her rippling fair hair. Though she is capable of suddenly transforming herself within hours, in autumn and winter, into a roaring monster bursting its banks, overflowing the high dykes built all along its course with a dirty yellowish flood spreading catastrophe.

The same gentleness of climate graces the regions of Poitou, Aunis and Saintonge, crossed next by the A10 before one reaches the **Entre-Deux-Mers** part of the Bordelais (the part between the **River Dordogne** and the **River Garonne**). The soothing influence of the **Atlantic Ocean** brings a characteristically mild and humid climate in which the flat fertile land basks, enabling rich crops and vineyards to flourish, while in the lush fields the white Charolais cattle and the black and white Friesians are fattened. Sheep and goats inhabit the poorer lands of the Poitou.

The **Charente**, east of the Saintonge, is the home of **Cognac**, the world-famous brandy, and its low hills are taken over by rich vineyards. Vineyards, of course, are the most important feature of the Bordelais area. The A10 passes by such great names as **St Emilion** (a red wine of distinction, full-bodied and with a powerful aroma), while the **Entre-Deux-Mers** produces dry white wines, to be drunk young and particularly delicious with seafood. The region of the **Médoc**, with its world-famous wines such as **Château-Lafite, Mouton-Rothschild** and **Château-Latour** is unfortunately out of reach of the *autoroute*.

To cross the Orléanais, the Loire Valley and the Touraine is to make a journey back in time. Medieval cities, châteaux, churches, forests and rivers are the threads in the rich tapestry of a golden, often turbulent, past. A thousand years of history are locked in the stones of the Gallo-Roman ruins, the abbeys and churches, the châteaux and the simple village houses.

Even in Roman times the Loire Valley stood firm in a proud independent spirit, the local tribe of the *Carnutes* being the first to resist the Roman legions. In the 3rd century, Christianity triumphed with **St Martin**, a former Roman legion officer, at **Tours**, which soon became a centre of pilgrimage.

In the Middle Ages the division of France into fiefdoms brought about endless internecine wars between the Touraine, Blésois and Anjou, Orléans being part of the Kingdom of France. From these times date the first châteaux. As Jules Lemaitre wrote:

> The Loire is a Queen and Kings have long loved her,
> They have jealously endowed her azure flow,
> With castles as preciously chased as jewels,
> And from these priceless gems her Crown is formed.

With the Hundred Years War and the English invasion, the enemy occupying Orléans, the fate of France was sombre indeed. But the radiant faith and courage of **Joan of Arc**, a young shepherdess from Domremy in Lorraine, rallied the vacillating strength of the French kingdom. On 8 May 1429, she delivered the city, an event still commemorated every year in Orléans, with a young girl entering the city on horseback, acting the part of the patron saint of France.

The English claim to the throne of France by marriage and the ensuing occupation of Paris by **Henry V of England**, after the French defeat at **Agincourt**, favoured the flourishing of the Loire Valley. **Charles VII** of France was king only of Bourges and settled with his small court at **Chinon**, a medieval fortress on the **River Vienne**, some 80 miles from Tours, until 1450. Paris was delivered from English occupation in 1453, and the king and court returned to the capital. But the attraction of the Val de Loire for the Valois Kings only grew stronger. **Amboise** was a royal seat under Louis XI, and **Blois** became a royal palace under Louis XII. François I embellished it even further, as well as building new châteaux such as Chambord (conceived as a hunting lodge).

The Wars of Religion at the end of the 16th century brought bloodshed and destruction, which were unfortunately perpetuated during the Revolution, the Franco-Prussian War and the two World Wars, as the Loire is a natural frontier of enormous strategic importance.

The south-western area crossed by the A10 was, from the 10th century, under the domination of the **Counts of Poitiers** and **Angoulême. Bordeaux** itself was a Gallic city which became the capital of the **Duchy of Aquitaine**, or, as it is now known, **Guyenne** (from the Anglicised pronunciation of Aquitaine). **Eleanor of Aquitaine** married **Henry Plantagenet**, Count of Anjou and suzerain overlord of Maine, Touraine and Normandy, after her divorce from **Louis VII** of France in 1152. She brought as her dowry nearly all the south-west of France: the Duchy of Aquitaine, the Périgord, the Limousin, Poitou, Angoumois, Saintonge and Gascogne, as well as suzerainty over Auvergne and the Comté of Toulouse. Politically their joint possessions presented a threat to the French kingdom. When, two months later, Henry Plantagenet inherited the English throne and became **Henry II of England**, there began a fight between France and England which was to last for two centuries.

The legendary **Black Prince**, son of **King Edward III of England**, established his headquarters at Bordeaux. He defeated **Jean le Bon** at the **Battle of Poiters** in 1356. However the English domination was thrown off a century later with the end of the 100 Years War.

During the Revolution the twenty-two *députés* (members of parliament) for Bordeaux, the **Girondins**, were executed for their moderate and federalist beliefs by their opponents, the **Montagnards**, who represented the people of Paris.

The Revolution also brought terrible bloodshed in Poitou and the surrounding region, called then the **Vendée Militaire** (Military Vendée).

In 1793 the **Catholic and Royal Army** rebelled against the revolutionary government, the **Convention**, after the execution of the King and the persecution of priests. A form of guerilla war ensued, with the land-owners joining and leading the peasantry, ambushing and massacring the **Bleus** (Blues), who were the Revolutionary forces massed behind the high hedges of the Poitou and Vendée regions. The battle cry of the **Blancs** (Whites), the Catholic and Royal Army, was, 'Rembarre. Vive la Religion, Vive le Roi' (Assault. Long Live the Church, Long Live the King) and their insignia was a scapula with a flaming heart surmounted by a Cross. After a year of ferocious fighting, counter-fighting and the execution of thousands of *Blancs*, the Convention negotiated a peace treaty, at the beginning of 1795.

During the Franco-Prussian War and the two World Wars, the French government took refuge at Bordeaux.

The long and rich historical past of the Loire Valley and the south-west is accompanied by an equally brilliant artistic tradition. Tours was already a great intellectual centre in the 6th century; **Bishop Grégoire of Tours** was the first Gallic historian with his *Historia Francorum*. **Charlemagne** had a school of calligraphy founded in the 9th century, while the Latin poems of **Baudin de Bourgueil**, in the 11th century, look forward to the tradition of the **Art Courtois** (courtly art). In the 12th century in the south-west region, the **troubadours**, itinerant poets and musicians of noble birth and education, created an original form of poetry in the **Langue d'Oc**, the language spoken south of the Loire, while north of the Loire the **Langue d'Oïl** reigned. (*Oc* and *Oïl* were the two different ways of saying *Oui*: Yes.) Going from court to court they recited their poetry to a lute accompaniment. Celebrating platonic love, beauty and women with lyricism, **l'Amour Courtois** (courtly love), was a civilising and refining influence on the uncouth manners of most men of the time, more prone to war and killing each other than reciting madrigals to the lady of their heart. This gallant ideal rapidly spread all over France. **Adela**, wife of the **Count of Blois**, and **Mary**, wife of the **Duke of Champagne**, were the founders of the famous **Courts of Love.** Their atmosphere, imbued with elegance, warmth of heart and fervour of soul, greatly influenced the artistic climate of the Middle Ages.

However, by the end of the 13th century, Scholasticism was super-seding lyricism, and the didactic *Roman de la Rose*, written by **Guillaume de Lorris** and finished at the beginning of the 14th century by **Jean de Meung**, codified love and faith and heralded the hair-splitting dialectics of the 15th century sophists, with the ensuing scepticism and unbelief.

Charles d'Orléans, royal prince and father of Louis XII, discovered his poetic gifts while imprisoned in England for twenty-five years after his capture at the Battle of Agincourt. Back in Blois he organised poetry competitions, which **François Villon** won in 1457. Charles d'Orléans's own poems were short, elegant, eminently courtly pieces celebrating an idyllic aristocratic way of life beautifully depicted in the **Mille Fleurs** (Thousand Flowers) **tapestries** produced by workshops in the Loire Valley around the turn of the century.

By then the rise of Humanism, prompted by the Italian influence, was introducing a more intellectual and scholarly approach to literature. Learning and scholarship had always been to the fore in the Loire Valley and the Touraine. The **universities** of Orléans (founded in 1365) and Angers (1364) attracted philosophers, writers and scholars like **Erasmus** and **Calvin. Rabelais**, an erudite Benedictine, a doctor and a philosopher, was born at Chinon. His works epitomised the enormous vitality and appetite for life which characterised the early Renaissance.

From the 16th century onwards the French language – all clarity, measure and balanced rhythm – acquired its lustre and radiance in this region of France, moulded in gentle harmony and wondrous beauty, propitious to artistic creativity. French language was truly born here in the country of the *Beau Parler* (beautiful speech). Here French is spoken at its purest and finest without the sunny accent of the south or the heavy drawl of the misty north. The language disengaged itself from the medieval multiplicity of local tongues, and the preference given to Latin by scholars and writers, under the creative impulse of a school founded in the Loire Valley by seven native poets who called themselves **La Pléiade.** Among them were **Ronsard**, the 'Prince of Poets', born in the Vendôme region, **du Bellay**, born in Anjou, **Baïf** and **Belleau.** In 1549 Joachim du Bellay published his *Défense et Illustration de la Langue Française* (Defence and Illustration of the French Language), a manifesto proclaiming the potential greatness of the French language and the necessity of making it so by a true emulation of the Ancients, a Humanism representing a genuine assimilation of classical ideas and forms within the context of an original French culture.

This true Renaissance was prompted and sustained by a king, **François I**, whose personality was as versatile, dynamic and larger-than-life as the ideas he promoted. In 1539, with the **Edict of Villers-Côtterets**, he declared French the official language, thereby uniting the kingdom linguistically. François I protected scholars, writers and poets, earning the title of *Père des Lettres* (Father of Literature). He attracted foreign artists such as **Cellini** and **Leonardo da Vinci** to his court, transforming the great medieval fortresses and endowing the Val de Loire with elegant pleasure palaces inspired by the Italian Renaissance, yet fundamentally French in the sense that they were designed for gracious living and pleasure rather than being dry exercises in the declination of aesthetic rules and laws. With the return of the court to Paris and the Wars of Religion, the artistic tone became more serious and prone to reflection.

The great philosopher **Descartes** was born at the edge of the Touraine, which gave to French literature one of its giants – the 19th century writer **Honoré de Balzac**.

The 20th century saw a blossoming of talent too in the poet **Charles Péguy** from Orléans and his love for his native Beauce, and in the Academician **Maurice Genevoix** and his lyrical description of the Loire and the nearby Sologne, as well as in many writers of international repute who came to the Touraine and the Val de Loire to sustain and renew their inspiration at the very heart of French culture.

GASTRONOMY

The Loire Valley and the Touraine, regions of varied landscapes, proud vineyards, glorious orchards and abundant rivers, provide a wide selection of riches for the table.

The wines are as varied as the lands which produce them. Of those bordering the A 10, **Vouvray** is one of the most famous names of the Loire whites. A white wine with a flavour of ripe grape, it can be mellow or dry. The **Montlouis**, a fruity wine with a delicate aroma and the **Touraine-Amboise** are produced like the Vouvray from the white **Pineau** grape. The **Breton** grape, a **Cabernet** variety from the Bordelais, produces the reds of the region, all light wines, easy to drink and full of the *Douceur de Vivre* of the region that nurtured them. **Bourgueil** is light and full of finesse while **Chinon** is a more scented wine, 'a wine for intellectuals' according to **Jules Romains**, with a class of its own and a distinctive raspberry flavour. **Gris-Meunier** is a pale red wine produced near Orléans, light and easy-going.

The local Bacchic societies such as the **Chantepleure of Vouvray** and the **Entonneurs Rabelaisiens of Chinon** gather regularly to keep alive the tradition of *Bien-Boire* (good drinking) and to initiate new members to the rites of Bacchus.

The Val de Loire is also the country of *Bien-Manger* (good eating). Its cuisine is a cuisine of harmony, lightness and measure, quintessentially French, simple, healthy and prepared with superb fresh ingredients. The exquisite fruit and vegetables are the basis of many dishes. Tender, young asparagus from **Vineuil**, cultivated on the left bank of the Loire at Blois only since 1870, delicious mushrooms stuffed or in a cream sauce, or delectable strawberries from market gardens, are delicate fare.

The Loire and its tributaries yield many varieties of **fish** which are prepared very simply with a *Beurre Blanc*, a light sauce made of emulsified melted butter with shallots and a little white wine or vinegar, served warm, to be poured over: *Saumon de la Loire* (fresh Loire salmon); *Brochet* (pike); *Carpe* (carp); *Mulet* (grey mullet); *Sandre* or *Perche* (perch); and *Alose* (shad).

Brème (bream) and *Carpe* (carp) are served stuffed with herbs and spices in a white wine sauce, while *Matelote d'Anguilles* (eel stew) is cooked with a red wine sauce with small onions and mushrooms.

Charcuterie is particularly prized. There are: *Rillons* (pieces of pork cooked very slowly); *Rillettes* (pork cooked in its own fat until the meat is reduced to shreds, and allowed to cool so that it solidifies into a sort of pâté eaten as a starter with bread); and *Boudin Blanc* (a very delicate sausage made of white meats such as chicken and veal and often containing small pieces of scented truffles).

Game from the deep forests of the nearby Sologne includes in season: *Sanglier* (wild boar) cooked usually in its own marinade of white wine, herbs and spices, or in pâté; *Chevreuil* (venison); *Lièvre* (hare) in pâté or as a *Civet* (red wine sauce with onions and served with potatoes). (*Lapin de Garenne* (wild rabbit) is also served as a *Civet*.)

Fricassée de Poulet is a chicken stew with a white wine cream sauce with onions and mushrooms, while the *Cul-de-Veau à l'Angevine* is a veal roast cooked in a casserole with the tender young vegetables of the region.

Most of the delicious **cheeses** of the region are goat cheeses, such as: *Valençay* (pyramid-shaped with a nutty taste); *Selles sur-Cher* (round with a bluish outside and a mild flavour); *Crottins de Chavignol* (small, hard, ball-shaped, with a musty flavour, delicious with *Sancerre* wine – it comes from the **Sancerre** area). As for cow's milk cheeses, try the *Crémets d'Anjou* (bland, soft and white, eaten with sugar and fresh cream). The *Olivet Bleu* cheese has a fruity taste and the *Olivet à la Cendre* is made using wood ashes, giving a strong savoury taste. The *Vendôme* is much of the same variety.

Sweets are very much fruit-based. Plums and prunes from Tours are eaten *Glacé* or in Cognac, and there are also the *Chaussons aux Pommes* (a sort of apple pie) and the *Tarte Tatin* (upside-down apple tart with caramel) from Sologne. *Cotignacs* are pieces of quince and apple jelly rolled in sugar and *Crêpes Angevines* are apple-filled pancakes with a dash of Cointreau (made in Angers) served hot with butter.

The Bordelais region offers a cuisine which is 'simple, honest and outright, peasant-like', according to Curnonsky, using the first-class fresh products of the region. The proximity of the sea ensures many seafood and fish specialities: *Mouclade* (mussels in cream or a white wine sauce with shallots); *Chaudrée* (fish soup with white wine, made with conger eel, whiting, plaice, sole etc); *Anguille* or *Lamproie à la Bordelaise* (eel or lamprey in a red wine sauce); *Esturgeon* (sturgeon), *Saumon* (salmon) and *Alose* (shad) from the Gironde, and of course *Huîtres* (oysters).

Oie (goose) is prepared in many different ways and all the parts of the bird are eaten separately, including *foie gras* and *Cou d'Oie* (goose neck). *Chevreau* (kid), *Mouton* and *Agneau* (mutton and lamb) all appear on menus, while the *Salmis de Palombes* is a dish made of wood pigeons partly cooked then sautéed with red wine, mushrooms and ham.

Of the vegetables the *Cèpes* (Cèpe mushrooms) are the most typically prepared *à la Bordelaise* (sautéed in oil with shallots or garlic). *Fèves à la Crème* are broad beans in a cream sauce.

Chabichou is a nutty goat **cheese** from Poitou. Of the **fruit** produced in the area the Charentais melon, with its luscious flesh and musky flavour, is renowned. Sweets are simple, such as *Clafoutis aux Cerises* (a creamy flan with cherries) or *Tourteaux au Fromage* (a goat-cheese-based cake). *Marguerites* and *Duchesses* are chocolates.

Of the five great wine areas of the Bordelais – the **Médoc, Graves, Pomerol, St Emilion** and **Sauternes** – only the regions of St Emilion and Pomerol are reached by the A10.

St Emilion produces full-bodied red wines with great personality and a strong aroma. The two most distinguished names are **Ausone** and **Cheval-Blanc.** Like all good **clarets** they are drier than **Burgundy**, not as high in alcohol content, and mature remarkably well. (As they say in the area, 'all the angles are rounded off in the bottle'.)

Pomerol, like St. Emilion, is a full-bodied wine with a distinctive flavour and personality. **Château-Petrus** is the best-known name.

DOURDAN
From Paris, Dourdan exit, N836 and N838, 6Km
From Bordeaux, Dourdan exit, N836 and N838, 6Km
Inhabitants: 7,487
Office de Tourisme: Place du Général de Gaulle, closed Sunday afternoon and Monday.

Dourdan, the former capital of the **Hurepoix** region, is a very attractive old town 52Km from Paris, ideal for an overnight stop. Situated on the left bank of the **River Orge**, it was from earliest times a royal fortified city used to protect the grain route from the Beauce region to Paris and to keep the local noblemen under control. Until the 17th century its revenues went to high-ranking servants of the Crown. In 1661 it became part of the apanage of the royal Orléans family. In the centre of the small town built on a slope, the fortified castle, the church and the 18th century **Hospital** are gathered, together with the picturesque 13th century wood-covered market, restored in the 19th century. The **château** now houses a **municipal museum** with collections relating to local history.

Only the lower half of the **outer walls**, built in 1222 by Philippe Auguste on the defensive plan of the Louvre, remains. The **keep** still stands 25m high. It marks an advance in defensive architecture by having its entrance door at ground level. (Before the door was awkwardly placed on the first floor.) The keep used to protect the most vulnerable point of the fortress and was surrounded by a moat, now filled in. (Open 2–6pm Wednesday, Saturday and Sunday.)

The **Church of St Germain**, dating from the 12th and 13th centuries, has suffered greatly from its proximity to the château during successive sieges. Partly destroyed at the siege of 1428, it was rebuilt in the late 15th century. The two spires of the bell tower and the north portal, in Flamboyant Gothic style, date from this time. Inside, the impression of height is enhanced by the narrowness of the arches. The tomb of the poet Regnard is behind the main altar. He died ignominiously of indigestion at Dourdan in 1709.

Hotels and Restaurants
Hostellerie Blanche de Castille A very comfortable hotel in a lovely house, in the middle of a garden with tennis court and swimming pool at the edge of the ancient Forest of Dourdan. The restaurant is excellent and offers classical gourmet cuisine with a dash of individuality. Sample the *Raie à la Moutarde* (skate with mustard sauce) the *Navarin d'Agneau de la Beauce* (lamb stew with young vegetables) and the delicious *Tarte à la Framboise* (raspberry tart). Place des Halles, 91410, Dourdan, Essone. Tel: (6) 492.92.72. 40 rooms 150–250F. Meals 130–200F. Closed 1–15 August. Credit cards: DC, VISA.

Garages
Citroën: Tel: (6) 459.64.00.
Ford/Lancia/Toyota: Tel: (6) 459.66.65.
Peugeot: Tel: (6) 459.71.86.
Renault: Tel: (6) 492.70.83.

ÉTAMPES
From Paris, Allainville exit, N191, 20Km
From Bordeaux, Allainville-Étampes exit, N191, 20Km
Inhabitants: 19,755
Office de Tourisme: Maison Anne de Pisseleu, Place de l'Hôtel de Ville, closed Sunday and Monday

Étampes is an historic town, with many beautiful buildings, stretching along the Valley of the **River Chalouette** and the **River Juine.** A very comfortable hotel and delicious restaurant make it a very pleasant stopping place.

A royal city until the 14th century, Étampes reached a par with Paris when Suger, Abbot of St Denis, was given the responsibilities and title of Regent of the Kingdom while the King was on a Crusade. Despite successive wars over the centuries, Étampes has remained a market town.

In the 15th century, the **River of Étampes**, wider than it is today, was used to carry barges of wine and grain to the **Ile de France**. The **Promenade du Pont** is a remnant from that time.

Arriving by the N191 take **Rue Louis Moreau** on the right after the station and look at the **Church of St Basile**, founded by Robert le Pieux. Its façade with a Romanesque portal, the transept and the main tower all date from the 12th century. The rest was built between the 15th and the 16th centuries.

Behind St Basile, the **Rue de la Cordonnerie** leads to the **Church of Notre Dame-du-Fort.** Built in the 12th century and fortified in the 13th, its elegant Romanesque bell tower is 62m high and the south portal displays some statue-columns in the same style as the **Royal Portal of Chartres.** Inside the plan is irregular, as a result of successive alterations. Yet the height of the vaults and columns and the quality of the carvings are noteworthy. The glass windows date from the 16th century.

Walking down the **Rue du Pont Doré** one can enjoy an attractive view over the old washhouse, and from the **Rue du Rampart** over the old fortified port of Étampes.

Notice at the corner of Rue Louis Moreau, opposite the south portal of St Basile, the **Renaissance house**, with sculptures by **Jean Goujon**, built in 1554 by **Diane de Poitiers**, second Duchesse d'Étampes. The **Place de l'Hôtel de Ville**, near the **Maison d'Anne de Pisseleu**, now the *Office de Tourisme*, was built in 1583 by François I for Anne de Pisseleu, for whom he changed the *Comté* (county) of Étampes into a *Duché* (duchy).

The **Hôtel de Ville** dates from the 15th century and was finished in the 16th century. It now houses a **museum** with collections of documents and artefacts related to local history. (Open 9–12am and 2–5.30pm in summer.)

Opposite the Church of St Basile the **Rue du Château Guinette** leads to the station and a walkway to the **Tour Guinette**, a former royal keep built in the 12th century by Philippe Auguste on a rare four-lobed plan. The name comes from *guigner* (to watch). From the public garden around the tower there is an extensive view over Étampes.

Going down the Rue St-Jacques, one passes the **Church of St Gilles** on the left. It has a Romanesque façade and 15th and 16th century additions. On the **Place St Gilles**, where the gallows and guillotine used to stand, notice an old house dating from the 13th century with a wooden gallery and stone pillars. Take the **Rue de l'Abreuvoir du Mouton** and turn left into the **Boulevard Berchère** to rejoin the **Avenue T. Charpentier** on the right and get a glimpse of the 14th century fortifications on the promenade called **Les Portereaux**, which runs along the River Chalouette where the washhouses still survive.

At the south end of the town the **Church of St Martin** (12th century, completed in the 16th century) has a bizarre leaning tower (16th century).

Hotels and Restaurants

At **Fontaine-la-Rivière** (9Km south of Étampes by the N721) is the **Auberge de Courpain.** A very comfortable hotel, beautifully furnished with antique furniture, in the depths of the Beauce countryside. Very quiet and with an excellent restaurant offering delicious food. Try the *Escargots à la Menthe Fraîche* (snails with fresh mint) or the *Tarte Tatin* (upside-down apple tart). Court-Pain, 91690, Saclas, Essonne. Tel: (6) 495.67.04. 17 rooms, 130–320F. meals 85–180F. Open all year. Credit cards: AE, DC.

L'Europe 'A l'Escargot' A small family hotel in a street near the Church of St Gilles. With restaurant. Very good value. 71 Rue St-Jacques, 91150, Étampes, Essonne. Tel: (6) 494.02.96. 24 rooms, 50–120F. Meals 33–40F. Closed 20 June–25 July and 20 September–4 October. Credit card: VISA.

Garages

Austin/Morris/Rover: Tel: (6) 494.90 00.
Citroën: 146 Rue St-Jacques. Tel: (6) 494.01.81.
Fiat/Lancia/Autobianchi: 90 Rue St-Jacques. Tel: (6) 494.57.27.
Peugeot/Talbot: Tel: (6) 494.16.72.
Renault: Rue Plisson. Tel: (6) 494.52.22.

OLIVET

From Paris, Orléans–Ouest exit, A71, N20, D14, 6Km
From Bordeaux, Orléans–Ouest exit, A71, N20, D14, 6Km
Inhabitants: 12,830
Office de Tourisme: Place de la Mairie, 15 May–15 September, closed Thursday afternoon

Olivet, on the right bank of the **Loiret**, is a delightful spot in beautiful surroundings for fishing, rowing or just strolling along the river banks, which mostly consist in the strip of land between the **Loire** and the Loiret, where there are nurseries and fields of roses, gladioli, carnations etc according to season. Near the bridge a floral clock is made of 5,000 flowers. Very comfortable hotels and excellent restaurants provide relaxing and satisfying halts for the traveller.

Walk along the **quays** by the Loiret, and admire the fine old houses in their gardens and the remaining old mills. Follow the **Rue de la Source** to the **Parc Floral de la Source (floral park).** The Parc Floral was created in 1967, for the flower festival, on 35Ha around the 17th century **Château de la Source.** A branch of the River Loire goes underground at **St Benoît** and reappears in the park here, in the form of two different springs which join to create the short tributary of the Loire called the Loiret. The first spring or *bouillon* comes to light in the circular ornamental lake which flows into a channel and then spreads out in a *miroir* (lake) in front of the terraces of the château. At the very end of the lake the **Grande Source** gushes from an 18m deep whirlpool. The whole park, with its glassy water surfaces, small zoo, games and attractions, and a few modern sculptures dotted about, is a very pleasant and entertaining family excursion. As for the gardens, they provide a sumptuous sight with colours, shapes and scents constantly changing according to the season. From spring to autumn, tulips, irises, roses, dahlias and chrysanthemums form a richly woven carpet of varied hues. The Rose Garden is particularly renowned for its 200,000 rose trees and the quality and beauty of their blooms. Competitions are held here regularly, the mild climate and the sunny skies of the valley being especially favourable for the full blossoming of flowers.

South of the Floral Park a **university campus** on the lines of American ones, the first of its kind in France, has been laid out in the countryside around a 7Ha lake and welcomes some 10,000 students.

Hotels and Restaurants

Le Beauvoir A very comfortable modern hotel with a garden overlooking the Loiret, near the Parc Floral, with a very good restaurant offering dishes with a light *nouvelle cuisine* touch: *Filet de Turbot à l'Estragon* (turbot fillet with tarragon) and *Raie à la Menthe* (skate with mint). 43 Rue du Beauvoir, 45160, Olivet, Loiret. Tel: (38) 63.57.57. 23 rooms, 60–160F. Meals 65–170F. Open all year. Credit cards: AE, DC, EC, VISA.

Le Rivage A very pleasant, comfortable hotel with a garden overlooking the river and a good restaurant offering: *Friture de Loire* (fresh-water whitebait) or *Pigeonneau aux Raisins Frais* (pigeon with fresh grapes). 638 Rue de la Reine Blanche, 45160, Olivet, Loiret. Tel: (38) 66.02.93. 21 rooms, 50–132F. Meals 60–170F. Closed Sunday night (November–April) and 1–15 February. Credit cards: AE, DC, VISA.

A Madagascar A very reasonably priced restaurant with a terrace overlooking the river and offering honest food. Try the *Assiette Scandinave* (assorted smoked fish and roes) or the *Pâté de Grives* (thrush pâté, an Orléanais speciality). 402 Rue de la Reine Blanche, 45160, Olivet, Loiret. Tel: (38) 66.12.58. Meals 58–160F. Closed Wednesday and 15 January–15 February. Credit cards: AE, VISA.

Le Manderley An excellent restaurant, with a terrace overlooking the river, offering delicious Loire specialities such as *Matelote* (fish stew with red wine) or *Perche Sauce Ravigote* (perch with a sauce made of onions, mushrooms and vinegar). Very good value. 117 Sentier des Prés, 45160, Olivet, Loiret. Tel: (38) 66.19.85. Meals 48–150F. Closed Monday night and Tuesday (May–October) or Tuesday night and Wednesday (October–May), and 1–20 November. Credit cards: AE, DC, EC, VISA.

MEUNG-SUR-LOIRE/CLÉRY-ST-ANDRÉ

From Paris, Meung exit, D2 to Meung (2Km) then cross the river to Cléry (D18, 5Km)
From Bordeaux, Meung exit, D2 to Meung (2Km) then cross the river to Cléry (D18, 5Km)
Inhabitants: 4,630

Meung is a small town stretched out on the right bank of the River Loire. It has the quiet provincial charm of all the smaller Loire Valley towns and is well worth a visit to soak up the atmosphere before crossing the river to Cléry, where an excellent hotel and restaurant in a peaceful park await the weary traveller.

The main building of Meung is its **château**, built in the 13th century and belonging to the **Bishops of Orléans** until the end of the 18th century. An extensive network of underground passages and dungeons can be visited. (Open 8.30–12am and 2–6pm Easter–1 November. Otherwise at weekends only.)

The **Church of St Liphard** near the château was built from the 11th to the 13th century. The most notable features are the bell tower, a semi-circular chevet and a transept with rounded ends. Next to the bell tower, the 12th century ruined keep was one of many prisons where the poet **François Villon** spent some time.

Walk in the narrow picturesque streets around the centre of the town and then on to the **Mail**, a promenade along the river banks, and the avenue lined with lime trees which follows the **Mauves**, small tributary of the Loire and a fisherman's delight.

A statue of **Jean de Meung** stands in the Mail. The 14th century poet added some 18,000 lines to **Guillaume de Lorris**'s 4,000 and completed the famous medieval poetic work the *Roman de la Rose* (The Romance of the Rose), an allegory of Love.

From Meung cross the river to **Cléry**. Cléry's claim to fame lies in the **Basilica of Notre Dame**, where King Louis XI is buried. The actual church was built on the site of a humble country chapel where, in 1280, peasants brought a wooden statue of the Virgin they had found lying in a nearby bush. The legend of the statue grew and a pilgrimage built up around it. In 1428 the Earl of Salisbury, marching towards Orléans, destroyed it. Charles VII of France provided funds to rebuild it, but it was his son, Louis XI, who became its greatest benefactor. While still prince he vowed to endow Notre Dame de Cléry if victorious at the siege of Dieppe. Once king he dedicated himself to the Virgin and kept his word. His tomb is inside the basilica and the house where he used to stay, now a school, still stands at the side of the church.

Completed by Charles VIII, Notre Dame is a 15th century building except for the square tower dating from the earlier church. The inside reflects the sober and stern character of its main donor, Louis XI. It is elegant but rather cold in its frigid whiteness, no decorations impeding the travel of the eye. However the stained-glass windows and the tapestries which used to hang in medieval churches on feast days would no doubt have provided a rich note of colour.

Notice the **tomb of Louis XI** and his wife, Charlotte de Savoie, with the skulls rather gruesomely exhibited separately in a glass case. Nearby stands the **King's mausoleum** without any luxurious trimmings. The marble statue is a 17th century replacement of the bronze original which was melted down by Huguenots.

The **Chapel of St James of Compostella** in the right aisle is richly decorated in Renaissance style, Notre Dame de Cléry being on the pilgrimage route which drew droves of pilgrims in the Middle Ages, as well as merchants, highwaymen, entertainers etc. The two wooden statues of St James and St Sebastian, together with a lovely stone Virgin date from the 16th century.

The pews given by **Henri II of France** bear his monogram together, rather inappropriately, with that of his mistress **Diane de Poitiers.** On the main altar stands the wooden long-venerated statue of **Notre Dame de Cléry**.

Hotels and Restaurants

Hostellerie des Bordes A very comfortable hotel in its own park, with very quiet rooms decorated in a country-house style to match the homeliness and succulence of the cuisine. Sample the *Lapin Sauté Chasseur* (rabbit with wine sauce, onions and mushrooms) and the *Brochet au Beurre Blanc* (pike with butter sauce, shallots and white wine, a Loire speciality). A lovely place in lovely countryside, and very good value. 9 Rue des Bordes, 45370, Cléry-St-André, Loiret. Tel: (38) 45.71.25. 23 rooms, 45–180F. Meals 32–90F. Closed Sunday night, Monday (September–April) and 15 January–15 February.

BEAUGENCY
From Paris, Meung exit, D2 and N152, 9Km
From Bordeaux, Meung exit, D2 and N152, 9Km
Inhabitants: 6,814
Office de Tourisme: 28 Place du Martroi, closed 1 December–28 February

To visit and stay at Beaugency is to get a generous glimpse of the Middle Ages. Despite the many sieges it suffered, Beaugency has a wealth of monuments harmoniously disposed against a typical Loire Valley background of clear waters and lush vegetation. Some comfortable hotels and restaurants cater for the needs of the modern traveller.

Beaugency played a very important part in the history of France and England. The two **Councils of Beaugency** in the 12th century had to resolve the marital problems of the French Crown. In 1104 the first Council excommunicated **Philippe I of France** for having repudiated his wife and eloped with a married woman, the wife of the **Count of Anjou**. In 1152 the second Council annulled the marriage of **Louis VII** to **Eleanor of Aquitaine.** It was one of the most decisive events of medieval history. Eleanor married **Henry Plantagenet** who became King of England two months later. Eleanor's dowry, nearly all the south-west region of France, and Henry's own lands, went to England and triggered off centuries of disputes and wars between the two countries.

Strategically Beaugency was an important place as it commanded, until modern times, the only bridge over the Loire between **Blois** and **Orléans.** During the 100 Years War the town was occupied four times by the English, in 1356, 1412, 1421 and 1429. The last time it was delivered by **Joan of Arc.** The Wars of Religion brought further bloodshed.

Arriving from the *autoroute* by the N152, go down the **Rue du Pont** to the **château.** Built in the 15th century, it houses a museum, **Le Musée des Arts et Traditions de l'Orléanais** (museum of the arts and traditions of the Orléanais region), with collections ranging from local archaeology to furniture and costumes, and rooms dedicated to the wine of the Orléanais and the bridges of the Loire. (Open 9–12am and 2–6pm. Closed Tuesday and 1 November–31 March.) Behind the château an 11th century **keep** still stands.

The **Church of Notre Dame** nearby dates from the 12th century, the wooden false Gothic vaults replacing the Romanesque vaulting burnt in 1567. It was the church of the former **Abbey of Notre Dame**, an 18th century building partly converted into a hotel on the **Quai de l'Abbaye.** Walk along the Quai to the **Petit Mail**, a lovely promenade lined with trees and overlooking the Loire.

Go back via **Porte Tavers**, a vestige of the old **ramparts** to **Place St-Firmin** where the **tower** of a 16th century **church** still stands. Place St-Firmin and **Place Dunois** form a picturesque corner of Beaugency, particularly at night when old lampposts light up the whole scene, taking one back through the centuries.

Continue to the **Place du Martroi** and on to the **Rue du Change** to visit the **Hôtel de Ville.** A lovely Renaissance building, it has on exhibition some 17th century embroidered hangings from the former Abbey of Notre Dame. (Open 9–12am and 2–6pm. Closed Wednesday.) Nearby, in the same street, the **Tour de l'Horloge** (clock tower) was one of the entrances to the 12th century fortress.

Hotels and Restaurants

Hostellerie de l'Écu de Bretagne A very comfortable hotel with large homely rooms overlooking a garden, with a very good restaurant serving delectable regional specialities, but with originality and individuality: *Côtelette de Brochet aux Noix* (pike with walnuts) and *Lapereau au Miel* (rabbit in honey sauce). Place du Martroi, 45190, Beaugency, Loiret. Tel: (38) 44.67.60. 26 rooms, 70–180F. Meals 60–140F. Closed February. Credit cards:. AE, DC, EC, VISA.

At **Tavers** (2.5Km from Beaugency by the N152) is **La Tonnellerie**. A really lovely hotel, beautifully decorated with antique furniture, in a peaceful green setting with a garden and heated swimming pool, a warm welcome and a cuisine to match the refinement of the rest. Try the specialities of the Loire, the fish and the delicious cheeses. Truly a place in which to relax. 12 Rue des Eaux Bleues, Tavers, 45190, Beaugency, Loiret. Tel: (38) 44.68.15. 30 rooms and suites, 110–240F. Meals 95–150F. Closed 1 November–2 April.

Garages
Citroën: 30 Avenue de Blois. Tel: (38) 44.52.33.
Opel: N152. Tel: (38) 44.57.59.
Peugeot: 49 Avenue de Blois. Tel: (38) 44.53.20.
Renault: Avenue d'Orléans. Tel: (38) 44.50.40.

Festivals, Fairs and Sporting Events
Whitsun Saturday–1 September: **son et lumière** – 'La Cité des Sires de Beaugency' (The city of the Lords of Beaugency), an evocation of the city's medieval past.

BLOIS
From Paris exit, Blois, 5Km
From Bordeaux exit, Blois, 5Km
Inhabitants: 51,950
Office de Tourisme: Pavillon Anne De Bretagne, 3 Avenue Jean-Laigret

Blois 'Ville des Rois' (City of Kings) was the usual residence of the Valois Court until the end of the 16th century, when the king was not in residence at his Parisian palace of the Louvre. **Blois** has kept the Château which epitomises the whole history and art of the **Loire Valley**. The old town itself despite successive wars has retained much atmosphere with its narrow cobbled streets lined with fine houses.

But it is a city turned towards the 20th century as well and the Lac de Loire at 2Km on the left bank by D951 direction **Orléans**, is a modern resort built on the artificial lake created by a dam on the River Loire. A beach, a marina with restaurant and shop, a camping site and organised water sports such as sailing, wind surfing etc. make it a pleasant spot to unwind and enjoy the golden atmosphere of the Loire.

Blois itself has one pretty inn on the Loire quays and very comfortable quiet hotels within easy distance.

Blois was an important strategic place during the Middle Ages, the capital of a Comté. In the 14th century it was bought by the **Duc Louis d'Orléans**, brother of **King Charles VI**. **Blois** became the favourite residence of the Orléans family and the poet **Charles d'Orléans** spent the rest of his life at the château writing courtly poems, at his return from captivity in England. His son, who became **King Louis XII**, made **Blois** a Royal Palace with an importance equal to **Versaille** a century later. The château was further embellished by **François I** who delighted in magnificence. The Wars of Religion saw much political activity at Blois. The **Etats Généraux** (General Assembly of the Kingdom's representatives from the clergy, the nobility and the third party consisting of a cross-section of bourgeoisie, peasantry etc.) are held twice to try to contain the spreading of Protestantism. Henri de Guise, Lieutenant Général du Royaume (Lord Lieutenant of the Kingdom), tried to pressurise the King who, to be rid of opposition, had Henri and his brother the Cardinal de Guise both murdered at the château. Catherine de Medici, the King's mother, and counsellor, died there a few days later.

A century later, the Orléans family was back and Gaston d'Orléans, the brother of Louis XIII, was there in semi-exile. He tried to amuse himself in the château by commissioning Mansart to build a completely new wing, part of an ambitious rebuilding programme never to be completed. The château, the town's property since the time of Napoléon, is like an open history book. In its very structure can be read the various chapters of the sumptuous, turbulent or peaceful past. Reached via the **Place Victor Hugo** the château is built on a promontory dominating the valley. Of the old medieval château little remains except the **Tour du Foix**, in the inner courtyard on the **Terrasse du Foix** overlooking the lower part of the town and the Loire, and the **Grande Salle des Etats** in the 13th century building between the wings of Louis XII and François I. The entrance opens into the lovely Gothic façade of the Louis XII wing, built in pink brick and stone with an equestrian statue of the King by Guido Mazzoni over the gateway. The rich interiors and the **Chapel of St Calais** in the courtyard date from the same period (1498–1508). The private apartments of the Louis XII wing house a **museum** with an extensive collection of furniture, paintings and sculpture from the 15th to the 20th century.

The porcupine symbol belonging to the King and the pilgrim's cord and ermine of his wife, Anne de Bretagne, are used as decorative motifs all over this part of the building.

The left-hand gallery in the courtyard dates from the time of Charles d'Orléans, while the right-hand side is occupied by the Italianate wing of

François I. The magnificent octagonal **staircase** is as much a masterpiece of sculpture as of architecture. Designed to serve as a balcony for the Court on grand state occasions, its rich decoration uses the royal symbols conspicuous all over the château: François I's salamander and the swan of Claude de France, his queen, as well as the usual Renaissance grotesque motifs. The interior of this wing is empty of furniture and has been heavily restored. On the first floor look at Catherine of Medici's room with its secret cupboards for concealing valuables or (legend would have us believe) poisons! On the second floor, the Duc de Guise was murdered on the 23 December 1588 by the King's guards and on his order. (Open 9–12am and 2–5pm; 5.30pm 1 February–15 March; 6.30pm 16 March–30 September. Closed 1 January and Christmas Day.)

The farside building of classical style designed by Mansart brings a note of restraint after the exuberance of the François I wing. It houses the **municipal library** and the town **Grand Reception Rooms** where functions and concerts take place regularly. The grand staircase was built only in 1932.

In order to enjoy the façades of the château, walk from the **Place du Château**, a lovely open square with old houses standing in their gardens and a small café-restaurant, the whole overlooking a sweeping vista over the roofs of the lower town and the glittering river.

Go down the staircase at the side of the château to reach the **Rue St-Lubin**, with fine old houses, and the **Rue des Fossés du Château**, the former moat of the medieval structure. From there look up to the majestic façade of Mansart's 17th century building.

Go down to the **Place Victor Hugo** and admire the rhythmical alternation of bays and niches, inspired by Bramante and used on the elegant loggia of the François I façade, very much in the French Renaissance taste in its asymmetry and its love of decorative details.

From the Place Victor Hugo go up to the **Jardin des Lices** by the **Contrescape**, a ramp leading to the remnants of the vast terraced gardens laid out by the Italian gardener from Amboise on Louis XII's orders. Nearby, in the **Avenue Jean Laigret**, the **Pavilion of Anne de Bretagne** (now the Office de Tourisme) used to stand in the middle of the gardens. Louis XII and his queen used to come here to pray for an heir for the realm in the small adjacent oratory.

The **Church of St Vincent** on the far side of the Place Victor Hugo is a good example of the French 17th century Classical Jesuit style. Take the Rue des Fossés du Château again to get to the **Church of St Nicholas**, an interesting church which used to belong to the Benedictine **Abbey of St Laumer**, now a hospital. **St Nicolas** has a Romanesque choir and transept, with fascinating column capitals in the choir. The rest of the building dates from the Gothic era.

From the church walk down to the **Quai Abbé Grégoire** and along the river to the 18th century bridge, the Pont Gabriel, built by the father of the architect of the Place de la Concorde in Paris, and deemed 'the most beautiful bridge in the Kingdom of France' ever since.

From the bridge look back at the view of the **Rue Denis Papin** with its monumental staircase, and take in the most attractive all-embracing view of the town with its houses tumbling down to the river and its many church towers, spires and steeples piercing the skyline. On the left the massive form of the château broods on its promontory, while on the right the **Cathedral of St Louis**, destroyed by a storm and rebuilt in the 17th century in Gothic style over a crypt dating from the 10th and 11th centuries, dominates the lovely terraced gardens of the Evêché. The former **Archbishop's palace** nearby, built by Gabriel in the 18th century, is now the **Hôtel de Ville**. Away from this old part of the city, with its steep, narrow cobbled streets lined with fascinating old houses, the modern **Basilica of Notre Dame de La Trinité** (1937–49) stands out with its pink mass and campanile 60m high. The *carillon*, one of the best in Europe, consists of forty-eight bells, and regular concerts are given.

The **Chocolaterie Poulain**, a family-run chocolate factory situated near the station, off the **Avenue Gambetta**, can be visited and delicious samples of chocolates and sweets are distributed as part of the visit. (Enquiries: Tel: (54) 78.39.21, extension 339.)

Hotels and Restaurants

Hostellerie de la Loire A fine restaurant, with simple rooms, serving excellent regional cuisine with a gastronomic touch: *Mousse de Saumon à l'Oseille* (salmon mousse with sorrel); *Carré d'Agneau Rôti aux Primeurs* (lamp chops with young vegetables). 8 Rue du Maréchal-de-Lattre-de-Tassigny, 41000, Blois, Loir-et-Cher. Tel: (54) 74.26.60. 17 rooms, 50–150F. Meals 60–180F. Closed Sunday and 15 January–15 February. Credit cards: AE, DC.

La Péniche A lovely place for a special fish dinner on a barge converted into a very cosy restaurant, on the Loire itself about half a kilometre from the bridge. Very good sea food platter and Loire salmon etc. Promenade du Mail, 41000, Blois, Loir-et-Cher. Tel: (54) 74.37.23. Meals 100–150F. Credit card: VISA.

At **Chitenay** (12Km from Blois by the D956; turn right beyond Cellettes) is: **La Clé des Champs** A simple comfortable hotel in a large park with a lovely garden. A very quiet retreat with an excellent restaurant offering specialities of the Loire and the nearby Sologne, such as *Terrine de Poissons à l'Ail* (fish pâté with garlic) and *Salade de Lapereau Tiède aux Mâches* (hot rabbit salad with corn lettuce). Chitenay, 41120, Les Montils, Loir-et-Cher. Tel: (54) 44.22.03. 10 rooms, 55–90F. Meals 77–140F. Closed Monday night, Tuesday and 15 January–15 February. Credit card: VISA.

Garages

Austin/Morris/Rover/Triumph: 12bis Avenue du Président Wilson. Tel: (54) 78.02.15.
BMW/Lancia: 44 Avenue Maréchal-de-Lattre-de-Tassigny. Tel: (54) 78.77.06.
Citroën: Route de Châteaudun. Tel: (54) 78.42.22.
Fiat: 42 Avenue Maunoury. Tel: (54) 78.04.62.
Ford: 20 Avenue Maunoury. Tel: (54) 74.06.34.
Renault: 148 Avenue Maunoury. Tel: (54) 78.42.85.

Festivals, Fairs and Sporting Events

March, April, end August–end September: **son et lumière** at the château – 'Les Esprits Aiment la Nuit' (Spirits Like the Night), an evocation of the history of the château through the women connected with it: Joan of Arc, Anne de Bretagne, Claude de France, Catherine de Medici. The son et lumière performances were initiated by Jean Eugène Robert Houdin, a famous illusionist and conjurer who lived and died at Blois (1805–71). A small **museum** is kept at his former house near the château. (Not open to the public at the moment.)

CHAMBORD

From Paris, Blois exit, D951 and D112B, 23Km
From Bordeaux, Blois exit, D951 and D112B, 23Km
Inhabitants: 230

Take the D951 along the left bank of the Loire. After 8Km admire, on the opposite bank, the **Château de Ménars** (17th and 18th century) which belonged to Madame de Pompadour.

Chambord is one of the masterpieces of the French Renaissance and not to be missed. Standing in a 5,500Ha park which since 1948 has also been a nature reserve (**Parc National Cygénétique**), where stags, wild boars and deer can be spotted under the magnificent trees, Chambord is a marvellous place for a family excursion, a picnic or a stay and a meal at the simple hotel just opposite the château or in a comfortable hotel just outside the wall surrounding the park (at 32Km, it is the longest in France).

The **château** itself, built on a medieval square plan with four corner towers and a central keep, is surrounded by a moat in which flow the channelled waters of the River Cosson. It truly is a magnificent sight with its impressive proportions, which herald **Versailles**, its intricately decorated roof-line and the harmony of its parts, built in that lovely white Loire tufa stone. Built in 1519 on the site of a former hunting lodge by François I, who enjoyed entertaining on a lavish scale surrounded by his elegant court, Chambord saw many a grand occasion. Charles V Emperor

186

of Austria was received here in 1539. Grand receptions followed hunting parties, all graced with the presence of the beautiful women the king loved so, with the courtiers learning impeccable manners and courtesy towards the ladies, as decreed and insisted upon by the King himself. All this beautiful company, gorgeously arrayed in brilliant costumes and resplendent with jewels, would gather on the terraced roof to follow the events of the hunt, the pastime of kings, with the famous royal hounds and 300 falcons.

French kings throughout the centuries have enjoyed the beauty of this fairy-tale **château** and its lovely site, after its return from the Orléans family to the French Crown under Louis XIV. In the 17th century Lully and Molière both stayed at Chambord. Molière's *Le Bourgeois Gentilhomme* was first performed here.

From royal hands the château passed, under Louis XV, to the Maréchal de Saxe, as a reward for his victory at Fontenay. At his death, Chambord fell into disrepair and the Revolutionaries destroyed what was left of the furnishings. Napoléon gave the estate to the Prince of Wagram whose wife sold it. It now belongs to the state.

Despite its medieval plan the château is designed entirely for pleasure and enjoyment. The most outstanding feature of the outside building is the terraced roof inspired by Italy, yet fundamentally French with its maze of lanterns, dormers, gables, some 800 capitals and 365 chimneys with spires and turrets, all richly decorated with royal symbols and insignia as well as a multiplicity of ornamental motifs. Under the lustrous sky of the Loire Valley, the brilliant court of François I spent much time on the extraordinary roof, conceived as a small-scale city.

Inside, the central building contains the famous **Grand Staircase**, supposedly designed by Leonardo da Vinci, in the monumental **guard room.** Built in an Italianate style, it is designed so that two separate groups of people, going up and down respectively, do not meet or even see each other (most useful in a time famed for gallant affairs and love trysts!)

The interior has unfortunately lost all its original furnishings, but the state has slowly been refurbishing some of the apartments. On the first floor, the Louis XV apartments, occupied by King Stanislas ex-King of Poland and the Maréchal de Saxe, have furniture and tapestries of the period. (Open 9.30–12.30am and 2–6.30pm 1 April–31 October; and 10–12.30am and 2–4.30pm 1 November–31 March. Closed 1 January, 1 November, Christmas Day.)

Hotels and Restaurants

St Michel Just opposite the château, a very simple hotel with quiet rooms and of course a magnificent view. With restaurant. Chambord, 41250, Bracieux, Loir-et-Cher. Tel: (54) 46.31.31. 38 rooms, 80–210F. Meals 65–120F. Closed 15 November–24 December. Credit card: VISA.

At **St-Dyé-sur-Loire** (3Km from Chambord by the D112B) is the **Manoir Bel Air**. A beautiful country house converted into a very comfortable hotel overlooking the Loire on one side and a garden on the other, with a good restaurant offering regional specialities such as *Cailles Solognotes* (quails) and *Rillettes de Saumon* (salmon pâté). St-Dye-sur-Loire, 41500, Mer, Loir-et-Cher. Tel: (54) 87.60.10. 28 rooms, 60–130F. Meals 62–130F. Closed January–15 February.

Festivals, Fairs and Sporting Events
Easter–September: **son et lumière** – 'Le Combat du Jour et de la Nuit' (The Fight between Day and Night), an evocation of Chambord's history. (The first ever son et lumière performance was given at Chambord in 1952.)

CHAUMONT
From Paris, Blois exit, N152, 22Km
From Bordeaux, Blois exit, N152, 22Km
Inhabitants: 793

Chaumont is a small village on the left bank of the Loire with a 15th century *château* admirably situated on a hill overlooking the river. A very comfortable and peaceful hotel at Chaumont itself and another one at Onzain, on the right bank across the bridge, with excellent restaurants, make of Chaumont a perfect overnight stay.

A very old fortress several times destroyed, Chaumont was rebuilt in the late 15th century by Pierre d'Amboise and his successors. Catherine of Medici, widow of King Henri II, bought it in 1560 in order to force her husband's former mistress, Diane de Poitiers, to give her **Chenonceaux** in exchange. The site of Chaumont is outstanding. A walk through the park up to the château enables the visitor to experience the full impact of the rather forbidding west façade. Diane de Poitiers left her cipher here as at everywhere she owned: two interlocked 'D's and the hunting attributes of Diana the goddess of the hunt (a horn, quiver and arrows). However the main gateway behind the drawbridge displays the royal insignia with the initials of Louis XII and Anne of Bretagne.

All over the building Gothic style is tempered by the Italian Renaissance in the architectural decorative details.

Inside the **apartments** of the two famous rivals in love and power, Catherine and Diane, have tapestries, furniture and a collection of terracotta medallions modelled by Nini, a famous 18th century Italian potter and glass-engraver who lived at the château.

The **stables** nearby are of a magnificence equal to that of the princely apartments.

From the **Terrace**, built in the 18th century, there is a sweeping view of the Loire and its valley.

Hotels and Restaurants

Hostellerie du Château A very comfortable hotel with beautiful, peaceful rooms overlooking a lovely garden with a swimming pool. A very good restaurant offers delicious food. Try the *Foie de Canard Chaud aux Pommes* (duck's liver with apples) and one of the wonderful unusual *Sorbets au Thé* (tea sorbet), *à la Poire* (pear) or *au Pamplemousse* (grapefruit). 2 Rue du Maréchal de Lattre, 41150, Onzain, Loir-et-Cher. Tel: (54) 46.98.04. 15 rooms, 150–340F. Meals 70–150F. Closed 15 December–15 March. Credit cards: AE, DC, VISA.

At **Onzain**, just across the Loire on the right bank, is the **Domaine des Hauts-de-Loire**. A beautiful old manor house converted into a luxurious hotel in the absolute peace and quiet of a 70Ha park with a lake for fishing and tennis courts. A place to dream of with a restaurant offering a cuisine to match the superlative surroundings, such as the *Escalope de Saumon à l'Oseille* (salmon escalope with sorrel sauce) and *Pigeonneau à l'Ancienne* (stewed pigeon). 41150, Onzain, Loir-et-Cher. Tel: (54) 79.72.57. 37 rooms and suites, 380–600F. Meals 150–250F. Closed Thursday and 1 December–1 March. Credit cards: AE, DC, VISA.

Also at Onzain is the **Pont d'Ouchet.** Excellent small restaurant with simple rooms, offering very good regional dishes such as *Poulet au Vouvray* (chicken with a Vouvray wine sauce) or *Raie au Beurre Noir* (skate with browned butter sauce with capers). Very good value. 50 Grande Rue, 41150, Onzain, Loir-et-Cher. Tel: (54) 79.70.33. 10 rooms, 48–72F. Meals 37–120F. Closed Sunday night, Monday, and 27 September–3 October and 15 January–1 March.

At **Seillac** (7Km north of Onzain by the D45 and D131) is the **Domaine de Seillac.** A very peaceful comfortable hotel with individual bungalows in a beautiful park with an Olympic swimming pool, tennis courts and a lake with fishing. The château has an excellent restaurant serving specialities such as *Filet de Turbot en Papillote* (turbot fillet) or *Magret de Canard au Miel* (duck fillet in honey sauce). In the summer a barbecue provides meals by the swimming pool. A real holiday place. Seillac, 41150, Onzain, Loir-et-Cher. Tel: (54) 79.72.11. 81 rooms, 180–280F. Meals 85–170F. Closed Sunday night, Monday (15 November–15 March) and 20 December–15 January. Credit cards: AE, DC, VISA.

Garages

Peugeot/Talbot: Onzain. Tel: (54) 79.70.37.
Renault: Chaumont. Tel: (54) 46.98.65.
Renault: Onzain. Tel: (54) 79.70.45.

AMBOISE
From Paris, Amboise/Château-Renault exit, D31, 15Km
From Bordeaux, Amboise/Château-Renault exit, D31, 15Km
Inhabitants: 11,116
Office de Tourisme: Quai Général de Gaulle

Amboise is a most attractive town on the left bank of the Loire with its **château** picturesquely perched on a promontory. An historic place, it also has much to offer to the modern traveller, with very comfortable hotels and quality restaurants.

The strategic importance of Amboise dates from Gallo-Roman times, and a fortress has existed on the rocky promontory since the 11th century. After it had been confiscated by Charles VII from the Comte d'Amboise, King Louis XI gave it to his queen as a royal palace. The Dauphin Charles VIII was born here. During his campaigns in Italy in 1495 he acquired a taste for a more luxurious and sumptuous way of life. Together with an enormous amount of looted treasure, he brought back with him scholars, artists, architects, clothmakers, gardeners and all sorts of craftsmen, to make Amboise equal in spendour to the Italian *palazzi* he had seen and certainly a most magnificent royal palace. However the King did not enjoy his earthly possessions very long. In 1498 he died after banging his head against a low door lintel.

François I spent his childhood at Amboise and lived there during the first three years of his reign, which he spent pursuing the life of pleasure typical of the Renaissance courts. The emulation of Italy promoted by Charles VIII was carried on by François I. He brought over Italian artists, including the aged Leonardo da Vinci who spent his last years at Amboise at the manor house of the Clos-Luce nearby.

Amboise, like Blois, saw the bloodshed engendered by the Wars of Religion. In 1560, Huguenot conspirators were killed at the château and hung from the grand balcony overlooking the river. The young Mary Stuart, wife of François II of France, was staying at the château at the time.

In the 17th century, Amboise – together with **Blois** and **Chambord** – belonged to the tiresome Gaston d'Orléans, brother of Louis XIII, an inveterate conspirator and father of the no less tiresome Grande Mademoiselle. At his death Amboise came back to the French Crown and was used for a time as a state prison. It now belongs to the Comte de Paris, heir apparent to the throne of France, and is part of the **Fondation de St Louis**, a charitable body founded by the Comte de Paris in order to safeguard the French national heritage.

Much of the château was destroyed in the 19th century.

From the ramp leading up to the château one reaches a terrace from which the luminous Loire landscape is revealed. This terrace used to be an enclosed courtyard, in Charles VIII's time, surrounded on four sides by buildings similar to the lovely **Logis du Roi.** Receptions and wild-animal fights used to take place here.

The **Chapel of St Hubert** was the queen's oratory. Perched at the extreme end of the rampart, this preciously chased masterpiece of Flamboyant Gothic art was the creation of Flemish artists brought to the court by Louis XII. The lintel of the doorway is remarkable for the quality of its carvings, which depict St Christopher and St Hubert. Leonardo da Vinci's remains are buried in the left side chapel.

The interior of the château is beautifully furnished in various styles. The most remarkable feature of the château is the **Tour des Minimes** or **des Cavaliers** (riders), so named because of the wide ramp which horsemen could climb. From the top of the tower there is a wonderful view over the Loire. (Château open 9–12am and 2–7pm; 5.30pm 1 November–14 March.)

From the château take the mounting **Rue Victor Hugo** to the **Manoir du Clos-Lucé**, the 15th century house where Leonardo da Vinci lived, and died in 1519. It is a most attractive medieval house which has retained much atmosphere. The chapel, with the cipher of Charles VIII and Anne de Bretagne, has some interesting Italian frescoes. The rooms where Leonardo lived are open to the public. In the basement, a fascinating collection of models executed in 1952 by IBM France following drawings by Leonardo show the sheer genius and versatility of a man who was a painter, sculptor, muscian, poet, architect, military engineer and a scientist. Here at the Clos-Lucé, given to him by François I, he found peace, affection and friendship, and carried on his studies in geometry, architecture and urban development at the same time as planning and organising the court festivities and drawing (many of the Windsor drawings seem to have been executed here between 1517 and 1519). (Open 9–12am and 2–7pm. Closed in January.)

Walk down the Rue Victor Hugo to the river and the **Musée de l'Hôtel de Ville.** It has on exhibition royal documents, 19th century paintings and a 14th century Virgin, in a 16th century building. (Open 9–12am and 2–6pm.)

The **Musée de la Poste** in the **Rue d'Orange**, reached from the quay by the Rue J.J. Rousseau, in a Renaissance building – the **Hôtel Joyeuse** – is dedicated to the memory of the age of the stage coach, with postillions' and postmasters' uniforms, insignias etc. (Open 9.30–12am and 2–6.30pm 1 April–30 September. Otherwise 10–12am and 2–5pm.)

Walk along the animated Rue Nationale, parallel to the river, to the **Church of St Denis**, dating mostly from the 12th century and noteworthy for its vaulting and the Romanesque capitals in the nave.

Going 3Km south of Amboise by the **Route de Bléré** and the D31, take a look at a curious 18th century folly, the only vestige of a magnificent

château built by the Duc de Choiseul, a minister under Louis XV, in emulation of Versailles. The château was destroyed in 1823 but the **Pagoda of Chantelou**, built from 1775 to 1778 by Choiseul to commemorate the devotion of his friends still stands with its seven storeys 44m high. The visitor can climb the 149 steps to enjoy a sweeping view over the Loire Valley and the neighbouring Forest of Amboise. (On the way to the pagoda stop at the Chanteloup hotel for a quiet night in the countryside.)

Hotels and Restaurants

Château de Pray (2Km from Amboise by the D751). A beautifully comfortable hotel in an historic château in a large park, with a formal garden and a terrace overlooking the valley. With restaurant. 37400, Amboise, Indre-et-Loire. Tel: (47) 57.23.67. 16 rooms, 180–240F. Meals 95–120F. Closed January. Credit cards: AE, DC, EC, VISA.

Le Choiseul A small 18th century manor house converted into a very comfortable hotel with period interior decoration and furniture. No restaurant. 36 Quai Ch. Guinot, 37400, Amboise, Indre-et-Loire. Tel: (47) 57.23.83. 18 rooms, 330–410F. Closed December–March. Credit card: AE.

Le Lion d'Or A comfortable old-fashioned hotel with an excellent restaurant serving traditional fare such as *Terrine de Lapin aux Pruneaux* (rabbit pâté with prunes) and *Volaille aux Girolles* (chicken with chanterelles mushrooms). 17 Quai Ch. Guinot, 37400, Amboise, Indre-et-Loire. Tel: (47) 51.00.23. 22 rooms, 65–140F. Meals 75–150F. Closed Friday and November–March.

Le Mail Very good restaurant offering delicious food such as *Foie Confit au Vouvray* (liver marinated in Vouvray) and *Truite Farcie au Roquefort* (trout stuffed with Roquefort cheese). 32 Quai du Général de Gaulle, 37400, Amboise, Indre-et-Loire. Tel: (47) 57.60.39. Meals 65–150F. Closed Tuesday night, Wednesday lunch-time, and January and February.

Chanteloup A small family-run hotel. Very quiet. No restaurant. Route de Bléré, 37400, Amboise, Indre-et-Loire. Tel: (47) 57.10.90. 22 rooms, 160–230F. Closed 25 August–12 September and 15 December–April.

Garages

Ford/Lancia: Route de Chenonceaux. Tel: (47) 57.07.64.
Ford/Volvo: Boulevard Anatole France. Tel: (47) 57.11.30.
Opel: 12 Rue de Blois. Tel: (47) 57.11.32.
Peugeot: 108 Rue de St-Denis. Tel: (47) 57.42.82.
Renault: Route de Bléré. Tel: (47) 57.06.54.

Festivals, Fairs and Sporting Events

July and August: **son-et-lumière** – 'Soirées à la Cour du Roy François I'

('An Evening at the Court of François I').

Camping

ROCHECORBON/VOUVRAY
From Paris, Tours-Nord/St Symphorien exit, 10Km to Rochecorbon by
the N10 and D77, then 9Km to Vouvray by the N152.
From Bordeaux, Tours-Nord/St Symphorien exit, 10Km to Rochecorbon
by the N10 and D77, then 9Km to Vouvray by the N152.

Turn off before **Tours** to the picturesque village of Rochecorbon and
have a meal in a delicious restaurant in a superb position overlooking the
Loire before going to Vouvray to taste the lovely fragrant white wine and
to spend the night in a small comfortable hotel.

Rochecorbon (2,216 inhabitants), situated at the foot of a high cliff
dominated by the Lanterne de Rochecorbon, a 15th century watch tower,
has a wine museum in an 18th century folly at the end of the village. **Le
Musée d'Espelosin ou du Vin** offers tasting of the various Loire *crus* in its
cellars. Notice in the garden some Gallo-Roman stones used as a wine
press. (Open 9–12am and 2–6pm. Closed Tuesday.)

Vouvray (2,746 inhabitants) is a small village on the right bank of the
Loire which has produced the most famous wines in Touraine since the
15th century. Tasting is available in the local *caves*, dug into the soft white
tufa stone. Curious ancient *Troglodytique* houses, dug in the rock, give
the inhabitants the same environmental conditions as are required for the
storage of the wine. In the **Cave de la Bonne Dame** wine festivals take
place at the beginning of January and on 15 August.

Hotels and Restaurants
L'Oubliette In a restaurant with a superb view over the river and a
dining-room dug in the cliff of soft white tufa, enjoy a delicious meal and
an unusual setting. Try the *Fricassée de Sole et de Lotte aux Huîtres* (sole
and monkfish stew with oyster sauce) or the *Salade de Foie Gras*. 34 Rue
des Clouets, Rochecorbon, 37210, Vouvray, Indre-et-Loire. Tel: (47)
52.50.49. Meals 85–170F. Closed Sunday night and Monday, and 15–29
February and 1–15 October. Credit card: EC.
Les Fontaines A small quiet hotel with a garden. No restaurant.
Rochecorbon, 37210, Vouvray, Indre-et-Loire. Tel: (47) 52.50.86. 15
rooms, 70–150F. Open all year. Credit cards: AE, DC, VISA.

Garages
Renault: Tel: (47) 52.73.36.

VILLANDRY
From Paris, St Avertin/Vierzon/Chinon exit, D7, 16Km
From Bordeaux, Chambray/Tours-Sud exit, D7, 16Km
Inhabitants: 680

Villandry is a tiny village on the left bank of the **River Cher** with a Renaissance Château and famous 16th century formal gardens. A small comfortable family hotel with a very good restaurant makes it a very pleasant overnight stop in the peace of the French countryside.

The **château** was built in 1532 by Jean le Breton on the site of a medieval castle of which only the keep still stands, in the south-west corner. The three wings surrounding the inner courtyard are of the finest Renaissance style – elegant and graceful, full of nobility. The whole was restored by **Dr Carvallo** in the 1930s. He also collected the works of art exhibited inside and recreated the 16th century formal **gardens**, unique in France. On three superimposed terraces three different forms of garden are laid out: the lower level is the **vegetable garden**, planted with the vegetables known at the time; the middle terrace is the **ornamental garden** with box hedges forming symbols of the various forms of love (faithful, passionate, treacherous etc); and the upper terrace is a **water garden** with a magnificent lake. This harmonious and majestic creation, enlivened with fountains and canals, can be enjoyed fully from the terraced hill behind the château. (Open 9am–7pm April–October. Gardens open every day until 6pm; until 8pm July–September.)

Hotels and Restaurants
Le Cheval Rouge Excellent family-run establishment with delicious food such as *Ris de Veau aux Morilles* (sweetbreads with morilles mushrooms) and *Filet de Barbue aux Légumes* (brill fillet with vegetables). Comfortable rooms. Villandry, 37300, Joué-les-Tours, Indre-et-Loire. Tel: (47) 50.02.07. 20 rooms, 123–180F. Meals 65–200F. Closed Sunday night, Monday, and January and February. Credit card: VISA.

AZAY-LE-RIDEAU
From Paris, Chambray/Montbazon exit, D751, 23Km
From Bordeaux, Chambray/Montbazon exit, N10 and D751, 25Km
Inhabitants: 2,749
Office de Tourisme: 26 Rue Gambetta, 15 March–15 September, closed Sunday and public holidays

Azay-le-Rideau is a small village on the **River Indre** with one of the finest French Renaissance châteaux. An excellent hotel in the village itself and a fine restaurant in a delightful setting a few kilometres away make Azay a very enjoyable halt in the midst of a green and peaceful countryside.

Built from 1518 to 1529 by the financier Gilles Berthelot, the **château** at Azay-le-Rideau shows the Renaissance development from defensive architecture to a residence built for enjoyment. The Gothic outline with its high-pitched roofs, its monumental chimneys and pointed turrets, is tempered by an Italianate feeling for symmetry and classically inspired decorative motifs.

The most remarkable feature of the château is the impressive **Grand Staircase** which, following **Chambord** and **Blois**, marks a definite improvement in the interior plan of grand houses.

The château is now a **Renaissance museum** with period furniture, tapestries and paintings. (Open 9–12am and 2–6.30pm Palm Sunday–30 September; 9–12am and 2–5pm October–mid November; 9.30–12am and 2–4.45pm mid November–Palm Sunday. Closed 1 January, 1 May, 1 November and Christmas Day.)

Hotels and Restaurants

Le Grand Monarque A very attractive hotel in the centre of this lovely village, two minutes from the château, with an excellent restaurant serving delicious regional specialities such as *Quenelle de Brochet* (pike dumpling) and *Canard Sauvage au Citron* (mallard with lemon). Place de la République, 37190, Azay-le-Rideau, Indre-et-Loire. Tel: (47) 43.30.08. 30 rooms, 70–220F. Meals 75–150F. Closed 1 December–28 February. Credit cards: AE, EC.

At **Saché** (6.5Km by the D17) is the **Auberge du 12e Siècle** In medieval surroundings, just by the château de Saché, where the writer Balzac used to stay as a friend of the family and where he wrote many of his books, including *Le Père Goriot* and the *Le Lys dans la Vallée*, a delicious restaurant offers fare to vie with the surroundings, such as *Magret de Canard au Poivre Vert* (thin slices of duck with green pepper). Saché, 37190, Azay-le-Rideau, Indre-et-Loire. Tel: (47) 26.86.58. Meals 120–160F. Closed Tuesday and February. Credit cards: AE, VISA.

Garages

Citroën: Tel: (47) 43.30.26.
Renault: N751. Tel: (47) 43.36.89.

MONTBAZON

From Paris, Chambray/Montbazon exit, N10, 9Km
From Bordeaux, Chambray/Tours-Sud exit, N10, 9Km
Inhabitants: 2,688

Montbazon is a small town on the left bank of the **River Indre**, gathered around one of the twenty fortresses erected by Foulques Nerra (the

Black), Count of Anjou, in the 12th century. A bloodthirsty, violent unscrupulous man, he spread destruction all over the **Anjou**, the **Touraine** and the **Blésois.**

Montbazon is a very pleasant halt with its luxurious hotel nearby and delicious restaurant.

The **keep** of the fortress can be visited. (From the **Hôtel de Ville** follow the Rue des Moulins and, beyond the old gateway, a path on the right.) An enormous rectangular tower, it is dominated by a gigantic copper statue of the Virgin (1866). (Open 9–12am and 2–7pm 15 May–15 September.)

Hotels and Restaurants

Château d'Artigny (2Km by the D17) A very luxurious hotel in a converted château standing in a large park, with swimming pool, tennis courts etc, overlooking the Indre Valley. From October to March concerts are organised. A fine restaurant with an excellent cellar offers *Salade d'Ecrevisses aux Haricots Verts* (fresh-water crayfish with French beans) or *Foie Gras Cru au Poivre* (raw *foie gras* with pepper). Route d'Azay-le-Rideau, 37250, Montbazon, Indre-et-Loire. Tel: (47) 26.24.24. 51 rooms and 6 suites, 240–550F. Meals 115–250F. Closed 28 November–8 January. Credit card: VISA.
8 January. Credit card: VISA.

La Chancelière Simple small inn with a very good restaurant offering regional specialities and a warm welcome. 1 Place des Marronniers, 37250, Montbazon, Indre-et-Loire. Tel: (47) 26.00.67. 10 rooms, 80–140F. Meals 60–150F. Credit card: VISA.

Garage

Peugeot/Talbot: Tel: (47) 26.06.50.

VOUILLÉ

From Paris, Poitiers–Sud exit, N149, 12Km
From Bordeaux, Poitiers exit, N149, 12Km
Inhabitants: 2,040

Hotels and Restaurants

Château de Périgny Situated in a beautiful setting on the bank of the River Auxance and at the edge of the forest, this luxuriously comfortable hotel offers tennis, riding and trout fishing for its guests when they are not enjoying the exquisite food: *Matelote d'Anguilles* (eel stew) or *Tarte aux Reinettes* (apple tart). 86190, Vouillé, Vienne. Tel: (49) 51.80.43. 38 rooms, 190–580F. Meals 100–200F. Open all year. Credit cards: AE, DC, EC, VISA.

NIORT
From Paris, Niort exit, N11, 13Km
From Bordeaux, St-Maixent-L'Ecole exit, N11, 14Km
Inhabitants: 63,965
Office de Tourisme: Place de la Poste, closed Sunday

Niort is an attractive town with a smiling atmosphere on the left bank of the **Sèvre Niortaise.** An excellent hotel-restaurant with very reasonable prices makes it a pleasant overnight stop.

Built on an old Roman site, Niort has kept the medieval lay-out of the older city. Stretched on two slopes facing each other, the narrow windings lined with low houses tumble down the **Rue Victor Hugo**, which stands on the former open market.

Because of its geographical position, Niort has always been an important commercial centre. Eleanor of Aquitaine granted civic freedom to the town and its trade subsequently developed. The port exported salt, fish, corn and wood and imported pelts and skins to cure and transform into gloves and other leather clothing, from the 14th century onwards. Today Niort is an important industrial centre for a varied range of products, including leatherware, clothes, wood, electric appliances etc. An important **trade fair** is held here every year at the beginning of May.

Angelica, the plant used in jam, candied or made into a liqueur (*Sève d'Angélique*), and the **Tourteau Fromager** (goat's cheese cake) are the two gastronomic specialities of the town.

Arriving from the N11, head for the **Place de la Brèche**, formerly part of the **ramparts.** Walk down the **Rue Victor Hugo** to the Donjon stopping *en route* on the right at the **Pilori**, former Hôtel de Ville (1530–5) of Gothic and Renaissance styles housing the **Musée du Pilori** with various collections including tombstones, from the Middle Ages to the 16th century, Gallo-Roman jewels, coins and various other artefacts. (Open 9–12am and 2–6pm. Closed Tuesday.)

The **Donjon (keep)**, dominating the left bank of the River Sèvre, was built by Henry Plantagenet (Henry II of England) and finished by Richard the Lion Heart. It consists of two enormous square towers (12th and 13th centuries) linked by a 15th century wing with an **ethnographic museum** exhibiting local works of art and artefacts. (Open 9–12am and 2–6pm. Closed Tuesday.)

Follow the **Quai Cronstadt** and take the **Rue de l'Abreuvoir** to the **Musée des Beaux Arts**, which has extensive collections of the decorative arts, including ivories, enamels, bronzes etc and some paintings. (Open 9–12am and 2–6pm. Closed Tuesday.)

Go down the Rue de l'Abreuvoir again to reach the **Rue du Tourniquet** and the **Church of Notre Dame** dating from the late 15th/early 16th century with an elegant Flamboyant Gothic spire, and a portal in the same style. Inside, the Aubussons tapestries are noteworthy, together with some 17th century mausoleums.

Number 5 **Rue du Pont**, off the bridge, is the house where **Madame de Maintenon**, the famous mistress of Louis XIV, was born.

Hotels and Restaurants

Le Terminus An excellent restaurant offering a wide choice of delicious regional specialities, such as *Moules à la Charentaise* (mussels) or *Anguilles à l'Ail* (eels with garlic) and exquisite seafood. Comfortable rooms. Good value. 82 Rue de la Gare, 7900, Niort, Deux-Sèvres. Tel: (49) 24.00.38. 43 rooms, 55–160F. Meals 55–170F. Closed Friday night, Saturday and 20 December–5 January. Credit cards: AE, DC, EC, VISA.

At **Chavagne** (11Km by the D5 from Niort, 3Km from the *autoroute* by the N11) is the **Motel des Rocs**. A peaceful modern hotel with its own garden and tennis court. With restaurant. Chavagne, 79260, La Crèche, Deux-Sèvres. Tel: (49) 25.50.38. 23 rooms, 165F. Meals 70–180F. Closed Sunday (1 November–late March). Credit cards: AE, DC, EC, VISA.

Garages

Citroën: 80 Avenue St-Jean-d'Angely. Tel: (49) 75.55.10.
Fiat: Avenue de Paris. Tel: (49) 24.15.30.
Ford: 64 Avenue St-Jean. Tel: (49) 24.33.22.
BMW: 105 Rue de Goise. Tel: (49) 24.25.05.
Peugeot: 475 Avenue de Paris. Tel: (49) 24.38.05.
Renault: 214 Avenue de Paris. Tel: (49) 28.34.22.

SAINTES/COGNAC

From Paris, Saintes exit, N137, 5Km
From Bordeaux, Saintes exit, N137, 5Km
Inhabitants: 28,405
Office de Tourisme: Esplanade A. Malraux, closed Saturday afternoon and Sunday out of season

Saintes is a fascinating city with monuments dating from Roman times onwards. Several excellent restaurants and comfortable hotels make it a pleasant halt, while a visit to nearby Cognac, time permitting, is a must for any serious *gastronome*.

Named after the Gallic tribe of the *Santones*, Saintes soon became a Roman city with important buildings as befits the capital of western Aquitaine. The **Arch of Germanicus**, built in AD19, was a votive arch dedicated to Germanicus which used to stand on the main bridge. It was saved from destruction by the writer and Inspector of Historic Monuments **Prosper Mérimée** in 1842 and rebuilt on the right bank of the **River Charente**, on the other side of the **Pont Palissy** as one arrives from the *autoroute* by the N137.

Nearby a small **archaeological museum** houses Roman remains and carvings in a lovely garden beside the Charente lined with Doric columns. (Open 8.30–12am and 2–6pm.)

On the opposite bank, the **Quai de Verdun**, lies the old part of the town. The *Quai* itself is lined with 17th and 18th century houses, and their gardens stretch down to the river on which pleasure and rowing boats pass quietly by. Day boat-trips to La Rochelle, a lovely old port on the **Atlantic Ocean**, are available daily in the summer.

From the Quai de Verdun take the **Rue St-Pierre** to reach the **Cathedral of St Pierre**, a late Gothic building the belfry of which was never completed. The portal, decorated with angels, saints and prophets, is noteworthy. Damaged during the Wars of Religion, the interior was rebuilt in the 17th century. The statue of **Notre Dame des Miracles** (Our Lady of Miracles) is venerated here.

From the cathedral walk down **Rue Clemenceau** to the **Rue St-Maur** and turn towards the river to visit the **Musée Dupuy-Mestreau** in an 18th century house with an important collection of local art including some rare wood panelling attributed to Bérain. (Guided tour 2.30pm and 4.30pm; in July and August also 3pm, 3.30pm, 4pm and 5pm. Closed Monday and public holidays and 15 October–15 April.)

The nearly **Hôtel de la Bourse**, in the **Rue St-Maur**, has a handsomely carved portal. Walk through old Saintes to the **Rue Victor Hugo.** Number 2 is the **Présidial**, a 17th century building of classical style housing the **Musée des Beaux Arts** and various collections of local ceramics from the 11th century to modern times, as well as paintings. (Open 10–12am and 2–6pm. Closed Tuesday, Easter, Ascension Day, Whitsun, 14 July, 1 November, Christmas Day.)

Following the **Grande Rue** from the Présidial to the **Place de l'Echevinage**, the old **Echevinage (town hall)**, with its classical façade, exhibits 19th and 20th century collections from the Musée des Beaux Arts. The **belfry** dates from the 16th century.

From the Echevinage, turn right into the **Rue Alsace-Lorraine** to reach the **Rue Delage** to rejoin the **Rue Nationale**. Turn off in the **Cours** Flamboyant Gothic window. Nearby the **Hôtel Martineau** houses the **municipal library** and its collection of rare books. From the library take the **Rue Delage** to rejoin the **Rue Nationale**. Turn of in the **Cours Reverseaux**, taking the road for **Bordeaux**, the N137. The **Church of St Eutrope**, in the **Rue St-Eutrope**, lies on the right. It used to be one of the most important places of pilgrimage in the west of France and a stopping place for pilgrims on their way to **Santiago da Compostella**. St Eutrope was a bishop of Saintes and was supposed to work miracles. Louis XI attributed his recovery from dropsy to him and in gratitude added the 15th century **belfry** to the simple Romanesque church. The interior is also in the Flamboyant Gothic style. The Romanesque **crypt** is a subterranean church of impressive proportions, designed to welcome the many pilgrims to the sarcophagus of St Eutrope. The capitals, with their classically inspired carvings, are worth noting.

A little further down the **Rue St-Eutrope** and the **Rue Lacurie**, the **Roman amphitheatre** lies in a natural hollow in the hillside which descends to the Charente Valley. Built in the 1st century AD, one of the oldest in the Roman world, it could hold 20,000 spectators.

Cross the town again and the **Pont Bernard Palissy** to visit the **Abbaye aux Dames** on the way to Cognac. From the **Avenue Gambetta** take the **Rue du Pérat** and reach the **Place de la Caserne** where the abbey stands. Founded in 1047 by the Comte of Anjou, it was given to an order of nuns, for the education of the daughters of noble families. **Madame de Montespan**, Louis XIV's mistress, was educated there. The **abbatial church**, dedicated to Mary, is a good example of Romanesque style in the Saintonge, airy and simple with a richly decorated 12th century façade and friezes of flowers, animals and figures. The **central tower** is the most attractive part of the building with its harmoniously majestic proportions and the conical scaled roof, characteristic of south-western Romanesque, surmounting a graceful rotunda with slender columns.

To get to **Cognac** continue down the Avenue Gambetta and take the N141 (26Km).

Hotels and Restaurants

Relais du Bois St-Georges A very quiet lovely hotel on the outskirts of Saintes, with a large garden and a good view of the surrounding countryside. With restaurant – using their own vegetables. Rue de Royan, 17100, Saintes, Charente-Maritime. Tel: (46) 93.50.99. 21 rooms, 90–240F. Meals 65–100F. Open all year.

Mancini A very comfortable hotel with period furniture and an excellent restaurant offering delicious food with a hint of *nouvelle cuisine*, such as *Canard aux Pêches Fraîches* (duck with fresh peaches) and *Filet de Bar à la Menthe* (sea bass with mint). Rue des Messageries, 17100, Saintes, Charente-Maritime. Tel: (46) 93.06.61. 42 rooms, 90–185F. 6 suites, 220F. Meals 100–160F. Closed 15 December–15 January. Credit cards: AE, DC, EC.

Le Saintonge An excellent restaurant in an immense leisure complex, with swimming pool and a garden in which one can eat, just two minutes from the *autoroute*. Specialities include *Terrine de Poissons au Coulis de Tomates* (fish pâté with tomato sauce) and *Filet de Porc aux Pruneaux* (pork fillet with prunes). Good value. Complexe Saintes-Vegas, Route de Royan, 17100, Saintes, Charente-Maritime. Tel: (46) 93.42.76. Meals

45–150F. Credit cards: EC, VISA.

At **St-Hilaire-de-Villefranche** (8Km from Saintes by the N150) is the **Hostellerie du Château de Laléard**. A very quiet, comfortable hotel with a good restaurant offering regional specialities. 17720, St-Hilaire-de-Villefranche, Charente-Maritime. Tel: (46) 94.36.48. 16 rooms, 160–200F. Meals 70–100F. Closed 1 November–15 March.

Garages
Citroën: Route de Bordeaux. Tel: (46) 93.37.22.
Ford: Route de Bordeaux. Tel: (46) 93.43.44.
Peugeot/Talbot: Route de Royan. Tel: (46) 93.48.33.
Renault: 145 Avenue Gambetta. Tel: (46) 93.55.38.

Festivals, Fairs and Sporting Events
1 July: fortnight's **festival of ancient music**

COGNAC
26Km from Saintes by the N141
Inhabitants: 22,610
Office de Tourisme: Place J. Monnet, closed Sunday and public holidays

Although lying further away than Saintes from the *autoroute*, it is well worth making a detour to Cognac, to visit the cellars of the world-renowned brandy houses of **Martell, Otard, Hine** and **Hennessy.**

A pleasant town, Cognac is the birthplace of François I and was the seat of the Valois-Angoulême court from the end of the 14th century to the beginning of François I's reign.

Born in 1494 in the **château** overlooking the **Charente** on the right of the bridge as one approaches from **Saintes**, François I spent most of his youth here. Unfortunately much of the château has been destroyed or altered, so that little remains of the original medieval castle.

In 1795 a Scotsman named **Otard** bought the castle to use the favourable environment of its rooms for the maturing of brandy. Today the *chais* (cellars) of Otard Cognac can be visited together with the rest of the château. (Tours at 10am, 11am, 2pm, 3pm, 4pm, 5pm 1 April–30 September. Otherwise same times except Sundays and public holidays.)

Britain has always been closely involved with the production, distribution and consumption of Cognac and many firms have British names – Otard and Hennessy from Scotland and Hine from Dorset, for example. Other houses, apart from Otard's, can be visited. Martell is one of the most interesting, still standing in its original 1715 building off the **Place E. Martell.**

Dating from the 17th century the manufacture of Cognac starts with the local white wine, which is rather acid and of low alcoholic content. The wine is allowed to ferment but is not removed from its lees before being distilled. Once distilled it is stored in oak casks until bottling. The only additive is a little caramel for colour, Cognac being a white *eau de vie*. The English name 'brandy' comes from a Dutch word meaning 'burnt wine'.

Fine Champagne comes from the area next to Cognac, **Grande** and **Petite Champagne.** The terms of *Borderies, Fins Bois, Bons Bois* and *Bois Ordinaires* indicate in descending order the quality of the soil and thereby the quality of the spirit. *VSOP* stands for 'Very Superior Old Pale'. **Pineau** is an aperitive made from fresh grape juice with the addition of Cognac and drunk chilled.

Near the **Place François I**, at number 10 Place Jean Monnet, a **Cognatèque (Cognac exhibition)** presents and sells all the brands of Cognac. (Open all year; every day, Sunday included, during July and August.)

From the **Pont Neuf** follow the **Boulevard Denfert-Rochereau** to the Place François I. A **museum** in a lovely garden exhibits collections relating to local prehistory, ceramics and paintings from the 16th to the 20th century and the history of Cognac. (Open 10–12am and 2.30–6pm 1 June–15 September; otherwise 2.30–5.30pm. Closed Tuesday, 1 January, 1 May, Ascension Day, 14 July, 15 August, 1 November, 11 November, Christmas Day.)

The old part of Cognac around the château has many houses dating from the 15th to the 18th century. The **Rue Saunier** particularly recalls the ancient salt trade of Cognac, before brandy took over the economic activity of the town, and is most attractive with its aristocratic Renaissance houses.

LIBOURNE/ST-EMILION
From Paris, Libourne/St-André-de-Cubzac exit, D670, 18Km
From Bordeaux, St-André-de-Cubzac exit, D670, 18Km
Inhabitants: 22,988
Office de Tourisme: Place A. Surchamp, closed Monday morning, Sunday and public holidays

Libourne is an important market town for the wines of the neighbouring regions of **St-Emilion, Pomerol** and **Fronsac.** Two excellent restaurants make it an enjoyable halt on the way to the fascinating small city of St-Emilion 6.5Km away.

An important crossing point from earliest times Libourne is one of the largest *Bastides* (new medieval towns). It was founded in 1265 by an English Seneschal of Aquitaine, Roger de Leyburn, who gave it his name. Today only a tower remains of the old ramparts and the main square keep recalls its medieval past. Libourne used to be a port where Dutch and English vessels came up with the tide to stock up with the claret wine from the region.

The 15th century **town hall** was restored in the 19th century. Inside, a small **museum** contains works by Princeteau, Toulouse-Lautrec's first teacher.

Hotels and Restaurants

Loubat A quality restaurant offering exquisite clarets and exquisite cuisine. Try the *Foie de Canard aux Pommes* (duck liver with apple) and the *Boudin Noir du Pays* (Bordeaux black pudding). Very good value. 32 Rue Chanzy, 33500, Libourne, Gironde. Tel: (56) 51.17.58. Meals 25–200F. Closed Monday in winter. Credit cards: AE, DC.

L'Etrier An excellent restaurant in a lovely panelled room serving regional specialities with class. Try the delicious *Cèpes au Pomerol* (Cèpes mushrooms in wine sauce) or the *Salade Tiède de Homard* (hot lobster salad). 20 Place Decazes, 33500, Libourne, Gironde. Tel: (56) 51.13.59. Meals 70–200F. Closed Sunday night, Monday and 15 February–28 February and 1–15 July. Credit cards: AE, DC, VISA.

Garages

Citroën: 140 Avenue du Général de Gaulle. Tel: (56) 51.62.18.
Fiat: 12 Avenue Clemenceau. Tel: (56) 51.61.88.
Peugeot: 142 Avenue du Général de Gaulle. Tel: (56) 51.48.81.
Renault: Route d'Angoulême. Tel: (56) 51.52.53.

ST-EMILION
6.5Km from Libourne by the D17E
Inhabitants: 3,363
Office de Tourisme: Place des Créneaux

St-Emilion is a most picturesque and attractive city perched on two hills overlooking the **Dordogne** and the lush vineyard of its valley. Its name comes from a hermit monk who came to live in a grotto on this site in the 8th century.

The full-bodied red **wines of St-Emilion** are famous throughout the world. In the Middle Ages they used to be offered as state gifts to monarchs and people of rank. A municipal body called **La Jurade** used to be assembled to judge their quality. Reinstated in 1948, the Jurade still assumes the same responsibility every year in the spring. After hearing Mass, dressed in their robes of scarlet and ermine, they gather in the subterranean church and confer as to the quality of the year's production and whether to affix to it the seal of excellence.

In the autumn, they proclaim from the top of the **Tour du Roi** the opening of the festivities accompanying the *vendanges* (the grape harvest), which take place in the cloisters of the old collegiate church. Macaroons are the town's second speciality.

Coming from Libourne, the visitor reaches the town through the **Porte Bourgeoise**, part of the 13th century ramparts. Taking to the right inside the ramparts, the **Old Collegiate Church** stands out for its impressive proportions (79m long) with a 12th century nave and a Gothic choir and transept. The portal and the cloisters date from the 14th century. South of the church the 12th century bell tower of the intriguing subterranean church dominates the town. From it a vast panoramic view encompasses the whole valley.

Take the steep narrow street going down to the small picturesque **Place du Marché** to reach the **Eglise Monolithe (subterranean church)** dug from the very rock in the 9th century at a place where there was already a natural cave. The entrance is to the side of the Gothic doorway. The interior, with three naves, used to be vividly bright with frescoes and must have been a most impressive sight. Only a few survive, notably two Byzantine-style angels on the ceiling.

The cave where St Emilion is supposed to have lived is under the 13th century **Chapel of the Trinity** on the left of the subterranean church. There are catacombs in the rock near the chapel which is an elegant example of High Gothic.

From the Place du Marché take the narrow Rue de la Cadene to reach the **Rue Guadet.** Turn right to go up to the **Couvent des Cordeliers** (Franciscan monastery), where the **cloisters** present a romantic sight, smothered under vegetation. Opposite, the ruins of the **Commanderie** still include a gable with Romanesque details.

The **Château du Roi**, off the **Rue Loiseau**, was built in the 13th century by Henry Plantagenet (Henry III) and was the **Hôtel de Ville** until 1608.

Hotels and Restaurants

Auberge de la Commanderie A very comfortable hotel well decorated with a homely atmosphere. With restaurant. Rue des Cordeliers, 33330, St-Emilion, Gironde. Tel: (56) 24.70.19. 14 rooms, 90–160F. Meals 60–180F. Closed 20 November–10 January.

Logis de la Cadene Delicious food in a lovely 18th century house on the picturesque Place du Marché, with a small garden in a courtyard. Regional specialities such as *Lamproie au St-Emilion* (Lamprey in a red wine sauce) and *Confits de Canard* (duck pâté) are on the menu. Very good value. Place du Marché-au-Bois, 33330, St-Emilion, Gironde. Tel: (56) 24.71.40. Meals 35–100F. Lunch-time only. Closed Monday and 15–30 June and 1–15 September.

Garages
Renault: Tel: (56) 24.72.68.

Festivals, Fairs and Sporting Events
June, second Sunday: **Festival of the Jurade** (the local wine society)
September, a Sunday: **opening of the vendanges by the Jurade**
September–October: **crafts sale and exhibition** in the old collegiate cloisters.

Near Bordeaux

Hotels and Restaurants
On the *autoroute* around Bordeaux at **L'Alouette** (from Paris, Pessac/ L'Alouette exit, 1Km; from Bordeaux, L'Alouette exit, 1Km) is **La Réserve.** A modern comfortable hotel in its own park and lovely garden, with an excellent restaurant serving traditional cuisine such as *Escalope de Lotte au Xérès* (monkfish escalope with sherry sauce) and delicious sweets. Avenue Bourgailh, L'Alouette, 33600, Pessac, Gironde. 20 rooms, 100–330F. Meals 85–200F. Closed 20 December–20 January, and Friday night and Saturday (1 November–1 April). Credit cards: AE, DC.

Autoroute des Deux-Mers
Bordeaux–Narbonne (A61)

From **Bordeaux** to **Toulouse** the A61 follows the **Valley of the Garonne**. Towns and villages have grown on terraces and the tops of hills in order to avoid the devastating floods in winter and early spring. As far as **Langon** the limestone hills are covered with vineyards producing the wines of **Ste-Croix-du-Mont** and the **Entre-Deux-Mers**, while the lower country of **Graves** and **Sauternes** gives names to world-famous wines.

From Langon to **Agen** the large flow of the river, lined by poplar trees, spreads into a vast plain, yielding rich crops of cereals, market vegetables and fruit, punctuated by large farmhouse buildings. Peaches, Chasselas grapes, apricots and plums (particularly for prunes at Agen) are grown over large areas.

At **Moissac** the **River Tarn** joins the Garonne in a green landscape of wooded hills, vineyards and orchards, while the *autoroute* carries on down the alluvial plain to Toulouse.

At **Toulouse** the A61 enters the **High Languedoc**, a hilly country where the cultivation of cereals is pre-eminent, until **Carcassonne** where vineyards take over the valleys between the rocky hills of the **Garrigue** in **Lower Roussillon**.

The region crossed by the A61 is a place of transition where the great traffic axes, north–south and east–west, have always been the scene of invasions and warfare. From Roman times onwards successive waves of invaders swept over the country. In the 5th century Toulouse was the capital of the Visigoths, later to be conquered by Frankish tribes. In 719 the Saracens took over **Narbonne** but **Charles Martel** defeated the arabs at **Poitiers** in 732. Fifty years later Charlemagne's army was massacred by Basque mountain people at **Roncevaux**, an event which inspired the legendary *Chanson de Roland*, an epic poem dating from the 12th century and written in an Anglo-Norman dialect. (The **English** presence in **Aquitaine** is dealt with in the section on the Val de Loire and Aquitaine.)

The beginning of the Middle Ages saw an increase in traffic in the region with the start of the pilgrimage to **Santiago da Compostella.** The tomb of the Apostle **St James** in Spain attracted an enormous influx of pilgrims from all over Europe, after the first pilgrimage there had been made in 951 by the Bishop of **Le Puy.**

Dressed in a vast cloak displaying the insignia of the pilgrimage (the **scallop shell** and the **medal**), and leaning on the curved pilgrim's staff, the *Jacquet* or *Jacquot* (as these worshippers were called) traced his way from one of the main starting points: **Paris, Vézelay, Le Puy, Autun** or **Arles.**

Hospices (hostels) organised by the **Order of Cluny**, helped later by the

Cistercians and the **Knights of Malta**, welcomed the pilgrims along their route, enabling them to rest in congenial surroundings and to renew their spiritual fervour.

Back home the pilgrim achieved considerable status and was given entry to the exclusive **Confrérie de St-Jacques** (Order of St James), an independent body with its own chapel in various churches and a whole network of pilgrimage routes (even publishing a guide book for the pilgrim).

The pilgrimage route used to cross the frontier at the **Pass of Roncevaux** and there the pilgrim would plant a cross of green leaves he had been carrying. The pilgrimage carried on until the 16th century when it declined, virtually disappearing in the 18th century.

GASTRONOMY

As the A61 runs between two regions already dealt with in this guide, the gastronomic specialities can be found under the sections on the **Val de Loire** and **Aquitaine** for the area from **Bordeaux** to **Toulouse**, and on the **Languedoc** and **Roussillon** for the area between **Toulouse** and **Narbonne.** The wines, however, are particular to this part of the **Bordelais** and are fully described under the relevant entry (ie **Langon/Sauternes**).

LANGON/SAUTERNES

From Bordeaux, Langon exit, 2Km by the N113 to Langon, then 9Km by the D8 and D125 to Sauternes
From Narbonne, Langon exit, 2Km by the N113 to Langon, then 9Km by the D8 and D125 to Sauternes
Inhabitants: 6,124
Office de Tourisme: Parc Bordes, closed Tuesday out of season

Langon is a commercial centre for the wines of the following regions: the **Graves**, which stretches from north of Bordeaux to east of Langon; the **Entre-Deux-Mers**, from east of Bordeaux to Langon; and the **Sauternes**, south of Langon.

The Graves, the name of which comes from the gravelly soil, produces pleasant white wines from the **Sauvignon** grapes and some excellent red wines, the best being the **Château Haut-Brion**, already known in England in the 17th century and mentioned by both John Locke and Samuel Pepys in their diaries.

The Entre-Deux-Mers is well known for its dry white wines, to be drunk young, and some red *Grand Ordinaire* wines.

The Sauternes region and the neighbouring **Barsac** produce the best **Liquoreux** – sweet white wines. Obtained from the *Sémillon* and

Sauvignon grapes, the special quality and characteristic mellow sweetness of the *Liquoreux* wines come from the way the *vendange* (harvest) is performed. The grapes are left to mature, though the leaves are removed so that the sunshine falls directly on to them and a mould peculiar to the region called the **Pourriture Noble** develops. The whole process is exceedingly complex as any variation in weather conditions or timing can mean the success or total ruin of the whole *vendange*; hence the relative rarity of these wines and the very high prices they command. Of the great *Liquoreux* the Sauternes **Château Yquem** and **Barsac**, are world famous, while on the other side of the Garonne the **Loupiac, Cadillac** and **Ste-Croix-du-Mont** produce mellow fruity wines of varying degrees of sweetness.

From Langon take the D8 and N113 to **Sauternes** (580 inhabitants), a typical small village nestling in the middle of the famous vineyards, and enjoy a delicious meal in a lovely little inn.

From Langon, take the N113 to **Barsac** (11Km, 2,019 inhabitants), a small town with an **Office Viticole de Sauternes et Barsac** on the **Place de l'Eglise** where tasting of the wines of the region can be enjoyed. The **church** nearby is an interesting building dating from the beginning of the 17th century, with 18th century interior fittings.

From Langon take the N113 across the River Garonne and the D10 to **Ste-Croix-du-Mont** (7Km, 846 inhabitants). A very attractive drive along the river on the chalky hills overlooking the valley takes one to this small village sitting on a promontory among the vineyards.

From the **terrace of the château**, near the **church**, walk down the stairs on to a lower terrace where a **Cave de Dégustation (tasting cellar)** for the local *Liquoreux Ste-Croix-du-Mont* has been established in a most intriguing place of grottoes dug into a cliff of fossilised oysters dating from Prehistoric times. Sit on the terrace, beautifully set up with tables and parasols, and sip the lovely golden wine while admiring the vast panorama stretching towards the **Pyrenees** from the lush green valley of the Garonne.

Hotels and Restaurants

Claude Darroze Very quiet comfortable rooms and a wonderful restaurant make this a marvellous base from which to explore the nearby vineyards. Sample the delights of the *Mosaïque de Poissons* (various fish in tarragon aspic) and the *Agneau aux Girolles* (lamb with chanterelles mushrooms). 95 Cours du Général Leclerc, 33210, Langon, Gironde. Tel: (56) 63.00.48. 16 rooms, 70–180F. Meals 100–200F. Closed Monday, 10 October–5 November and 15–28 February.

Les Vignes Delicious traditional specialities at very good prices is the keynote of this friendly little place: *Lapin* (or *Caille*) *au Sauternes* (rabbit or quail with a Sauternes sauce) and *Poulet à la Broche* (barbecued

chicken). Place de l'Eglise, 33210, Langon, Gironde. Tel: (56) 62.60.06.
2 rooms 35F. Meals 32–120F. Closed Monday and February.
Château de Rolland On the N113, a beautiful former Carthusian monastery converted into a very comfortable hotel in a lovely garden. With restaurant. Barsac, 33720, Podensac, Gironde. Tel: (56) 25.17.75.
8 rooms, 130–200F. Meals 45–125F. Closed Wednesday. Credit cards:
AE, DC, VISA.

Garages

Peugeot/Talbot: 50 Rue J. Ferry, Langon. Tel: (56) 63.00.47.
Renault: 1 Place de la Libération, Langon. Tel: (56) 63.50.19.

BAZAS

From Bordeaux, Langon exit, D932, 15Km
From Narbonne, Langon exit, D932, 15Km
Inhabitants: 5,235
Office de Tourisme: Place de la Cathédrale, closed Sunday and Monday

Built on a rocky promontory and surrounded by medieval ramparts, Bazas is an attractive small town overlooking the **River Beuve** and its valley. A very comfortable hotel and excellent restaurant makes it an ideal overnight stop.

Founded by the Romans, Bazas was the seat of a diocese until the 18th century. The **Cathedral of St Jean** recalls this former importance and grandeur. It was built in the 13th and 14th centuries on the plan of the great northern Gothic cathedrals. The blood of St John the Baptist was particularly venerated here. Badly damaged during the Wars of Religion, it was restored in the 17th century and the façade is still impressive, despite the mixture of styles. The portal still retains the 13th century carvings, saved by the people of Bazas with a ransom of 10,000 *écus* (crowns), depicting the Last Judgement and the life of St John the Baptist. Inside, the nave without transept is very impressive with its elongated proportions. The **Gardens of the Evêché** provide a lovely view over the valley.

Hotels and Restaurants

Relais de Fompeyre A very quiet comfortable hotel in a wonderful situation in a park with a swimming pool and an excellent restaurant offering regional specialities, such as *Lamproie Bordelaise* (lamprey in a red wine sauce). Route de Mont-de-Marsan, 33430, Bazas, Gironde. Tel: (56) 24.04.60. 35 rooms and suites, 130–155F. Meals 75–180F. Closed 15 October–15 March. Credit cards: AE, EC, VISA.
Grill Mirambet Excellent grill restaurant offering *haute cuisine* as well as

simple grills: *Paupiette de Saumon au Concombre* (salmon with cucumber). Hôtel de France, 1 Cours du Général de Gaulle, 33430, Bazas, Gironde. Tel: (56) 25.02.37. Meals 45–180F. Closed January. Credit card: VISA.

Garages
Peugeot: Tel: (56) 25.00.73.
Renault: Tel: (56) 25.03.63.

CASTELJALOUX
From Bordeaux, Marmande exit, D933, 15Km
From Narbonne, Marmande exit, D933, 15Km
Inhabitants: 5,440

Casteljaloux, at the edge of **Gascony** and the region of the **Agen**, is a small town, once fortified, but nearly all destroyed in 1621 having become a Huguenot stronghold. Only few medieval houses and a 16th century **convent**, now a hospital, survive. A very comfortable hotel and excellent restaurant welcome the modern traveller.

Hotels and Restaurants
Les Cadets de Gascogne An old house standing in a beautiful garden has been converted into a very comfortable hotel, with a terrace covered with flowers on which one can sample delicious Gascogne specialities, such as *Foie Gras Frais aux Pommes et Raisins* (fresh foie gras with grapes and apples) and *Coquilles St Jacques aux Cèpes* (scallops with cèpe mushrooms). Good value. Place Gambetta, 47700, Casteljaloux, Lot-et-Garonne. Tel: (58) 93.00.59. 15 rooms, 70–150F. Meals 53–180F. Credit cards: EC, VISA.
La Vieille Auberge A rustic inn serving exceedingly good food at very good prices. Try the *Asperges du Pays* (fresh asparagus) and the *Faux Filet Grillé aux Echalottes* (fillet steak with a shallot sauce). 11 Rue Posterne, 47700, Casteljaloux, Lot-et-Garonne. Tel: (58) 93.01.36. Meals 40–130F. Closed Monday, Sunday night, one week in February and 15–30 October. Credit cards: AE, DC, EC, VISA.

Garages
Citroën: Tel: (58) 93.01.59.
Peugeot: Tel: (58) 93.05.96.

AIGUILLON
From Bordeaux, Aiguillon exit, D8, 7Km

From Narbonne, Aiguillon exit, D8, 7Km
Inhabitants: 4,066

Aiguillon is a small town, once the seat of a duchy, which retains the 18th century **château** of the Ducs d'Aiguillon, together with some fine old houses from its more glorious past. A comfortable modern hotel and excellent restaurant makes it a pleasant restful halt.

Hotels and Restaurants

Les Cygnes A comfortable modern hotel in a park with delicious food at low prices. Route de Villeneuve, 47190, Aiguillon, Lot-et-Garonne. Tel: (53) 79.60.02. 17 rooms, 90–145F. Meals 40–140F. Closed Saturday and 15 December–15 January.

AGEN

From Bordeaux, Agen exit, N21, 5Km
From Narbonne, Agen exit, N21, 5Km
Inhabitants: 35,839
Office de Tourisme: Boulevard Carnot, closed Saturday out of season

Agen is a busy modern market town, on the right bank of the **Garonne**, and the centre of an important trade in fruit: Chasselas grapes, peaches, plums and the famous prunes, Agen specialities, are all produced in the lush orchards on the slopes of the Garonne Valley. A quiet hotel-restaurant in the countryside and some excellent restaurants in the town centre cater for the traveller.

The **Agenais** region is truly a Garden of Eden. Its geographical position as a natural passageway between the **Atlantic Ocean** and the **Mediterranean**, and its situation on the rich silted soils of the valleys of the rivers Lot and Garonne, together with the mildness of its climate (subjected to oceanic influences as well as warmth from the south), have encouraged the flourishing of the most delicate vegetables and fruit from the Middle Ages onwards. The famous Agen prunes date from the time of the Crusades, and the monks at **Clairac** were already producing them commercially in the 16th century. Nowadays they are exported all over France and the EEC.

Agen was an important intellectual centre in the Renaissance, with the presence of Italian writers such as **Bandello** and **Scaliger.** It retains from this time some fine 16th century houses. Four of these houses have been restored and converted into a **museum.** The elegant Renaissance buildings house important collections ranging from Gallo-Roman archaeology to the picture collection of the Comte de Chaudordy, Ambassador to Madrid, which include some outstanding works by **Goya**, notably a self-portrait and the Capriccios. The most famous piece in the museum, however, is the **Vénus du Mas**, a gracefully proportioned Greek marble statue found in a field in 1876. To reach the museum, go from the **Place Jasmin** along the **Boulevard de la République** to the **Rue Voltaire** and the **Rue Chaudordy** where the museum stands. (Open 10–12am and 2–6pm. Closed Tuesday, 1 January, 1 May, 1 November, Christmas Day.)

Hotels and Restaurants

Le Voltaire A lovely modern restaurant offering exquisite food of regional inspiration, such as *Magret de Canard Grillé* (grilled fillet of duck), and some delicious fish, including *Bar aux Algues* (sea bass cooked in seaweed). 36 Rue Voltaire, 47000, Agen, Lot-et-Garonne. Tel: (53) 47.27.01. Meals 58–150F. Closed Sunday. Credit card: VISA.

At **Colayrac** (1.5Km by the N113) is **La Corne d'Or**. A wonderful view over the Garonne and the Pont-Canal of Agen from this hotel-restaurant with delicious dishes, such as *Cuisses de Grenouilles à la Menthe* (frog's legs with mint) and *Filet de Bar aux Légumes* (sea bass fillet with vegetables). Good value. Route de Marmande, 47450, Colayrac, Lot-et-Garonne. Tel: (53) 47.02.76. 14 rooms, 110–160F. Meals 50–180F. Closed Sunday and 15 July–15 August. Credit card: AE.

Garages

Austin/Morris/Rover/Triumph: 182 Boulevard Liberté. Tel: (53) 47.10.63.
Ford: Avenue du Général de Gaulle. Tel: (53) 47.32.07.
Peugeot: Rue Boillot. Tel: (53) 47.12.21.
Renault: 84 Avenue J. Jaurès. Tel: (53) 66.81.75.
Talbot: 14 Boulevard Liberté. Tel: (53) 47.20.84.

MOISSAC

From Bordeaux, Castelsarrasin/Moissac exit, N113, 6Km
From Narbonne, Montauban exit, D958 and N113, 29Km
Inhabitants: 12,138
Office de Tourisme: Place Delthil, 15 June–15 September, closed Sunday

Moissac is an attractive town on the **River Tarn**, nestling in the middle of green hills covered with orchards and vineyards around its famous abbey. It is one of the high spots of French Romanesque art and, with its lovely setting, a comfortable hotel overlooking the river and a camping site on a nearby lake, Moissac is a most pleasant halt.

Moissac Abbey was founded in the 7th century by Benedictine monks from Normandy. Charlemagne and his son were its benefactors in the 9th century. In 1047 it was attached to **Cluny Abbey** by St Odilon and Moissac radiated prosperity. However English troops occupied Moissac twice during the 100 Years War and the Wars of Religion further accelerated the decline. In the 17th century the abbey was secularised, and it was looted during the Revolution.

The **Church of St Pierre** is the former abbey church. The oldest part is the doorway to the tower, a sort of defensive keep which dates from the end of the 12th century. The two periods of the nave are obvious on the outside: the lower part in stone is Romanesque whereas the rest, in brick, is Gothic. However the most celebrated feature of the abbey is the southern portal.

The **tympanum** (1110–15) of this portal is a masterpiece of Romanesque sculpture in the Languedoc tradition. Its theme is the **Apocalyptic Vision of St John.** Christ as supreme judge dominates the whole composition through his powerful presence and impressive size. Majesty, awesome power and stern justice emanate from him over the twenty-four Elders of the Apocalypse disposed in two rows, endowing the ensemble with a psychological intensity of drama and holy fear rarely attained. The symbols of the four Evangelists surround the figure of Christ. The high quality and precision of the carving, the heightened spirituality expressed in beauty of form and elegance of conception make this tympanum a highlight of Western art. Its impact cannot be stressed enough.

The lintel on which the tympanum rests is just as outstanding for the decorative quality of the stylised lions, inspired by Eastern art and used in an entwined 'X' shape to constitute the central pillar or *trumeau*, on which two striking stylised figures of elders are carved. On either side of the portal scenes from the New Testament are depicted in the same powerful manner.

Inside the church the furniture and **altarpiece** date from the Renaissance. Notice a moving Romanesque 12th century Christ behind the altar. The **cloister**, built at the end of the 11th century, is the most remarkable in the whole of southern France for its elegance of forms and proportions, the subtle harmony of its coloured marble (pink, white, grey, green), and the richness of imagination and the quality of execution of its carved capitals. Subjects from the Old and New Testaments, the Apocalypse and the legends of the saints, together with purely decorative animal, vegetal and geometric motifs, are treated with a wealth of artistic virtuosity. (Open 9–12am and 2–6pm. Closed Christmas Day and 1 January.)

In the former **abbots' palace** a **Musée des Arts et Traditions Populaires** (museum of popular arts and traditions) presents a collection of local furniture, costumes and ceramics. (Open 9–12am and 2–6.30pm 15 June–15 September; otherwise 9.30–12am and 2.30–6pm. Closed Sunday morning, Tuesday, 1 May and 1 December–15 January.)

From Moissac take the N113 in the direction of **Agen**, driving on the right bank of the River Tarn along the hills bearing the vineyards producing the succulent golden **Chasselas** grapes, a particularly sweet type of grape, called *Moissac*. These choice grapes, growing in the rich soil of the Garonne Valley, are famous for their musky flavour and are exported to Paris and beyond.

4Km from Moissac, cross over the Garonne on the D15 for the **Lac de Vit** at **St-Nicolas-de-la-Grave**, a natural lake formed by the confluence of the Rivers Tarn and Garonne. A leisure centre has been established on its bank with a camp site, a marina, sailing, windsurfing, pedalos etc.

Hotels and Restaurants
Moulin de Moissac A splendid position over the River Tarn with a garden and a terrace makes this hotel an attractive place to stay. With restaurant. Place du Moulin, 82200, Moissac, Tarn-et-Garonne. Tel: (63) 04.03.55. 45 rooms, 180–325F. Meals 90–200F. Closed 15 December–1 February, Monday (1 October–15 December) and 1 February–1 April.

Garages
Peugeot: Place Ste-Blanche. Tel: (63) 04.18.31.
Talbot: Route de Bordeaux. Tel: (63) 04.01.51.

Camping

MONTAUBAN
From Bordeaux, Montauban exit, N20, 18Km
From Narbonne, Montauban exit, N20, 18Km
Inhabitants: 50,420
Office de Tourisme: 1 Rue du Collège, closed Sunday and public holidays except in July and August

Montauban is a city of pink brick built on a plateau dominating the right bank of the **River Tarn.** A peaceful and luxurious hotel in the countryside nearby makes it a very pleasant overnight stop.

Founded in the 12th century, Montauban was the scene of fierce fighting during the Wars of Religion. In 1570 it was recognised as a Calvinist stronghold and Henri de Navarre reinforced the ramparts. After three months of resistance King Louis XIII and his 20,000 men ended the siege in 1621, only to start again in 1628 and to subdue the city which welcomed him after the defeat of the Huguenot forces at **La Rochelle**. The ramparts of Montauban were then destroyed.

Two great artists were born at Montauban. The first was the painter **Ingres** (1780–1867), who was very fond of his native city and bequeathed part of his estate to form the basis of a museum. The other was a sculptor, **Bourdelle** (1861–1929), whose heroic style is illustrated by his *Centaure*

Mourant (dying centaur), which is in the garden opposite the museum.

From the *autoroute*, arriving from the left bank, cross the **Pont Vieux** (14th century), spanning the Tarn on seven arches. The sweeping view from the bridge of the right bank of the river, with its pink brick buildings, is a most attractive sight under a cloudless blue sky. The former bishop's palace on the right, the handsome 17th century houses and the fine tower of the **Church of St Jacques** form a very graceful ensemble.

The **bishop's palace**, built in the 17th century on the site of a medieval castle, is very impressive in the simplicity and massiveness of its forms. It now houses the **Musée Ingres et Bourdelle.**

The first floor of the museum is consecrated to Ingres and includes paintings, some 4,000 drawings, and personal mementoes, together with works by David, Chassériau, Géricault and Delacroix. The ground floor contains Bourdelle's works, notably some outstanding busts. The basement is dedicated to local history and medieval lapidary collections, while the second floor holds paintings from the 15th to the 20th century. (Open 10–12am and 2–6pm. Closed Sunday morning, Monday, 1 January, 1 May, 14 July, 1 November, 11 November, Christmas Day.)

The **Musée d'Histoire Naturelle (natural history museum)** stands on the other side of the **Place Bourdelle** and has extensive collections of birds, minerals and prehistoric animals. (Open 10–12am and 2–6pm. Closed Sunday morning, Monday and public holidays.)

The Place Général-Picq, opposite the museum, displays the **Centaure Mourant** by Bourdelle. The **Church of St Jacques** overlooks the garden and dates from the 14th and 15th centuries. Built in brick in southern Gothic style, it is a fortified church with a tower, characteristic of the Toulouse region.

From the Church of St Jacques go to the **Place Nationale**, a 17th century square, built in the lovely local pink brick, of harmonious proportions with a double-arcaded gallery and houses above. Every morning a flower market animates the graceful scene.

The **Cathedral of Notre Dame**, reached from the bridge by the Rue de la Mairie and the Avenue Lacaze, is a classical building. Inside, the famous picture by Ingres **Le Voeu de Louis XIII** (the oath of Louis XIII) is noteworthy.

Hotels and Restaurants

Hostellerie les Coulandrières 3Km from Montauban by the N658, a very comfortable luxuriously appointed modern hotel, with a swimming pool in a lovely garden in the middle of the countryside, offers delicious food, such as *Matelote d'Anguilles aux Pruneaux* (eel stew with prunes) or *Lotte aux Légumes* (monkfish with vegetables). Montbeton, Route de Castel-sarrasin, 82290, La Villedieu-du-Temple, Tarn-et-Garonne. Tel: (63)

03.18.09. 21 rooms 220–290F. Meals 80–180F. Closed January. Credit cards: AE, DC, EC, VISA.

Garages
Citroën: N20. Tel: (63) 03.15.30.
Datsun: 15 Avenue Jean Jaurès. Tel: (63) 63.08.00.
Ford: 1724 Avenue de Toulouse. Tel: (63) 63.04.83.
Peugeot/Talbot: Rue du Bac. Tel: (63) 63.03.33.
Renault: Route de Paris. Tel: (63) 03.23.23.

CASTELNAUDARY
From Bordeaux, Castelnaudary exit, D6, 3Km
From Narbonne, Castelnaudary exit, D6, 3Km
Inhabitants: 10,847
Office de Tourisme: Place de la République, closed morning out of season and Sunday.

Situated on the Midi Canal linking the Mediterranean with **Toulouse**, Castelnaudary is a pleasant resort with a large lake for sailing and other water sports. It is famous for its gastronomic speciality, *Cassoulet*. A comfortable, very quiet hotel-restaurant makes it an ideal overnight stop.

The idea of linking the Atlantic to the Mediterranean goes back to the Romans. After various attempts in the 16th century, it was eventually achieved by Pierre Paul Riquet, Baron de Bonrepos, in the late 17th century. The port of **Sète**, the Mediterranean end of the canal, was built at that time too. Having been a busy waterway for most of the period since, the canal is now given over to small-scale commercial traffic, consisting mostly of agricultural products and pleasure boats which enable the traveller to enjoy its attractive banks, the graceful pink brick bridges spanning it and the lovely Mediterranean landscape of widely spreading plane trees, darkly upright cypresses and homely maritime pines.

Castelnaudary's monuments consist of the 14th century **Collegiate Church of St Michel**, built in the southern Gothic style, and the **Moulin de Cugarel**, dating from the 17th century, the last survivor of a dozen mills built on the hills overlooking the town.

Cassoulet is a white bean stew, cooked in a clay *cassole* (casserole dish). The clay for the cassole comes from the village of Issel near Castelnaudary. In Castelnaudary, the original *Cassoulet* consists of ham, pork and *Saucisson* (dry sausage) added to the beans, whereas the Toulouse variety has *Saucisse de Toulouse* (a special sausage), conserve of goose and best end of lamb added, and Carcassonne's *Cassoulet* includes leg of lamb and partridges in season. A more than nourishing dish! Castelnaudary's second speciality is the *Alléluia* a cake made from a secret recipe and which was offered to Pope Pius VII on his visit to the city.

Hotels and Restaurants

Palmes et Industrie A very quiet very comfortable hotel with a fine restaurant serving regional specialities: *Cassoulet* (bean stew with pork etc) and *Confit d'Oie* (goose cooked in its own fat). Good value. 10 Rue du Maréchal Foch, 11400, Castelnaudary, Aude. Tel: (68) 23.03.10. 20 rooms, 80–170F. Meals 55–160F. Open all year. Credit cards: AE, DC, EC, VISA.

Grand Hôtel Fourcade An excellent restaurant, with rooms, whose *Cassoulet* is the main attraction. Called 'l'Incomparable', it is even tinned to be exported. Very good value. 14 Rue des Charmes, 11400, Castelnaudary, Aude. Tel: (68) 23.02.08. 19 rooms, 50–150F. Meals 40–120F. Closed Wednesday and 1 February–5 March.

At **Villemagne** (by the N113 and D103 from Castelnaudary) is the **Castel de Villemagne**. A 15th century manor house converted into a very comfortable hotel near the picturesque ruins of the Château of Saissac. Restaurant for guests. 11310, Villemagne-par-Saissac, Aude. Tel: (68) 60.22.95. 9 rooms, 90–180F. Closed Monday and January–April. Credit cards: DC, VISA.

Garages

Citroën: Route de Toulouse. Tel: (68) 23.00.78.
Fiat/Mazda: 10 quai du Port. Tel: (68) 23.33.49.
Opel: Route de Carcassonne. Tel: (68) 23.13.36.
Peugeot: Route de Toulouse. Tel: (68) 23.13.06.
Renault: Avenue Monseigneur de Langle. Tel: (68) 23.18.82.

CARCASSONNE

From Bordeaux, Carcassonne exit, 3Km
From Narbonne, Carcassonne exit, 3Km
Inhabitants (old town): 380
Inhabitants (new town): 46,329
Office de Tourisme (old town): Porte Narbonnaise, Easter and July–September; (new town) Boulevard Camille Pelletan, closed Sunday and public holidays except July and August

Carcassonne is two cities, the old fairy-tale fortress and the new town, centre of the wine region of the **Aude.** To the modern traveller the old city, with the medieval streets, shops, hotels and restaurants within its ramparts, is a unique experience.

The hill on which Carcassonne is built has always been a key position on the route between **Toulouse** and the **Mediterranean.** The Romans, the Visigoths and later the Franks successively occupied it. For 400 years Carcassonne was the capital of a *Comté* under the Comte de Toulouse. In the 13th century the **Albigensian Crusade** against the **Catharist Heresy** brought ferocious persecution, massacres and destruction. The Vicomte de Carcassonne, **Trencavel**, nephew of the Comte de Toulouse, refusing to yield to terror and intimidation from the papal and royal forces, offered asylum to the persecuted Cathars and brought about the downfall of Carcassonne. Lack of water brought the town to surrender to the assailants. The leader of the crusade, Simon of Montfort, took over the government of Carcassonne and Trencavel was murdered. In 1204 his son tried to regain his rightful inheritance but was defeated by the royal troups. Louis IX (St Louis) had all the villages outside the walls destroyed and their inhabitants sent into exile for seven years. At their return they built a new town on the other side of the River Aude – the modern Carcassonne.

In 1844 the architect **Viollet-le-Duc** restored old Carcassonne, the largest fortified city in Europe. The very structure of the old town illustrates its violent past. Composed of two series of ramparts round a fortified castle, the Château Comtal, the town still has 380 inhabitants together with lively shops, a school, bank, post office etc.

The Château Comtal is reached from the **Porte d'Aude**, leaving one's car in the car park near the **Church of St Gimer.** The view of the city's golden walls is most impressive and evocative. Turn left to visit the **Château Comtal** and its **museum** containing local medieval artefacts. (Guided tours 9–11am and 2–5.30pm 1 April–30 September; 10–11.30am and 2–4.30pm 1 October–31 March. Closed 1 January, 1 May, 14 July, 1 November, Christmas Day.)

Then follow the fortifications, walking on the ramparts and exploring the narrow cobbled streets. Dating from the 3rd to the 13th century the **ramparts** are punctuated at regular intervals by watch towers of various periods. The area between the two sets of fortifications is called the **Lices** and in peace-time provided an exercise and jousting place, as well as being a place to trap the enemy in time of war. Near the **Grand Théâtre**, where open-air performances are given during the summer, the Romanesque **Basilica of St Nazaire** has been greatly restored by Viollet-le-Duc and the façade does not fit in with the rest of the building.

The interior however retains much of the southern Romanesque style, bare and austere in its simplicity. The stained-glass windows (13th and 14th century) are noteworthy. In the right aisle, in the **Chapelle Rodier**, notice the **Pierre du Siège de Toulouse**, a medieval stone carving depicting the siege of Toulouse in 1218 in which Simon de Montfort died. It provides fascinating information on medieval war techniques.

In the new town the **Musée des Beaux Arts**, in the Rue de Verdun, houses a collection of Dutch and Flemish 17th and 18th century Old Masters together with porcelain of the period. (Open 9–11.45am and 2–5.45pm. Closed Sunday.)

Hotels and Restaurants
In the old town:

Hôtel de la Cité A luxury hotel opposite the Church of St Nazaire, with a lovely view over the gardens and ramparts, decorated in medieval style, with Gothic architecture, four-poster beds etc. No restaurant. Place St-Nazaire, 11000, Carcassonne, Aude. Tel: (68) 25.03.34. 54 rooms, 120–350F. Closed 15 October–Easter.

Le Sénéchal A very welcoming restaurant serving excellent regional specialities: *Cassoulet* (bean stew), *Gigot Rôti* (leg of lamb). 6 Rue Viollet-le-Duc, 11000, Carcassonne, Aude. Tel: (68) 25.00.15. Meals 55–100F. Closed October–April. Credit card: VISA.

Near the ramparts is the **Auberge du Pont-Levis**. An excellent restaurant with traditional fare, such as *Canard aux Cèpes* (duck with cèpes mushrooms) and *Pigeon Rôti à l'Ail* (roast pigeon with garlic). A wonderful view over the ramparts and the surrounding countryside from the terrace. Près de la Porte Narbonnaise, 11000, Carcassonne, Aude. Tel: (68) 25.55.23. Meals 90–170F. Closed Sunday night and Monday. Credit cards: AE, DC, EC, VISA.

In the new town:

Montségur A very comfortable family hotel with a homely atmosphere. No restaurant. 27 Allée d'Iena, 11000, Carcassonne, Aude. Tel: (68) 25.31.41. 21 rooms 100–200F. Closed 20 December–18 January. Credit cards: AE, DC, EC.

At **Auriac** (4Km south-east of Carcassonne by the D104) is the **Domaine d'Auriac.** In a beautiful park stretching between the River Aude and the old ramparts, a very comfortable hotel with swimming pool and tennis court offers a warm and sophisticated welcome with a fine restaurant serving regional dishes with a lot of refinement, such as *Canard aux Cèpes Secs* (duck with dry cèpes mushrooms) and *Sabayon à la Blanquette de Limoux* (syllabub with the local white wine). Route de St-Hilaire, 11000, Carcassonne, Aude. Tel: (68) 25.72.22. 23 rooms, 180–300F. Meals 100–180F. Closed Sunday night, Monday lunch-time, and October–June except for Easter and January. Credit card: AE.

Garages
BMW: 71 Allée D'Iena. Tel: (68) 47.14.14.
Citroën: 30 Avenue F. Roosevelt. Tel: (68) 25.75.36.
Datsun/Volvo: Plateau de Grazailles. Tel: (68) 25.33.34.

Just off the Autoroute

Fiat: Route de Montrel. Tel: (68) 25.81.31.
Ford: 47 Avenue H. Gout. Tel: (68) 25.11.50.
Peugeot: 133 Avenue F. Roosevelt. Tel: (68) 47.84.36.
Renault: Route de Narbonne. Tel: (68) 25.77.12.

KEY TO AUTOROUTE MAPS

AUTOROUTE DU NORD

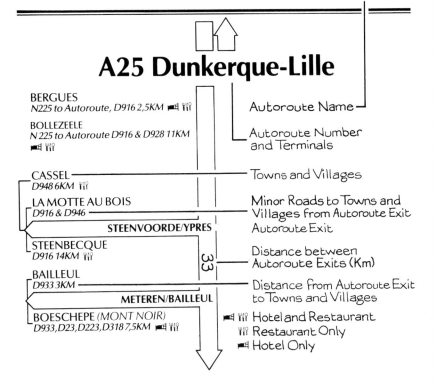

A25 Dunkerque-Lille

BERGUES
N225 to Autoroute, D916 2,5KM 🏨 🍴

BOLLEZEELE
N 225 to Autoroute D916 & D928 11KM
🏨 🍴

CASSEL
D948 6KM 🍴

LA MOTTE AU BOIS
D916 & D946

STEENVOORDE/YPRES

STEENBECQUE
D916 14KM 🍴

BAILLEUL
D933 3KM

METEREN/BAILLEUL

BOESCHEPE *(MONT NOIR)*
D933,D23,D223,D318 7,5KM 🏨 🍴

33

Autoroute Name

Autoroute Number
and Terminals

Towns and Villages

Minor Roads to Towns and
Villages from Autoroute Exit

Autoroute Exit

Distance between
Autoroute Exits (Km)

Distance from Autoroute Exit
to Towns and Villages

🏨 🍴 Hotel and Restaurant
🍴 Restaurant Only
🏨 Hotel Only

221

AUTOROUTE DU NORD

A25 Dunkerque-Lille

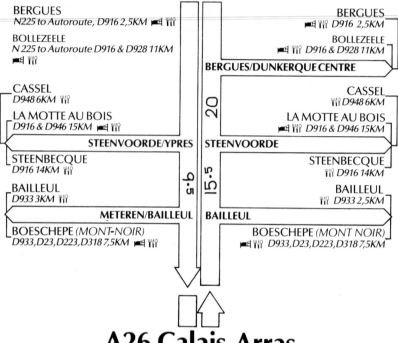

BERGUES
N225 to Autoroute, D916 2,5KM 🛏️ 🍴

BERGUES
🛏️ 🍴 *D916 2,5KM*

BOLLEZEELE
N 225 to Autoroute D916 & D928 11KM
🛏️ 🍴

BOLLEZEELE
🛏️ 🍴 *D916 & D928 11KM*

BERGUES/DUNKERQUE CENTRE

20

CASSEL
D948 6KM 🍴

CASSEL
🍴 *D948 6KM*

LA MOTTE AU BOIS
D916 & D946 15KM 🛏️ 🍴

LA MOTTE AU BOIS
🛏️ 🍴 *D916 & D946 15KM*

STEENVOORDE/YPRES | **STEENVOORDE**

STEENBECQUE
D916 14KM 🍴

STEENBECQUE
🍴 *D916 14KM*

9.5   15.5

BAILLEUL
D933 3KM 🍴

BAILLEUL
🍴 *D933 2,5KM*

METEREN/BAILLEUL | **BAILLEUL**

BOESCHEPE *(MONT-NOIR)*
D933,D23,D223,D318 7,5KM 🛏️ 🍴

BOESCHEPE *(MONT NOIR)*
🛏️ 🍴 *D933,D23,D223,D318 7,5KM*

A26 Calais-Arras

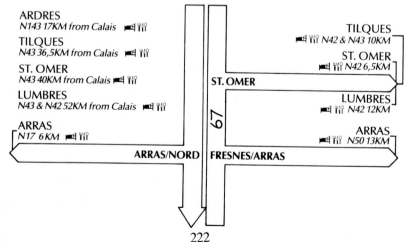

ARDRES
N143 17KM from Calais 🛏️ 🍴

TILQUES
N43 36,5KM from Calais 🛏️ 🍴

TILQUES
🛏️ 🍴 *N42 & N43 10KM*

ST. OMER
N43 40KM from Calais 🛏️ 🍴

ST. OMER
🛏️ 🍴 *N42 6,5KM*

ST. OMER

LUMBRES
N43 & N42 52KM from Calais 🛏️ 🍴

LUMBRES
🛏️ 🍴 *N42 12KM*

67

ARRAS
N17 6KM 🛏️ 🍴

ARRAS
🛏️ 🍴 *N50 13KM*

ARRAS/NORD | **FRESNES/ARRAS**

A1 Lille-Paris

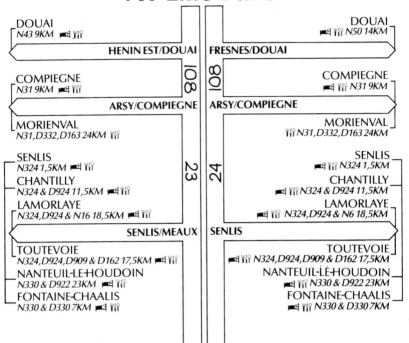

AUTOROUTE DU SOLEIL

A6 Paris-Lyon

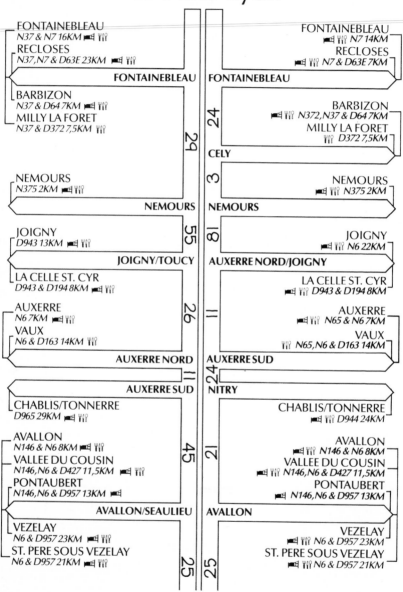

FONTAINEBLEAU
N37 & N7 16KM

RECLOSES
N37,N7 & D63E 23KM

FONTAINEBLEAU

FONTAINEBLEAU
N7 14KM

RECLOSES
N7 & D63E 7KM

FONTAINEBLEAU

BARBIZON
N37 & D64 7KM

MILLY LA FORET
N37 & D372 7,5KM

BARBIZON
N372,N37 & D64 7KM

MILLY LA FORET
D372 7,5KM

29

24

CELY

3

NEMOURS
N375 2KM

NEMOURS

NEMOURS
N375 2KM

NEMOURS

55

18

JOIGNY
D943 13KM

JOIGNY/TOUCY

JOIGNY
N6 22KM

AUXERRE NORD/JOIGNY

LA CELLE ST. CYR
D943 & D194 8KM

LA CELLE ST. CYR
D943 & D194 8KM

AUXERRE
N6 7KM

VAUX
N6 & D163 14KM

26

11

AUXERRE
N65 & N6 7KM

VAUX
N65,N6 & D163 14KM

AUXERRE NORD

11

AUXERRE SUD

24

AUXERRE SUD

NITRY

CHABLIS/TONNERRE
D965 29KM

CHABLIS/TONNERRE
D944 24KM

AVALLON
N146 & N6 8KM

VALLEE DU COUSIN
N146,N6 & D427 11,5KM

PONTAUBERT
N146,N6 & D957 13KM

45

21

AVALLON
N146 & N6 8KM

VALLEE DU COUSIN
N146,N6 & D427 11,5KM

PONTAUBERT
N146,N6 & D957 13KM

AVALLON/SEAULIEU

AVALLON

VEZELAY
N6 & D957 23KM

ST. PERE SOUS VEZELAY
N6 & D957 21KM

25

25

VEZELAY
N6 & D957 23KM

ST. PERE SOUS VEZELAY
N6 & D957 21KM

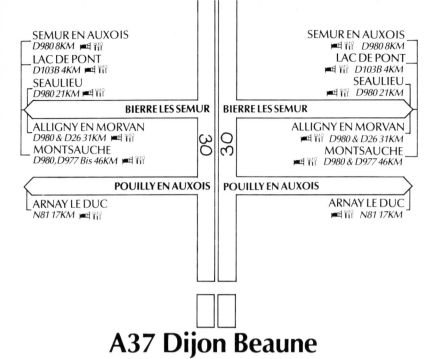

SEMUR EN AUXOIS
D980 8KM

LAC DE PONT
D103B 4KM

SEAULIEU
D980 21KM

BIERRE LES SEMUR

ALLIGNY EN MORVAN
D980 & D26 31KM

MONTSAUCHE
D980, D977 Bis 46KM

30

POUILLY EN AUXOIS

ARNAY LE DUC
N81 17KM

SEMUR EN AUXOIS
D980 8KM

LAC DE PONT
D103B 4KM

SEAULIEU
D980 21KM

BIERRE LES SEMUR

ALLIGNY EN MORVAN
D980 & D26 31KM

MONTSAUCHE
D980 & D977 46KM

30

POUILLY EN AUXOIS

ARNAY LE DUC
N81 17KM

A37 Dijon Beaune

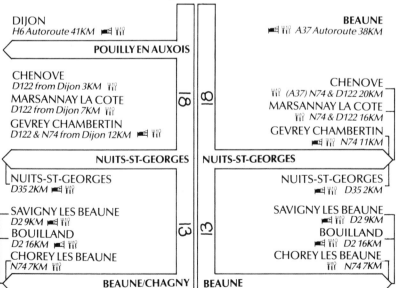

DIJON
H6 Autoroute 41KM

POUILLY EN AUXOIS

CHENOVE
D122 from Dijon 3KM

MARSANNAY LA COTE
D122 from Dijon 7KM

GEVREY CHAMBERTIN
D122 & N74 from Dijon 12KM

NUITS-ST-GEORGES

NUITS-ST-GEORGES
D35 2KM

SAVIGNY LES BEAUNE
D2 9KM

BOUILLAND
D2 16KM

CHOREY LES BEAUNE
N74 7KM

BEAUNE/CHAGNY

18

13

BEAUNE
A37 Autoroute 38KM

CHENOVE
(A37) N74 & D122 20KM

MARSANNAY LA COTE
N74 & D122 16KM

GEVREY CHAMBERTIN
N74 11KM

NUITS-ST-GEORGES

NUITS-ST-GEORGES
D35 2KM

SAVIGNY LES BEAUNE
D2 9KM

BOUILLAND
D2 16KM

CHOREY LES BEAUNE
N74 7KM

BEAUNE

18

13

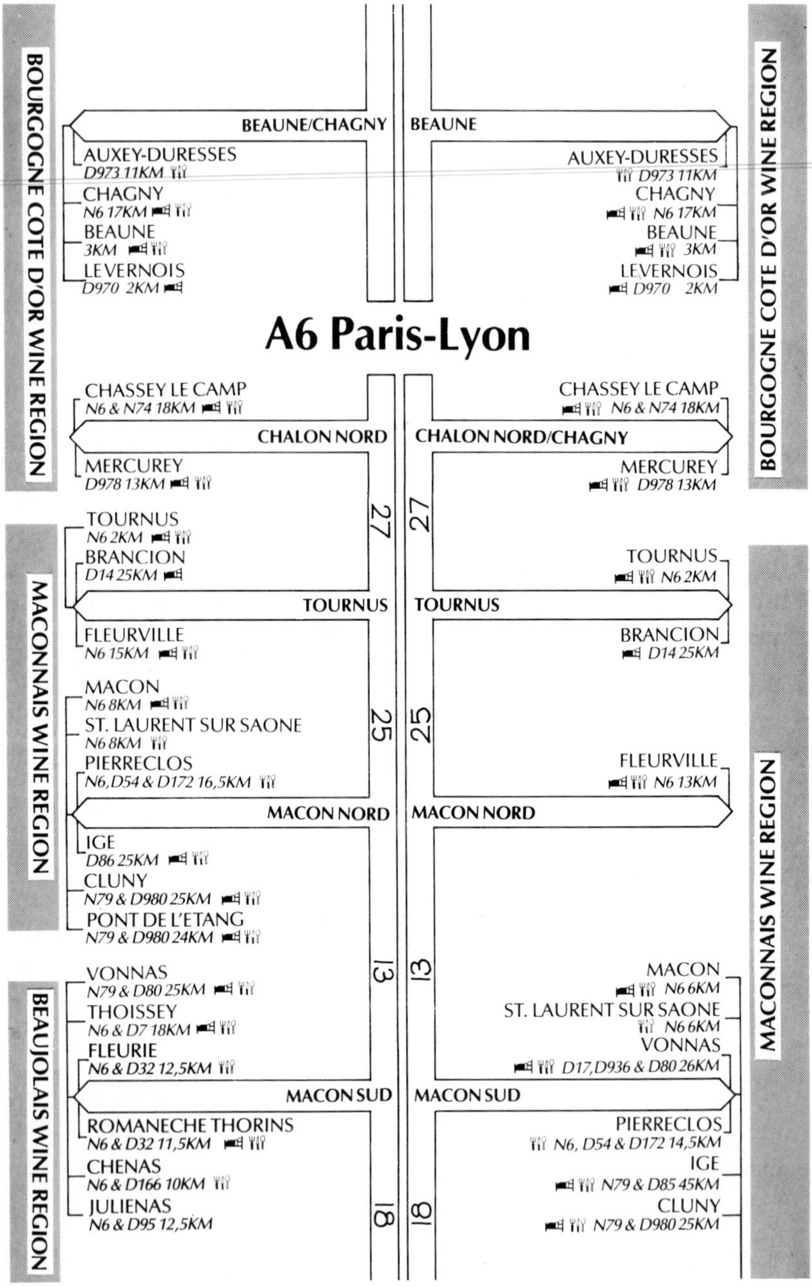

A6 Paris-Lyon
BOURGOGNE COTE D'OR WINE REGION
BEAUNE/CHAGNY
AUXEY-DURESSES
D973 11KM
CHAGNY
N6 17KM
BEAUNE
3KM
LEVERNOIS
D970 2KM
CHASSEY LE CAMP
N6 & N74 18KM
CHALON NORD
MERCUREY
D978 13KM
MACONNAIS WINE REGION
27
TOURNUS
N6 2KM
BRANCION
D14 25KM
TOURNUS
FLEURVILLE
N6 15KM
MACON
N6 8KM
ST. LAURENT SUR SAONE
N6 8KM
25
PIERRECLOS
N6, D54 & D172 16,5KM
MACON NORD
IGE
D86 25KM
CLUNY
N79 & D980 25KM
PONT DE L'ETANG
N79 & D980 24KM
BEAUJOLAIS WINE REGION
13
VONNAS
N79 & D80 25KM
THOISSEY
N6 & D7 18KM
FLEURIE
N6 & D32 12,5KM
MACON SUD
ROMANECHE THORINS
N6 & D32 11,5KM
CHENAS
N6 & D166 10KM
JULIENAS
N6 & D95 12,5KM
18
BOURGOGNE COTE D'OR WINE REGION
BEAUNE
AUXEY-DURESSES
D973 11KM
CHAGNY
N6 17KM
BEAUNE
3KM
LEVERNOIS
D970 2KM
CHASSEY LE CAMP
N6 & N74 18KM
CHALON NORD/CHAGNY
MERCUREY
D978 13KM
27
TOURNUS
N6 2KM
TOURNUS
BRANCION
D14 25KM
MACONNAIS WINE REGION
25
FLEURVILLE
N6 13KM
MACON NORD
13
MACON
N6 6KM
ST. LAURENT SUR SAONE
N6 6KM
VONNAS
D17, D936 & D80 26KM
MACON SUD
PIERRECLOS
N6, D54 & D172 14,5KM
IGE
N79 & D85 45KM
CLUNY
N79 & D980 25KM
18

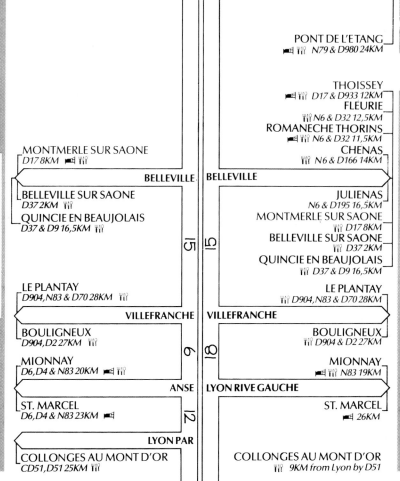

PONT DE L'ETANG
N79 & D980 24KM

THOISSEY
D17 & D933 12KM
FLEURIE
N6 & D32 12,5KM
ROMANECHE THORINS
N6 & D32 11,5KM
CHENAS
N6 & D166 14KM

MONTMERLE SUR SAONE
D17 8KM

BELLEVILLE | **BELLEVILLE**

BELLEVILLE SUR SAONE
D37 2KM

QUINCIE EN BEAUJOLAIS
D37 & D9 16,5KM

JULIENAS
N6 & D195 16,5KM
MONTMERLE SUR SAONE
D17 8KM
BELLEVILLE SUR SAONE
D37 2KM
QUINCIE EN BEAUJOLAIS
D37 & D9 16,5KM

LE PLANTAY
D904, N83 & D70 28KM

LE PLANTAY
D904, N83 & D70 28KM

VILLEFRANCHE | **VILLEFRANCHE**

BOULIGNEUX
D904, D2 27KM

BOULIGNEUX
D904 & D2 27KM

MIONNAY
D6, D4 & N83 20KM

MIONNAY
N83 19KM

ANSE | **LYON RIVE GAUCHE**

ST. MARCEL
D6, D4 & N83 23KM

ST. MARCEL
26KM

LYON PAR

COLLONGES AU MONT D'OR
CD51, D51 25KM

COLLONGES AU MONT D'OR
9KM from Lyon by D51

15   15   6   18   12

227

AUTOROUTE DU SOLEIL

A7 Lyon Salon de Provence

COTES DU RHONE WINE REGION

VIENNE
N7 5KM ⅋⅋

CONDRIEU
N86 12KM 🛏 ⅋⅋

CONDRIEU/AMPUIS

CHONAS L'AMBALLON
N7 4KM 🛏 ⅋⅋

LES ROCHES DE CONDRIEU
N86 11KM 🛏 ⅋⅋

MERCUROL
D532 4KM 🛏 ⅋⅋

TAIN L'HERMITAGE/TOURNON

SAINT ROMAIN DE LERPS
N7,N533 & D287 15KM 🛏 ⅋⅋

ST. PERAY
N7 & N533 10KM 🛏 ⅋⅋

VALENCE NORD

PONT DE L'ISERE
N7 5KM 🛏 ⅋⅋

VALENCE
N7 4KM 🛏 ⅋⅋

BAIX
N104 & N86 7KM 🛏 ⅋⅋

LORIOL/PRIVAS/CREST

MIRMANDE
N7 15KM 🛏 ⅋⅋

MONTELIMAR NORD

MONTELIMAR
N7 13KM 🛏 ⅋⅋

MONTBOUCHER SUR JABRON
N7 & D169 15KM 🛏 ⅋⅋

L'HOMME D'ARMES
N7 9KM 🛏 ⅋⅋

LE POET LAVAL
N7 & D540 35KM 🛏 ⅋⅋

52
11
27
9
44

VIENNE
⅋⅋ *N7 26KM*

CONDRIEU
🛏 ⅋⅋ *D519 & N86 20KM*

CHANAS/ANNONAY

CHONAS L'AMBALLON
🛏 ⅋⅋ *N7 17KM*

LES ROCHES DE CONDRIEU
🛏 ⅋⅋ *D519 & N86 20KM*

MERCUROL
🛏 ⅋⅋ *D532 4KM*

TAIN L'HERMITAGE/TOURNON

SAINT ROMAIN DE LERPS
🛏 ⅋⅋ *N7,N533 & D287 15KM*

ST. PERAY
🛏 ⅋⅋ *N7 & N533 10KM*

VALENCE SUD/GRENOBLE

PONT DE L'ISERE
🛏 ⅋⅋ *N7 13KM*

VALENCE
🛏 ⅋⅋ *N7 4KM*

BAIX
🛏 ⅋⅋ *N104 & N86 7KM*

LORIOL/PRIVAS/CREST

MIRMANDE
🛏 ⅋⅋ *N7 5KM*

MONTELIMAR NORD

MONTELIMAR
🛏 ⅋⅋ *N7 10KM*

MONTBOUCHER SUR JABRON
🛏 ⅋⅋ *N7 & D169 12KM*

MONTELIMAR SUD

L'HOMME D'ARMES
🛏 ⅋⅋ *N7 14KM*

LE POET LAVAL
🛏 ⅋⅋ *N7 & D540 32KM*

3
bl
bl
b
22
12

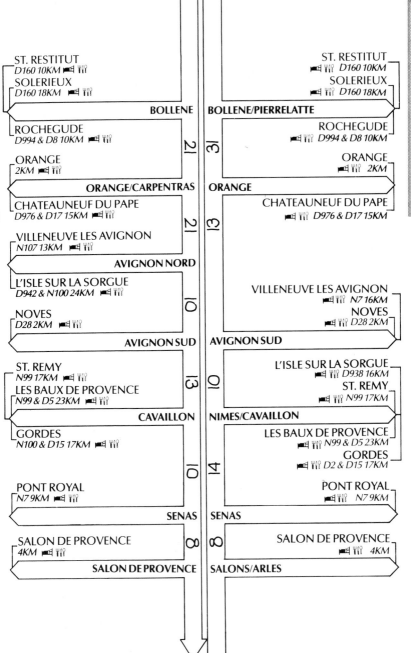

COTES DU RHONE WINE REGION

ST. RESTITUT
D160 10KM
SOLERIEUX
D160 18KM

BOLLENE

ROCHEGUDE
D994 & D8 10KM

ORANGE
2KM

ORANGE/CARPENTRAS

CHATEAUNEUF DU PAPE
D976 & D17 15KM

VILLENEUVE LES AVIGNON
N107 13KM

AVIGNON NORD

L'ISLE SUR LA SORGUE
D942 & N100 24KM

NOVES
D28 2KM

AVIGNON SUD

ST. REMY
N99 17KM
LES BAUX DE PROVENCE
N99 & D5 23KM

CAVAILLON

GORDES
N100 & D15 17KM

PONT ROYAL
N7 9KM

SENAS

SALON DE PROVENCE
4KM

SALON DE PROVENCE

21 · 21 · 10 · 13 · 10 · 8

13 · 13 · 10 · 10 · 14 · 8

ST. RESTITUT
D160 10KM
SOLERIEUX
D160 18KM

BOLLENE/PIERRELATTE

ROCHEGUDE
D994 & D8 10KM

ORANGE
2KM

ORANGE

CHATEAUNEUF DU PAPE
D976 & D17 15KM

VILLENEUVE LES AVIGNON
N7 16KM
NOVES
D28 2KM

AVIGNON SUD

L'ISLE SUR LA SORGUE
D938 16KM
ST. REMY
N99 17KM

NIMES/CAVAILLON

LES BAUX DE PROVENCE
N99 & D5 23KM
GORDES
D2 & D15 17KM

PONT ROYAL
N7 9KM

SENAS

SALON DE PROVENCE
4KM

SALONS/ARLES

229

LA PROVENCALE

A8 Salon de Provence/Menton

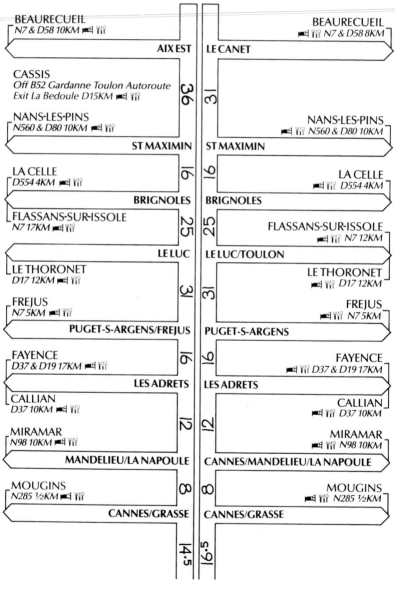

BEAURECUEIL
N7 & D58 10KM

AIX EST | LE CANET

BEAURECUEIL
N7 & D58 8KM

CASSIS
Off B52 Gardanne Toulon Autoroute
Exit La Bedoule D15KM

36 | 31

NANS-LES-PINS
N560 & D80 10KM

NANS-LES-PINS
N560 & D80 10KM

ST MAXIMIN | ST MAXIMIN

LA CELLE
D554 4KM

16 | 16

LA CELLE
D554 4KM

BRIGNOLES | BRIGNOLES

FLASSANS-SUR-ISSOLE
N7 17KM

25 | 25

FLASSANS-SUR-ISSOLE
N7 12KM

LE LUC | LE LUC/TOULON

LE THORONET
D17 12KM

31 | 31

LE THORONET
D17 12KM

FREJUS
N7 5KM

FREJUS
N7 5KM

PUGET-S-ARGENS/FREJUS | PUGET-S-ARGENS

FAYENCE
D37 & D19 17KM

16 | 16

FAYENCE
D37 & D19 17KM

LES ADRETS | LES ADRETS

CALLIAN
D37 10KM

CALLIAN
D37 10KM

MIRAMAR
N98 10KM

12 | 12

MIRAMAR
N98 10KM

MANDELIEU/LA NAPOULE | CANNES/MANDELIEU/LA NAPOULE

MOUGINS
N285 ½KM

8 | 8

MOUGINS
N285 ½KM

CANNES/GRASSE | CANNES/GRASSE

14.5 | 5.91

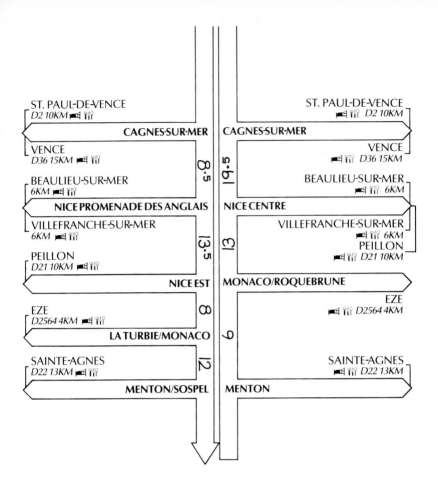

ST. PAUL-DE-VENCE
D2 10KM

CAGNES-SUR-MER

VENCE
D36 15KM

BEAULIEU-SUR-MER
6KM

NICE PROMENADE DES ANGLAIS

VILLEFRANCHE-SUR-MER
6KM

PEILLON
D21 10KM

NICE EST

EZE
D2564 4KM

LA TURBIE/MONACO

SAINTE-AGNES
D22 13KM

MENTON/SOSPEL

ST. PAUL-DE-VENCE
D2 10KM

CAGNES-SUR-MER

VENCE
D36 15KM

BEAULIEU-SUR-MER
6KM

NICE CENTRE

VILLEFRANCHE-SUR-MER
6KM

PEILLON
D21 10KM

MONACO/ROQUEBRUNE

EZE
D2564 4KM

SAINTE-AGNES
D22 13KM

MENTON

8.5
13.5
8
12

9.5
13
9

LA LANGUEDOCIENNE

A9 Orange-Collioure

UZES *N100,D19 & D981 19KM* 🛏️ 🍴	🛏️ 🍴 *N100,D19 & D981 19KM* UZES
PONT DU GARD *N100 & D981 4KM* 🛏️ 🍴	PONT DU GARD 🛏️ 🍴 *N100 & D981 4KM*
REMOULINS	**REMOULINS/AVIGNON**
CASTILLON-DU-GARD *N100 & D228 4KM* 🛏️ 🍴	CASTILLON-DU-GARD 🛏️ 🍴 *N100 & D228 4KM*
NIMES *N86 4KM* 🛏️ 🍴	NIMES 🛏️ 🍴 *N86 4KM*
NIMES EST 18	26 **NIMES OUEST/GARONS/MARSEILLE**
AIGUES-MORTES *N313 & D979 18KM* 🛏️ 🍴 26	81 AIGUES-MORTES 🛏️ 🍴 *N313 & D979 18KM*
GALLARGUES	**GALLARGUES**
PORT-CAMARGUE *N313,D979 21KM* 🛏️ 🍴	PORT-CAMARGUE 🛏️ 🍴 *N313 & D979 21KM*
PEZENAS *D13 12KM* 🛏️ 🍴 74	74 PEZENAS 🛏️ 🍴 *D13 12KM*
AGDE/PEZENAS	**AGDE/PEZENAS**
ORNAISONS *D113 & D24 15KM* 🛏️ 🍴 45	43 ORNAISONS 🛏️ 🍴 *D113 & D24 15KM*
NARBONNE SUD	**NARBONNE SUD**
SIGEAN *1KM* 🛏️ 🍴 14	9 SIGEAN 🛏️ 🍴 *1KM*
SIGEAN	**SIGEAN**
PORT-LA-NOUVELLE *D9B 10KM* 🛏️ 🍴	PORT-LA-NOUVELLE 🛏️ 🍴 *D9B 10KM*
ST. LAURENT-DE-LA-SALANQUE *D83 & D11 10KM* 🛏️ 🍴 33	33 ST. LAURENT-DE-LA-SALANQUE 🛏️ 🍴 *D83 & D11 10KM*
PERPIGNAN NORD	**PERPIGNAN NORD**
CERET *D115 8KM* 🛏️ 🍴 31	31 CERET 🛏️ 🍴 *D115 8KM*
LE BOULOU/LE PERTHUS	**LE BOULOU**
COLLIOURE *D618 & D114 28KM* 🛏️ 🍴	COLLIOURE 🛏️ 🍴 *D618 & D114 28KM*

L'AQUITAINE

A10 Paris-Bordeaux

DOURDAN		DOURDAN
N836 & N838 6KM ⊨ ⛏		⊨ ⛏ N836 & N838 6KM
DOURDAN	16 / 16	DOURDAN
ETAMPES		ETAMPES
N191 20KM ⊨ ⛏		⊨ ⛏ N191 20KM
ALLAINVILLE		ALLAINVILLE/ETAMPES
FONTAINE-LA-RIVIERE	71 / 57	FONTAINE-LA-RIVIERE
N191 & N721 29KM ⊨ ⛏		⊨ ⛏ N191 & N721 29KM
OLIVET		OLIVET
A71,N20 & D14 6KM ⊨ ⛏		⊨ ⛏ A71,N20 & D14 6KM
ORLEANS OUEST		ORLEANS OUEST
CLERY-ST. ANDRE	16 / 16	CLERY-ST. ANDRE
D2 & D18 7KM ⊨ ⛏		⊨ ⛏ D2 & D18 7KM
BEAUGENCY		BEAUGENCY
D2 & N152 9KM ⊨ ⛏		⊨ ⛏ D2 & N152 9KM
MEUNG		MEUNG
TAVERS		TAVERS
D2 & N152 13KM ⊨ ⛏		⊨ ⛏ D2 & N152 13KM
BLOIS	33 / 33	BLOIS
5KM ⊨ ⛏		⊨ ⛏ 5KM
CHITENAY		CHITENAY
D956 17KM ⊨ ⛏		⊨ ⛏ D956 17KM
CHAMBORD		CHAMBORD
D951 & D112B 23KM ⊨ ⛏		⊨ ⛏ D951 & D112B 23KM
ST. DYE SUR LOIRE		ST. DYE SUR LOIRE
D951 & D112B 20KM ⊨ ⛏		⊨ ⛏ D951 & D112B 20KM
BLOIS		BLOIS
CHAUMONT	30 / 30	CHAUMONT
N152 22KM ⊨ ⛏		⊨ ⛏ N152 22KM
ONZAIN		ONZAIN
N152 21KM ⊨ ⛏		⊨ ⛏ N152 21KM
SEILLAC		SEILLAC
N152,D135 & D131 15KM ⊨ ⛏		⊨ ⛏ N152,D135 & D131 15KM
AMBOISE		AMBOISE
D31 15KM ⊨ ⛏		⊨ ⛏ D31 15KM
AMBOISE/CHATEAU-RENAULT		AMBOISE/CHATEAU-RENAULT
CHANTELOUP	21 / 21	CHANTELOUP
D31 18KM ⊨		⊨ D31 18KM

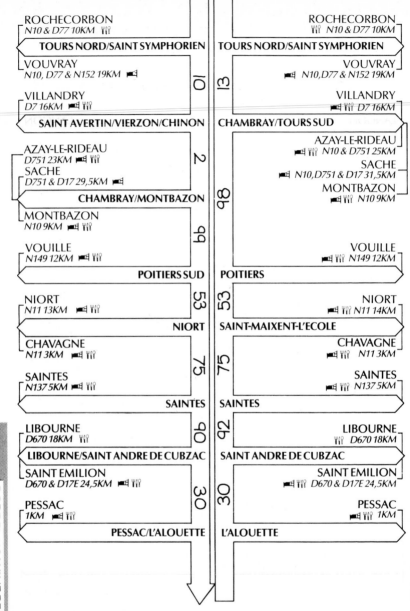

ROCHECORBON
N10 & D77 10KM 🍴

ROCHECORBON
🍴 *N10 & D77 10KM*

◁ **TOURS NORD/SAINT SYMPHORIEN** | **TOURS NORD/SAINT SYMPHORIEN** ▷

VOUVRAY
N10, D77 & N152 19KM 🛏

VOUVRAY
🛏 *N10, D77 & N152 19KM*

10   13

VILLANDRY
D7 16KM 🛏 🍴

VILLANDRY
🛏 🍴 *D7 16KM*

◁ **SAINT AVERTIN/VIERZON/CHINON** | **CHAMBRAY/TOURS SUD** ▷

AZAY-LE-RIDEAU
D751 23KM 🛏 🍴

AZAY-LE-RIDEAU
🛏 🍴 *N10 & D751 25KM*

2   8b

SACHE
D751 & D17 29,5KM 🛏

SACHE
🛏 *N10, D751 & D17 31,5KM*

◁ **CHAMBRAY/MONTBAZON**

MONTBAZON
🛏 🍴 *N10 9KM*

MONTBAZON
N10 9KM 🛏 🍴

9b

VOUILLE
N149 12KM 🛏 🍴

VOUILLE
🛏 🍴 *N149 12KM*

◁ **POITIERS SUD** | **POITIERS** ▷

NIORT
N11 13KM 🛏 🍴

53   53

NIORT
🛏 🍴 *N11 14KM*

◁ **NIORT** | **SAINT-MAIXENT-L'ECOLE** ▷

CHAVAGNE
N11 3KM 🛏 🍴

CHAVAGNE
🛏 🍴 *N11 3KM*

75   75

SAINTES
N137 5KM 🛏 🍴

SAINTES
🛏 🍴 *N137 5KM*

◁ **SAINTES** | **SAINTES** ▷

LIBOURNE
D670 18KM 🍴

90   92

LIBOURNE
🍴 *D670 18KM*

◁ **LIBOURNE/SAINT ANDRE DE CUBZAC** | **SAINT ANDRE DE CUBZAC** ▷

SAINT EMILION
D670 & D17E 24,5KM 🛏 🍴

SAINT EMILION
🛏 🍴 *D670 & D17E 24,5KM*

30   30

PESSAC
1KM 🛏 🍴

PESSAC
🛏 🍴 *1KM*

◁ **PESSAC/L'ALOUETTE** | **L'ALOUETTE** ▷

BORDELAIS WINE REGION

234

AUTOROUTE DES DEUX MERS

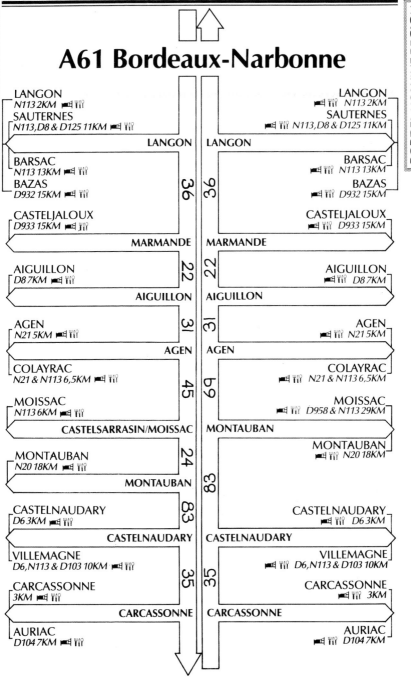

Index *(entries in italics are hotels)*